A CLASSICAL INTRODUCTION TO CRYPTOGRAPHY EXERCISE BOOK

A CLASSICAL INTRODUCTION TO CRYPTOGRAPHY EXERCISE BOOK

by

Thomas Baignères
EPFL, Switzerland

Pascal Junod
EPFL, Switzerland

Yi Lu
EPFL, Switzerland

Jean Monnerat
EPFL, Switzerland

Serge Vaudenay
EPFL, Switzerland

 Springer

Thomas Baignères
EPFL - I&C - LASEC
Lausanne, Switzerland

Pascal Junod
Lausanne, Switzerland

Yi Lu
EPFL - I&C - LASEC
Lausanne, Switzerland

Jean Monnerat
EPFL-I&C-LASEC
Lausanne, Switzerland

Serge Vaudenay
Lausanne, Switzerland

Library of Congress Cataloging-in-Publication Data

A C.I.P. Catalogue record for this book is available
from the Library of Congress.

A CLASSICAL INTRODUCTION TO CRYPTOGRAPHY EXERCISE BOOK
by Thomas Baignères, Palcal Junod, Yi Lu, Jean Monnerat and Serge Vaudenay

e-ISBN-10: 0-387-28835-X
ISBN-13: 978-1-4419-3912-8   e-ISBN-13: 978-0-387-28835-2

Printed on acid-free paper.

Printed in the United States of America.

springeronline.com

To Valérie and my parents

To Mimi and Chloé

To my parents

To Susan and my parents

To Christine and Emilien

Contents

12. FROM CRYPTOGRAPHY TO COMMUNICATION SECURITY

Foreword

As a companion book of Vaudenay's *A Classical Introduction to Cryptography*, this exercise book contains a carefully revised version of most of the material used in teaching by the authors or given as examinations to the undergraduate students of the *Cryptography and Security* lecture at EPFL from 2000 to mid-2005. It covers a majority of the subjects that make up today's cryptology, such as symmetric or public-key cryptography, cryptographic protocols, design, cryptanalysis, and implementation of cryptosystems.

Exercises do not require a large background in mathematics, since the most important notions are introduced and discussed in many of the exercises. We expect the readers to be comfortable with basic facts of discrete probability theory, discrete mathematics, calculus, algebra, as well as computer science. Following *A Classical Introduction to Cryptography*, exercises related to the more advanced parts of the textbook are marked with a star.

The difficulty of the exercises covers a broad spectrum. In some the student is expected to simply apply basic facts, while in others more intuition and reflexion will be necessary to find the solution. Nevertheless, the solutions accompanying the exercises have been written as clearly as possible. Some exercises are clearly research-oriented, like for instance the ones dedicated to decorrelation theory or to very recent results in the field of hash functions. The idea was to give to our readers a taste of this exciting research world.

Chapter 1 is dedicated to the prehistory of cryptology, exposing the design and the cryptanalysis of very simple and/or historical ciphers. Chapter 2 investigates basic facts of modern symmetric cryptography, focusing on the Data Encryption Standard, modes of operations, and stream ciphers. Chapter 3 handles the hash functions topic, while Chapter 4 describes some more involved notions of cryptanalysis of block ciphers. Chapter 5 considers protocols based on symmetric cryptography. Chapter 6 is based on some basic facts of algebra and on the algorithms used to compute within the usual algebraic structures used in cryptology, while Chapter 7 is devoted to number theory with a strong emphasis put on its algorithmic aspects. Chapter 8 is built around some elements of complexity theory. Chapter 9 treats the important subject of public-key encryption schemes and Chapter 10 contains exercises centered around the notion of digital signatures. Chapter 11 exposes some protocols using public-key cryptography, and Chapter 12 handles the case of hybrid protocols, combining both symmetric and public-key schemes.

A website (http://www.intro-to-crypto.info) has been set up as a companion of this book. It will contain inevitable errata as well as other material related to this book, like challenging tests and more exercises.

Finally, the authors would like to thank Gildas Avoine, Matthieu Finiasz, and all the EPFL students who attended at least one of our lectures, as well as the Springer-Verlag staff for having provided us so many useful comments on these exercises, their solutions, and on the textbook.

We wish the reader a wonderful trip in the exciting world of cryptology!

Chapter 1

PREHISTORY OF CRYPTOGRAPHY

Exercises

Exercise 1   Mappings, etc.

The goal of this exercise is to remind the notions of function, injection, surjection, bijection, permutation, and transposition. If any of those notions is not clear to you, keep reading!

Consider the two sets $\mathcal{X} = \{x_1, x_2, \ldots, x_n\}$ and $\mathcal{Y} = \{y_1, y_2, \ldots, y_m\}$, and a function $f : \mathcal{X} \longrightarrow \mathcal{Y}$. As f is a function, it assigns to each element of $\mathcal{X}$ a single element of $\mathcal{Y}$.

1 If $n < m$, can f be a function? What about the case where $n > m$?

2 Consider the case where $n = 3$ and $m = 4$. Which of the following diagrams represent a function? Explain why (or why not).

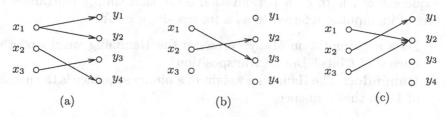

$\qquad\qquad$ (a) $\qquad\qquad\qquad\qquad\qquad$ (b) $\qquad\qquad\qquad\qquad\qquad$ (c)

3 A function f is said to be $1-1$ (one to one), or *injective*, if each element of $\mathcal{Y}$ is the image of at most one element of $\mathcal{X}$, i.e., for all $x_1, x_2 \in \mathcal{X}$,

$$f(x_1) = f(x_2) \Rightarrow x_1 = x_2.$$

Which of the following diagrams represent an injective function?

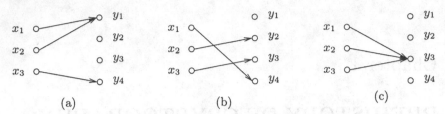

(a)   (b)   (c)

4 A function f is said to be *surjective* if each element of $\mathcal{Y}$ is the image of at least one element of $\mathcal{X}$, i.e., if for all $y \in \mathcal{Y}$ there exists an $x \in \mathcal{X}$ such that $f(x) = y$. When f is surjective, it is said to be a function from $\mathcal{X}$ *onto* $\mathcal{Y}$. Which of the following diagrams represent a surjective function?

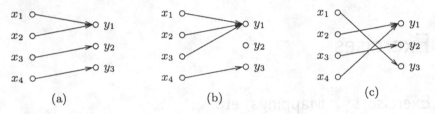

(a)   (b)   (c)

5 If every element of $\mathcal{Y}$ is the image of exactly one element of $\mathcal{X}$, then f is called a *bijection*, i.e., f is an injection *and* a surjection. Can f be a bijection if $n > m$? What about the case where $n < m$?

6 Show that if $\mathcal{X}$ and $\mathcal{Y}$ have the same cardinality and if f is an injection, then f is a bijection.

The last property is often used to show the bijectivity of a given function.

A *permutation* on $\mathcal{X}$ is a bijection from $\mathcal{X}$ onto itself, i.e., a rearrangement of the elements of $\mathcal{X}$. In order for f to be a permutation, we must have $\mathcal{X} = \mathcal{Y}$. Moreover, we let $\mathcal{X} = \{0, 1\}^{\ell}$, i.e., $\mathcal{X}$ is the set of all binary sequences of length ℓ. A permutation on $\mathcal{X}$ that simply rearranges the bits of its input is referred to as a *transposition* on $\mathcal{X}$.

7 Does a permutation always preserve the Hamming weight of a sequence of ℓ bits? Does a transposition?
   Reminder: The Hamming weight of a binary sequence is the number of 1's in that sequence.

8 Can we say that a transposition is just a permutation on the bit positions?

The Data Encryption Standard (DES) is a very famous and widely used block cipher. It maps 64-bit plaintext blocks $\mathbf{x} = (x_{63}x_{62} \ldots x_0)$ on

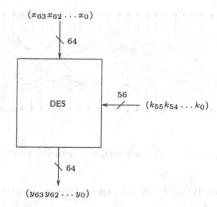

Figure 1.1. DES, a mapping of 64-bit plaintext blocks on 64-bit ciphertext block, depending on a 56-bit secret key

64-bit ciphertext blocks $\mathbf{y} = (y_{63}y_{62}\ldots y_0)$ using a 56-bit secret key $\mathbf{k} = (k_{55}k_{54}\ldots k_0)$ as a parameter (see Figure 1.1).

9 When the secret key $\mathbf{k}$ is fixed, DES defines a specific permutation on $\mathcal{X} = \{0,1\}^{64}$. Why do you think it is necessary for DES to be a bijection, and not a simple function?

10 How many permutations can you find on $\mathcal{X} = \{0,1\}^{64}$? How many different secret keys does DES have?

11 DES internal design involves a 32-bit transformation which is represented in Figure 1.2. Is this transformation a permutation and/or a transposition?

Consider now a *random* permutation on $\{0,1\}^{\ell}$ represented by a random variable C^*, uniformly distributed among all possible permutations of $\{0,1\}^{\ell}$.

12 Compute $\Pr[\mathsf{C}^* = c]$, where c is a fixed permutation on $\{0,1\}^{\ell}$.

13 Let $x, y \in \{0,1\}^{\ell}$ be two fixed ℓ-bit strings. Using the previous question, compute $\Pr[\mathsf{C}^*(x) = y]$. Compare this probability with $\Pr[Y = y]$ where Y is a random variable uniformly distributed in $\{0,1\}^{\ell}$.

14 Let $a, b \in \{0,1\}^{\ell}$ such that $a \neq 0$. We define the *differential probability* of C^* to be

$$\mathrm{DP}^{\mathsf{C}^*}(a, b) = \Pr_X[\mathsf{C}^*(X \oplus a) = \mathsf{C}^*(X) \oplus b],$$

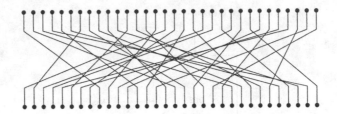

Figure 1.2. A transformation in DES on 32-bit strings

where the probability holds over the uniform distribution of X. For $b \neq 0$, show that

$$\mathrm{E}_{\mathsf{C}^*}(\mathrm{DP}^{\mathsf{C}^*}(a,b)) = \frac{1}{2^\ell - 1}.$$

▷ Solution on page 8

Exercise 2   A Simple Substitution Cryptogram

The following text is encrypted using a simple substitution method. The plaintext is part of an English text *encoded* in upper case characters without punctuation marks. Using the distribution of the characters in English texts (see Table 1.1), recover the plaintext.

```
ODQSOCL OW GIU BOEE QRROHOCS QV GIUR KIA QF Q DQCQSLR WIR
ICL IW CQFQF EIYQE YIDJUVLR FGFVLDF GIU SLV OCVI GIUR
IWWOYL IC VXQV DICPQG DIRCOCS VI WOCP VXL JXICLF ROCSOCS
LHLRG YQEELR OF Q POFVRQUSXV YICWUFLP CQFQ BIRMLR QCP
LHLRG YQEELR QFFURLF GIU VXQV XOF IR XLR WOEL IR
```

Table 1.1. Distribution of the characters in a typical English text

Letter	Probability	Letter	Probability	Letter	Probability
A	8.2 %	J	0.2 %	S	6.3 %
B	1.5 %	K	0.8 %	T	9.1 %
C	2.8 %	L	4.0 %	U	2.8 %
D	4.3 %	M	2.4 %	V	1.0 %
E	12.7 %	N	6.7 %	W	2.3 %
F	2.2 %	O	7.5 %	X	0.1 %
G	2.0 %	P	1.9 %	Y	2.0 %
H	6.1 %	Q	0.1 %	Z	0.1 %
I	7.0 %	R	6.0 %		

QYYIUCVOCS RLYIRP IR RLFLQRYX JRIKLYV LHLRG ICL IW BXOYX
OF DOFFOCS WRID VXL YIDJUVLR FGFVLD OF QAFIEUVLEG HOVQE

▷ Solution on page 11

Exercise 3   Product of Vigenère Ciphers

A group $(G, \diamond)$ consists of a set G with a binary operation $\diamond$ on G satisfying the following four properties:

- **(Closure)** $a \diamond b \in G$ for all $a, b \in G$

- **(Associativity)** $a \diamond (b \diamond c) = (a \diamond b) \diamond c$ for all $a, b, c \in G$

- **(Neutral element)** there exists $e \in G$ such that $a \diamond e = e \diamond a = a$ for all $a \in G$

- **(Inverse element)** for any element $a \in G$ there exists $a^{-1} \in G$ such that $a \diamond a^{-1} = a^{-1} \diamond a = 1$

1 Let ℓ be a positive integer. Let $\mathcal{V}$ be the set of all Vigenère ciphers of key length ℓ. Denoting $\circ$ the composition of two functions, prove that $(\mathcal{V}, \circ)$ is a group.

2 What is the product cipher of two Vigenère ciphers with distinct key length?

▷ Solution on page 12

Exercise 4   ⋆One-Time Pad

The *One-Time Pad* (also known as the *Vernam Cipher* and often abbreviated as OTP) is defined as follows. A plaintext is considered as a random variable $X \in \{0, 1\}^n$, where n is some positive integer. It is encrypted with a uniformly distributed random key $K \in \{0, 1\}^n$, independent of X, using a bitwise XOR operation. The ciphertext is thus $Y = X \oplus K$.

1 Prove that the OTP provides perfect secrecy.

2 Show why the OTP is insecure if the key is used more than once.

3 Show that the OTP does not provide information-theoretic security if the key is not uniformly distributed in $\{0, 1\}^n$.

▷ Solution on page 13

Exercise 5   ⋆Latin Squares

Let n be a positive integer. A *Latin square* of order n is an $n \times n$ matrix $L = (\ell_{i,j})_{1 \le i,j \le n}$ with entries $\ell_{i,j} \in \{1, \ldots, n\}$, such that each element of the set $\{1, \ldots, n\}$ appears exactly once in each row and each column of L. A Latin square defines a cipher over the message space $\mathcal{X} = \{1, \ldots, n\}$ and the key space $\mathcal{K} = \{1, \ldots, n\}$, for which the encryption of a plaintext $x \in \mathcal{X}$ under a key $k \in \mathcal{K}$ is defined by $y = C_k(x) = \ell_{k,x}$.

1 Find a Latin square L of order 4. Using this matrix, encrypt the plaintext $x = 3$ with the key $k = 2$.

2 Prove that a Latin square defines a cipher which achieves perfect secrecy if the key is uniformly distributed, independent from the plaintext, and used only once.

▷ Solution on page 13

Exercise 6   Enigma

The Enigma machine is a symmetric electromechanical encryption device which was used by the German army during World War II. The secret key consists of the initial position of three rotors (each rotor has 26 different positions), and an electric connection which represents a permutation on $\{a, b, c, \ldots, z\}$ with 14 fixed points and 6 non-overlapping exchanges of two characters. For example,

$$[b \leftrightarrow t, e \leftrightarrow q, g \leftrightarrow z, h \leftrightarrow i, k \leftrightarrow p, m \leftrightarrow s]$$

lets $a, c, d, f, j, \ell, n, o, r, u, v, w, x, y$ unchanged, maps b to t and t to b, e to q and q to e, etc. A toy Enigma machine (limited to 6 letters) is represented in Figure 1.3.

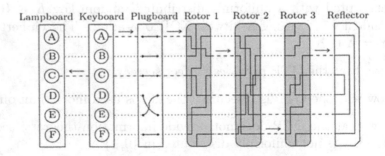

Figure 1.3.   An Enigma machine limited to 6 letters

1 How many different keys does the Enigma machine have?

2 What is the corresponding key length in terms of bits?

3 What is the average complexity of an exhaustive key search?

▷ Solution on page 14

Solutions

Solution 1   Mappings, etc.

1 The mapping f can be a function regardless of the cardinalities of $\mathcal{X}$ and $\mathcal{Y}$. The answer is *yes* in both cases.

2 Diagram (a) does not represent a function as x_1 is mapped on two different elements of $\mathcal{Y}$. Diagram (b) represents a function which is not defined on $\mathcal{X}$ but only on a subset of $\mathcal{X}$. Diagram (c) does represent a function (which is not injective by the way ...).

3 Diagram (a) does not represent an injective function as both x_1 and x_2 are mapped on y_1, i.e., $f(x_1) = f(x_2)$ with $x_1 \neq x_2$. Diagram (b) does represent an injection but Diagram (c) does not.

4 Diagrams (a) and (c) do not represent a surjective function. Diagram (b) is not a surjection as y_2 is not the image of any element of $\mathcal{X}$.

5 It is impossible to find a bijection between two sets of different cardinalities. The answer is *no* in both cases. Note that a usual way to prove that two given finite sets have the same cardinality is to explicitly construct a bijection from one onto the other. Also note that proving that a function is a bijection can be done by finding its inverse, i.e., finding a map $f^{-1} : \mathcal{Y} \to \mathcal{X}$ such that $(f^{-1} \circ f)(x) = x$ for all $x \in \mathcal{X}$.

6 First note that in a general case, if $\mathcal{A}$ and $\mathcal{B}$ are two finite sets such that $\mathcal{A} \subset \mathcal{B}$ and $|\mathcal{A}| = |\mathcal{B}|$, then $\mathcal{A} = \mathcal{B}$. Now, as f is injective, if $x_1, x_2 \in \mathcal{X}$ such that $x_1 \neq x_2$, we have $f(x_1) \neq f(x_2)$. If $n = |\mathcal{X}| = |\mathcal{Y}|$, taking the image of the elements of $\mathcal{X} = \{x_1, x_2, \ldots, x_n\}$, we obtain a list of n elements $\{f(x_1), f(x_2), \ldots, f(x_n)\} \subseteq \mathcal{Y}$. As f is injective, we know that these n elements are distinct. Therefore

$$\{f(x_1), f(x_2), \ldots, f(x_n)\} = \mathcal{Y}.$$

We have shown that every element of $\mathcal{Y}$ is the image of an element of $\mathcal{X}$ which makes f a surjective function. As f was also assumed to be injective, it is finally bijective.

7 A permutation does not always preserve the Hamming weight of a sequence. Here is a counterexample. Take

$$f: \quad \{0,1\}^\ell \quad \longrightarrow \quad \{0,1\}^\ell$$
$$x \quad \longmapsto \quad y = x \oplus k,$$

where k is the binary representation of 1, i.e., $k = \overbrace{0\ldots01}^{\ell \text{ bits}}$. This function is indeed a permutation. This should be clear from the fact that $f^{-1} = f$ (this is called an *involution*). We note that f maps the binary representation of 0 onto the binary representation of 1. As these two sequences do not have the same Hamming weight, we have found a counterexample. Finally, as a transposition is a particular permutation which simply rearranges the bits of an input string, it should be clear that a transposition preserves the Hamming weight.

8 Yes. Formally, we recall that a permutation P on $\{0,1\}^\ell$ is a bijection from $\{0,1\}^\ell$ to $\{0,1\}^\ell$. We also give the definition of a transposition thereafter, in a formal way. Let $T : \{0,1\}^\ell \rightarrow \{0,1\}^\ell$ be a permutation. We say that T is a transposition if and only if there exists a permutation σ on $\{1,2,3\ldots,\ell\}$ such that

$$T(a_1 a_2 \ldots a_\ell) = a_{\sigma(1)} a_{\sigma(2)} \ldots a_{\sigma(\ell)} \quad \forall a_1, a_2, \ldots a_\ell \in \{0,1\}.$$

Moreover, we notice that the number of transpositions on $\{0,1\}^\ell$ is equal to the number of all permutations on $\{1,2,3\ldots,\ell\}$, namely $\ell!$.

9 One desired property of a block cipher is to have the ability to decrypt what it can encrypt, and this should be done with no ambiguity. Therefore, for each $\mathbf{k}$ defining a permutation $\mathsf{DES_k}$, there should exist $\mathsf{DES_k^{-1}}$ such that $\mathsf{DES_k^{-1}}(\mathsf{DES_k}(\mathbf{x})) = \mathbf{x}$ for all $\mathbf{x} \in \{0,1\}^{64}$. This property can only be guaranteed if $\mathsf{DES_k}$ is a bijection for any key.

10 The number of permutations on a set of N elements is $N!$. Therefore, there are $2^{64}!$ permutations on $\mathcal{X} = \{0,1\}^{64}$. There are 2^{56} DES secret keys.

11 This transformation is a simple reordering of the input bits. It is a transposition. Strangely, it is always referred as *the* DES *permutation* on 32 bits.

12 The random variable C^* is uniformly distributed among a set of $2^\ell!$ elements (i.e., the permutations of $\{0,1\}^\ell$). Therefore

$$\Pr[C^* = c] = \frac{1}{2^\ell!}.$$

13 Using the chain formula, we can see that

$$\Pr[C^*(x) = y] = \sum_c \mathbf{1}_{c(x)=y} \Pr[C^* = c]$$

$$= \frac{1}{2^\ell!} \sum_c \mathbf{1}_{c(x)=y}.$$

Obviously, $\sum_c \mathbf{1}_{c(x)=y}$ is the number of permutations of $\{0,1\}^\ell$ having the property to map x onto y.

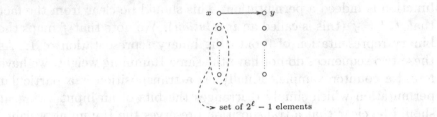

set of $2^\ell - 1$ elements

Noticing that this number is exactly the number of permutations of a set of $2^\ell - 1$ elements, that is $(2^\ell - 1)!$, we obtain

$$\Pr[\mathsf{C}^*(x) = y] = \frac{(2^\ell - 1)!}{2^\ell!}$$
$$= \frac{1}{2^\ell}$$
$$= \Pr[Y = y].$$

14 If $b = 0$, then it is easy to see that $\mathrm{DP}^{\mathsf{C}^*}(a,b) = 0$, and thus $\mathrm{E}_{\mathsf{C}^*}(\mathrm{DP}^{\mathsf{C}^*}(a,b)) = 0$. We now assume that $b \neq 0$. We have

$$\mathrm{E}_{\mathsf{C}^*}\left(\mathrm{DP}^{\mathsf{C}^*}(a,b)\right) = \mathrm{E}_{\mathsf{C}^*}\left(\Pr_X[\mathsf{C}^*(X \oplus a) = \mathsf{C}^*(X) \oplus b]\right)$$
$$= \sum_c \Pr_X[c(X \oplus a) = c(X) \oplus b]\Pr[\mathsf{C}^* = c]$$
$$= \sum_c \sum_x \mathbf{1}_{c(x \oplus a) = c(x) \oplus b}\Pr[X = x]\Pr[\mathsf{C}^* = c]$$
$$= \frac{1}{(2^\ell)!}\sum_x \Pr[X = x]\sum_c \mathbf{1}_{c(x \oplus a) = c(x) \oplus b},$$

as C^* is uniformly distributed. We denote $y = x \oplus a$. As $a \neq 0$, $y \neq x$. With this notation,

$$\sum_c \mathbf{1}_{c(x \oplus a) = c(x) \oplus b} = \sum_c \left(\sum_\alpha \mathbf{1}_{c(x) = \alpha}\right)\mathbf{1}_{c(y) = c(x) \oplus b}$$
$$= \sum_\alpha \left(\sum_{\substack{c \\ c(y) = \alpha \oplus b}} \mathbf{1}_{c(x) = \alpha}\right).$$

As $b \neq 0$, the inner sum is the number of permutations mapping x onto α and y onto $\alpha \oplus \beta$, which is $(2^\ell - 2)!$. Consequently,

$$\sum_c \mathbf{1}_{c(x \oplus a) = c(x) \oplus b} = 2^\ell(2^\ell - 2)! = \frac{(2^\ell)!}{2^\ell - 1}.$$

We conclude that

$$E_{C^*}(DP^{C^*}(a,b)) = \frac{1}{2^{\ell}-1}.$$

Solution 2 A Simple Substitution Cryptogram

The character distribution in the ciphertext is given in Table 1.2. Using this information and comparing it with the character frequency table, it is possible to isolate the most frequent characters in the ciphertext. If we consider the digrams and trigrams frequency mentioned in the textbook [56] and if we take advantage of the fact that there are not that many 2 letter and 3 letter words in English, we get (not without work!) the key represented on Table 1.3. The decrypted ciphertext [16] is

Table 1.2. Distribution of the characters in the ciphertext

Letter	Probability	Letter	Probability	Letter	Probability
A	0.63 %	J	1.27 %	S	3.16 %
B	0.95 %	K	0.63 %	T	0.00 %
C	6.65 %	L	9.81 %	U	3.80 %
D	3.16 %	M	0.32 %	V	6.33 %
E	3.80 %	N	0.00 %	W	3.16 %
F	7.28 %	O	7.28 %	X	3.48 %
G	3.80 %	P	1.90 %	Y	4.11 %
H	1.58 %	Q	7.91 %	Z	0.00 %
I	9.81 %	R	9.18 %		

is

```
IMAGINE IF YOU WILL ARRIVING AT YOUR JOB AS A MANAGER FOR
ONE OF NASAS LOCAL COMPUTER SYSTEMS YOU GET INTO YOUR
OFFICE ON THAT MONDAY MORNING TO FIND THE PHONES RINGING
EVERY CALLER IS A DISTRAUGHT CONFUSED NASA WORKER AND
EVERY CALLER ASSURES YOU THAT HIS OR HER FILE OR
ACCOUNTING RECORD OR RESEARCH PROJECT EVERY ONE OF WHICH
IS MISSING FROM THE COMPUTER SYSTEM IS ABSOLUTELY VITAL
```

or, in a more formatted manner:

> Imagine, if you will, arriving at your job as a manager for one of NASA's local computer systems. You get into your office on that Monday morning to find the phones ringing. Every caller is a distraught, confused NASA worker. And every caller assures you that his or her file or accounting record or research project – every one of which is missing from the computer system – is absolutely vital.

Table 1.3.   The key of the simple substitution

A → Q	G → S	M → D	S → F	Y → G
B → A	H → X	N → C	T → V	Z → Z
C → Y	I → O	O → I	U → U	
D → P	J → K	P → J	V → H	
E → L	K → M	Q → N	W → B	
F → W	L → E	R → R	X → T	

Solution 3   Product of Vigenère Ciphers

Let k and k' denote two keys of ℓ characters and let C_k and $C_{k'}$ denote their corresponding Vigenère ciphers. A Vigenère cipher encrypts a message x by adding character-wise a key modulo 26. If x is some plaintext of length d, then $y = C_k(x)$ where

$$y_i = x_i + k_{i \bmod \ell} \bmod 26$$

for all $i = 0, \ldots, d-1$.

1 In order to prove that $(\mathcal{V}, \circ)$ is a group, we have to check *four* properties:

- **(Closure)** We have to show that there exists some key k'' such that $C_{k''} = C_{k'} \circ C_k$. As the addition modulo 26 is an associative operation, if $y = (C_{k'} \circ C_k)(x) = C_{k'}(C_k(x))$ then

  $$y_i = x_i + (k_{i \bmod \ell} + k'_{i \bmod \ell} \bmod 26) \bmod 26$$

  for all $i = 0, \ldots, d-1$. Thus, if $k'' = k + k' \bmod 26$ (the modular addition being evaluated character-wise), $C_{k''} = C_{k'} \circ C_k$. This proves that encrypting twice with the Vigenère cipher is not more secure than a single encryption.

- **(Associativity)** The fact that $(C_k \circ C_{k'}) \circ C_{k''} = C_k \circ (C_{k'} \circ C_{k''})$ is a direct consequence of the associativity of the modular addition.

- **(Neutral element)** We have to show that there exists a key under which a Vigenère encryption is the identity function. It is easy to check that this is the case of the key $k_e = \mathtt{AA} \ldots \mathtt{A}$.

- **(Inverse element)** We have to show that to each key k corresponds a key k' such that $C_{k'} \circ C_k$ is the identity. This is the case when $k'_i = -k_i \bmod 26$ for all $i = 0, \ldots, \ell - 1$. Encrypting with the inverse is thus equivalent to decryption.

2 The product cipher of two Vigenère ciphers C_k and $C_{k'}$ having key length ℓ and ℓ' respectively is equivalent to a Vigenère cipher $C_{k''}$ with a key length $\ell'' = \mathrm{lcm}(\ell, \ell')$. Namely, ℓ'' must be a multiple of both ℓ, ℓ' and must be the smallest integer satisfying this property.

Solution 4   ⋆One-Time Pad

1 The OTP provides perfect secrecy if the plaintext and the ciphertext are independent, i.e., if $\Pr[X, Y] = \Pr[X] \cdot \Pr[Y]$. If n denotes the size of the key, we have

$$
\begin{aligned}
\Pr[X = x, Y = y] &= \Pr[X = x, K = x \oplus y] \\
&= \Pr[X = x] \cdot \Pr[K = x \oplus y] \\
&= \frac{\Pr[X = x]}{2^n},
\end{aligned}
$$

where the independence of X and K was used in the second equality. Moreover,

$$
\Pr[Y = y] = \sum_x \Pr[X = x] \cdot \Pr[K = x \oplus y] = \frac{1}{2^n}
$$

which concludes the proof.

2 Suppose we encrypt two messages x and x' with the same key k. If we add the two corresponding ciphertexts, we get $x \oplus k \oplus x' \oplus k = x \oplus x'$. If x and x' are ASCII texts written in a certain language (for instance), it is possible for an adversary to recover x and x' by exploiting their natural redundancy.

3 From information theory we know that $H(K) \leq n$, with equality if and only if K is uniformly distributed. Since perfect secrecy implies that $H(X) \leq H(K)$ (for any distribution of X), there is a contradiction if $H(K) < n$, as $H(X) \leq H(K)$ would not hold for a uniform distribution of X.

Solution 5   ⋆Latin Squares

1 An example of Latin square of order 4 is

$$
L = \begin{pmatrix} 1 & 4 & 3 & 2 \\ 4 & 2 & 1 & 3 \\ 2 & 3 & 4 & 1 \\ 3 & 1 & 2 & 4 \end{pmatrix}
$$

and $C_2(3) = \ell_{2,3} = 1$.

2 Let X be the random variable corresponding to the plaintext, Y be the random variable corresponding to the ciphertext, and K be the random variable corresponding to the key. We have

$$\Pr[X = x, Y = y] = \sum_{k=1}^{n} \Pr[X = x, Y = y \mid K = k] \Pr[K = k]$$

$$= \frac{1}{n} \sum_{k=1}^{n} \Pr[X = x, Y = y \mid K = k],$$

since the key is uniformly distributed. Moreover

$$\Pr[X = x, Y = y \mid K = k] = \mathbf{1}_{\ell_{k,x}=y} \Pr[X = x \mid K = k],$$

as for a given message x and key k there is only one corresponding ciphertext y. Finally, as X and K are independent,

$$\Pr[X = x, Y = y] = \frac{1}{n} \sum_{k=1}^{n} \mathbf{1}_{\ell_{k,x}=y} \Pr[X = x]$$

$$= \frac{\Pr[X = x]}{n} \sum_{k=1}^{n} \mathbf{1}_{\ell_{k,x}=y}$$

$$= \frac{\Pr[X = x]}{n},$$

because, as L is a Latin square, for any x and y there is one, and only one value k such that $\ell_{k,x} = y$. On the other hand

$$\Pr[Y = y] = \sum_{x=1}^{n} \Pr[Y = y, X = x]$$

$$= \frac{1}{n} \sum_{x=1}^{n} \Pr[X = x]$$

$$= \frac{1}{n}.$$

We conclude that $\Pr[X = x \mid Y = y] = \Pr[X = x]$ which concludes the proof.

Solution 6   Enigma

1 As each rotor allows 26 different positions, and as there are 3 rotors, the number of possible rotors starting positions is 26^3. For the

plugboard, we start by choosing the 14 fixed points. There are $\binom{26}{14}$ possibilities. We are left with 12 letters. We place them in a table:

$$[\cdot \leftrightarrow \cdot, \cdot \leftrightarrow \cdot, \cdot \leftrightarrow \cdot, \cdot \leftrightarrow \cdot, \cdot \leftrightarrow \cdot, \cdot \leftrightarrow \cdot]$$

There are 12! ways to place the letters. But among these possibilities, several are equivalent. We have to consider that *couples* of letter can be permuted (6! possibilities) and that among one couple, the two letters can be permuted (this gives 2^6 possibilities). Finally, there are

$$\frac{12!}{2^6 \cdot 6!}$$

ways to connect the 12 letters. In total there are

$$26^3 \cdot \binom{26}{14} \cdot \frac{12!}{2^6 \cdot 6!} = 1,764,486,127,404,000 \approx 1.76 \cdot 10^{15}$$

possibilities.

We now suggest an alternative to the previous solution. The three rotors allow $26^3 = 17,576$ different combinations. The plugboard allows

$$\frac{1}{6!} \cdot \binom{26}{2} \cdot \binom{24}{2} \cdot \binom{22}{2} \cdot \binom{20}{2} \cdot \binom{18}{2} \cdot \binom{16}{2} = 100,391,791,500$$

different possibilities. This makes a total number of different keys approximately equal to $1.76 \cdot 10^{15}$.

2 The key length in bits is equal to

$$\log_2\left(1.76 \cdot 10^{15}\right) \approx 50.65,$$

i.e., one can encode the key with 51 bits.

3 An exhaustive search on a 51-bit key requires 2^{50} attempts in average.

Simon Singh's *Code Book* [51] is a good reference on the history of the Enigma machine.

Chapter 2

CONVENTIONAL CRYPTOGRAPHY

Exercises

Exercise 1   Weak Keys of DES

We say that a DES key k is *weak* if DES_k is an involution. Exhibit four weak keys for DES.
Reminder: Let $\mathcal{S}$ be a finite set and let f be a bijection from $\mathcal{S}$ to $\mathcal{S}$. The function f is an *involution* if $f(f(x)) = x$ for all $x \in \mathcal{S}$.

▷ Solution on page 34

Exercise 2   Semi-Weak Keys of DES

We say that a DES key k is *semi-weak* if it is not weak and if there exists a key k' such that

$$\text{DES}_k^{-1} = \text{DES}_{k'}.$$

Exhibit four semi-weak keys for DES.

▷ Solution on page 34

Exercise 3   Complementation Property of DES

Given a bitstring x we let $\overline{x}$ denote the bitwise complement, i.e., the bitstring obtained by flipping all bits of x.

1 Prove that
$$\mathrm{DES}_{\overline{K}}(\overline{x}) = \overline{\mathrm{DES}_K(x)}$$
for any x and K.

2 Deduce a brute force attack against DES with average complexity of 2^{54} DES encryptions.

Hint: Assume that the adversary who is looking for K is given a plaintext block x and the two values corresponding to $\mathrm{DES}_K(x)$ and $\mathrm{DES}_K(\overline{x})$.

▷ Solution on page 35

Exercise 4   3DES Exhaustive Search

1 What is the average complexity of an exhaustive search against the two-key 3DES?

2 How can an adversary take advantage of the complementation property $\mathrm{DES}_{\overline{K}}(\overline{x}) = \overline{\mathrm{DES}_K(x)}$? What is the complexity now?

▷ Solution on page 36

Exercise 5   2DES and Two-Key 3DES

1 2DES encrypts a 64-bit message M in the following manner.

$$C = \mathrm{DES}_{K_1}(\mathrm{DES}_{K_2}(M)).$$

Here, K_1 and K_2 are bitstrings of 56 bits each.

(a) Give the average complexity of a "naive" exhaustive key search?

(b) We perform now a meet-in-the-middle attack. Give an approximate of the time and memory complexities.

2 Two-Key 3DES encrypts a 64-bit message M in the following manner.

$$C = \mathrm{DES}_{K_1}(\mathrm{DES}_{K_2}^{-1}(\mathrm{DES}_{K_1}(M))). \qquad (2.1)$$

Here, K_1 and K_2 are strings of 56 bits each.

(a) What is the average complexity of a "naive" exhaustive search?

(b) We are given a box that encrypts a message M according to (2.1). We may use the box to encrypt plaintexts of our choice. Denoting 0 the all-zero message, we first build a table containing the standard DES decryption of the message 0 under all 2^{56} keys. Then we use a chosen-plaintext attack to build a second table containing the 2^{56} ciphertexts resulting from box encryptions of the elements of the first table. Given these two tables, one can find both K_1 and K_2 used by the encryption box. Explain how one may proceed. The whole attack should take no more than 2^{60} DES encryptions (or decryptions) and no more than 2^{61} bytes of memory.

▷ Solution on page 37

Exercise 6 ⋆Exhaustive Search on 3DES

We consider 3DES with three independent keys. Let $P, C \in \{0,1\}^{64}$ be

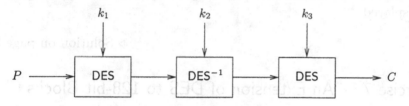

Figure 2.1. 3DES with three independent keys

a plaintext/ciphertext pair, where $C = 3\text{DES}_k(P)$ for some unknown key $k = (k_1, k_2, k_3)$ (see Figure 2.1). We want to recover k by an exhaustive search.

1 What is the number of DES encryptions/decryptions of Algorithm 1?

Algorithm 1 Exhaustive key search algorithm on 3DES

Input: a plaintext/ciphertext couple (P, C)
Output: key candidate(s) for $k = (k_1, k_2, k_3)$
Processing:
1: **for** each possible key $K = (K_1, K_2, K_3)$ **do**
2:    **if** $C = 3\text{DES}_K(P)$ **then**
3:       display $K = (K_1, K_2, K_3)$
4:    **end if**
5: **end for**

---

2 Let $C^* : \{0,1\}^{64} \to \{0,1\}^{64}$ denote a uniformly distributed random permutation. What is the probability that $C^*(P) = C$.

3 Assuming that $3DES_K$ roughly behaves like C^* when K is a uniformly distributed random key, estimate the number of wrong keys (i.e., different from k) displayed by Algorithm 1.

4 Assume that an adversary has t distinct plaintext/ciphertext pairs denoted (P_i, C_i) for $i = 1, \ldots, t$, all encrypted under the same (still unknown) key k (so that $C_i = 3DES_k(P_i)$). Write an algorithm similar to Algorithm 1 that reduces the number of wrong keys that are displayed (but which does at least display k). What is the total number of DES encryptions/decryptions of this algorithm?

5 Express the average number of wrong keys that are displayed by your algorithm in function of t (which is the number of available plaintext/ciphertext couples). Evaluate the necessary number of couples in order to be almost sure that *only* the good key $k = (k_1, k_2, k_3)$ is displayed.

▷ Solution on page 37

Exercise 7   An Extension of DES to 128-bit Blocks

DES is a 64-bit plaintext block cipher which uses a 56 bit key.

1 What is the complexity of exhaustive search against DES?

We can increase the security against exhaustive search in a triple mode by using two-key 3DES.

2 What is the complexity of exhaustive search against 3DES?

3 We now consider the CBC mode of operation. We want to mount a "collision attack". Show how a collision on encrypted blocks in CBC mode can leak some information on the plaintexts. What is the complexity of this attack when the block cipher used is DES? What is the complexity if we replace DES by 3DES? How can we protect ourselves against this attack?

We now try to transform DES into a block cipher with 128-bit plaintext blocks, that we denote ExtDES. We use a 112-bit key which is split into two DES keys K_1 and K_2. For this, we define the encryption of a 128-bit block x as follows:

- we split x into two 64-bit halves x_L and x_R such that $x = x_L \| x_R$
- we let $u_L = DES_{K_1}(x_L)$ and $u_R = DES_{K_1}(x_R)$

- we split $u_L \| u_R$ into four 32-bit quarters u_1, u_2, u_3, u_4 such that $u_L = u_1 \| u_2$ and $u_R = u_3 \| u_4$
- we let $v_L = \mathrm{DES}_{K_2}^{-1}(u_1 \| u_4)$ and $v_R = \mathrm{DES}_{K_2}^{-1}(u_3 \| u_2)$
- we split $v_L \| v_R$ into four 32-bit quarters v_1, v_2, v_3, v_4 such that $v_L = v_1 \| v_2$ and $v_R = v_3 \| v_4$
- we let $y_L = \mathrm{DES}_{K_1}(v_1 \| v_4)$ and $y_R = \mathrm{DES}_{K_1}(v_3 \| v_2)$
- we define $y = y_L \| y_R$ as the encryption $\mathrm{ExtDES}_{K_1 \| K_2}(x)$ of x

4 Draw a diagram of ExtDES.

5 Explain how this special mode is retro-compatible with 3DES: if an embedded system implements it, how can it simulate a 3DES device? Same question with DES: how is this special mode retro-compatible with DES?

6 Do you think that the new scheme is more secure than 3DES? Do you think that it is more secure than DES?

7 Let x and x' be two plaintexts, and let $y = \mathrm{ExtDES}_{K_1 \| K_2}(x)$ and $y' = \mathrm{ExtDES}_{K_1 \| K_2}(x')$ be the corresponding known ciphertexts. Explain how a smart choice of x and x' allows us to detect that we have $u_4 = u'_4$ and $v_4 = v'_4$ simultaneously (here u'_4 and v'_4 are the internal intermediate values for computing y').

8 Use the previous question to mount a chosen plaintext attack whose goal is to find a (x, x') pair with $u_4 = u'_4$ and $v_4 = v'_4$ simultaneously. What is the complexity of this attack?

9 Explain how to use this attack in order to reduce the security of ExtDES to the security of DES against exhaustive search? What can you say about the security of ExtDES now?

▷ Solution on page 40

Exercise 8   Attack Against the OFB Mode

Assume that someone sends encrypted messages by using DES in the OFB mode of operation with a secret (but fixed) IV value.

1 Show how to perform a known plaintext attack in order to decrypt transmitted messages.

2 Is it better with the CFB mode?

3 What about the CBC mode?

▷ Solution on page 42

Exercise 9   ⋆Linear Feedback Shift Registers

We consider the ring $\mathbf{Z}_2[X]$ of polynomials with coefficients in $\mathbf{Z}_2$ with the usual addition and multiplication. In the whole exercise, we consider an *irreducible* polynomial $P(X) \in \mathbf{Z}_2[X]$ of degree d. We define the finite field $\mathbf{K} = \mathbf{Z}_2[X]/(P(X))$ of the polynomials with a degree at most $(d-1)$ with coefficients in $\mathbf{Z}_2$, with the usual addition and with the multiplication between $a(X), b(X) \in \mathbf{Z}_2[X]$ defined by

$$a(X) * b(X) = a(X) \times b(X) \bmod P(X).$$

We build a sequence $s_0(X), s_1(X), \ldots$ in $\mathbf{K}$ defined by $s_0(X) = 1$ and $s_{t+1}(X) = X * s_t(X)$ for all $t \geq 0$. We have

$$s_t(X) = X^t \bmod P(X) \quad \text{for all } t \geq 0.$$

1 Compute the first eight elements of the sequence when $P(X) = X^3 + X + 1$. What is the period of the sequence?

2 To each element $q(X) = q_0 + \cdots + q_{d-1}X^{d-1}$ of $\mathbf{K}$ we assign an integer $\tilde{q}$ defined by
$$\tilde{q} = q_0 + q_1 \cdot 2 \cdots + q_{d-1} \cdot 2^{d-1}.$$
How is it possible to implement the computation of $\tilde{s}_{t+1}$ from $\tilde{s}_t$ with the usual instructions available in a microprocessor?

3 We define $c_{t,j}$ as being the coefficient of X^j in $s_t(X)$ and the $d \times d$ matrix M_t with elements in $\mathbf{Z}_2$ as

$$(M_t)_{i,j} = c_{i+t-1,j-1}$$

for $1 \leq i, j \leq d$ and $t \geq 0$.

- Show that there exists a relation $M_{t+1} = B \times M_t$ and compute the matrix B.

- Show that for a given $0 \leq j \leq d-1$, there exists an order-d linear recurrence relation for the sequence $c_{t+d,j}$ for all $t \geq 0$, i.e., from $c_{t,j}, c_{t+1,j}, \ldots, c_{t+d-1,j}$ one can linearly compute $c_{t+d,j}$.

- How is it possible to build an electronic circuit which computes the sequence defined in the first question with 1-bit registers and 1-bit adders?

4 What are the possible values of the period of the sequence $s_i(X)$ for $i \geq 0$? When is it maximal?

▷ Solution on page 42

Exercise 10   ⋆Attacks on Cascade Ciphers

In this exercise, we consider a block cipher of block length n and of key length ℓ. The encryption function of the block cipher is denoted E. If $P \in \{0,1\}^n$ denotes a plaintext and $k \in \{0,1\}^\ell$ is an encryption key, then $\mathsf{E}_k(P) = C \in \{0,1\}^n$ is the ciphertext obtained by encrypting P under the key k. We denote D the corresponding decryption function, such that $\mathsf{D}_k(\mathsf{E}_k(P)) = P$ for any plaintext $P \in \{0,1\}^n$ and any key $k \in \{0,1\}^\ell$. A *cascade cipher* is the concatenation of $L > 1$ identical block ciphers with *independent* keys, denoted $k_1, \ldots, k_L$. In this configuration, the output of block cipher i is the input of block cipher $i+1$. The plaintext is the input of the first block cipher and the ciphertext is the output of the last block cipher. For simplicity, we denote E_{k_i} and D_{k_i} by E_i and D_i respectively (see Figure 2.2).

1 What is the complexity (in terms of number of encryptions) of the exhaustive key search of Algorithm 2 on the block cipher? What is the complexity of a similar exhaustive key search on a cascade of L block ciphers? Give the name of an attack which reduces this complexity for the specific case where $L = 2$. Recall its complexity.

Algorithm 2 Exhaustive key search algorithm

Input: a plaintext/ciphertext pair (P, C) such that $C = \mathsf{E}_k(P)$
Output: key candidate(s) for k
Processing:
 1: **for** each possible key K **do**
 2:     **if** $C = \mathsf{E}_K(P)$ **then**
 3:         display K
 4:     **end if**
 5: **end for**

We now wonder how many (wrong) keys are displayed by Algorithm 2.

2 Let $\mathsf{C}^* : \{0,1\}^n \to \{0,1\}^n$ denote a uniformly distributed random permutation. Let x and y be some fixed elements of $\{0,1\}^n$. What is the probability that $\mathsf{C}^*(x) = y$? Let $K \in \{0,1\}^\ell$ be a random

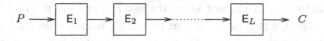

Figure 2.2. A cascade of L block ciphers

variable. Assuming that E_K roughly behaves like C^*, compute an estimation of the amount of wrong keys displayed by Algorithm 2. How many wrong keys are displayed for a similar algorithm on a cascade of L ciphers?

Assume that the adversary knows t plaintext/ciphertext pairs, all corresponding to the same key k.

3 Write an optimized algorithm, similar to Algorithm 2, which exploits these t pairs to reduce the number of wrong guesses. Estimate the number of wrong keys that are displayed.

4 If you replace the block cipher by a cascade of L block ciphers in your algorithm, what would be an estimation of the number of wrong keys which are displayed? Using your approximation, how should t be selected in order to be almost sure to have only one good key candidate after an exhaustive search on 3DES (with 3 independent keys)?

▷ Solution on page 44

Exercise 11   Attacks on Encryption Modes I

In this exercise, we consider a block cipher of block length n and of key length ℓ. The encryption function of the block cipher is denoted E. If $P \in \{0,1\}^n$ denotes a plaintext, and $k \in \{0,1\}^\ell$ is an encryption key, then $\mathsf{E}_k(P) = C \in \{0,1\}^n$ is the ciphertext obtained by encrypting P under the key k. We denote by D the corresponding decryption function, such that $\mathsf{D}_k(\mathsf{E}_k(P)) = P$ for any plaintext $P \in \{0,1\}^n$ and any key $k \in \{0,1\}^\ell$. Instead of using a simple cascade of block ciphers, we consider so called *multiple modes of operation*. The four modes of operation we will consider are ECB, CBC, OFB, and CFB (represented on Figure 2.3). Just as cascade of block ciphers consists in concatenating block ciphers, multiple modes of operation consist in concatenating modes of operations. For example, the notation CBC|CFB refers to the mode where the output of the CBC mode is the input of the CFB mode (see Figure 2.4).

Note that two independent keys are used here, one in the CBC mode, the other in the CFB mode. In this exercise, we assume that $n > \ell$ (i.e., that the block length is larger than the key length) and that *all the IV's are known to the adversary*. For simplicity, we denote E_{k_i} and D_{k_i} by E_i and D_i respectively.

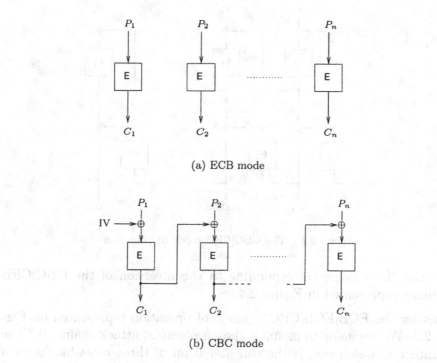

(a) ECB mode

(b) CBC mode

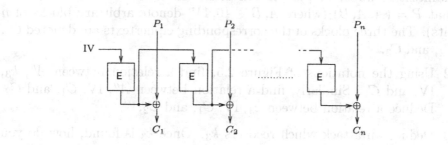

(c) OFB mode

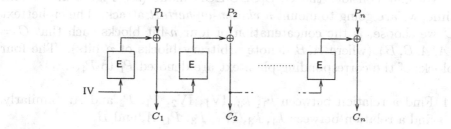

(d) CFB mode

Figure 2.3. Basic modes of operation

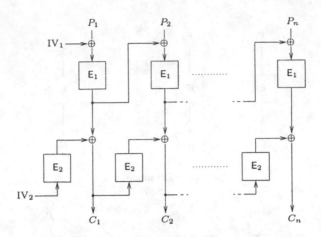

Figure 2.4. The CBC|CFB mode of operation

1 Draw the scheme corresponding to the inversion of the CBC|CFB mode represented in Figure 2.4.

Consider the ECB|ECB|CBC^{-1} mode of operation represented on Figure 2.5. We are going to mount a chosen *plaintext* attack against it. The plaintext P we choose, is the concatenation of three n-bit blocks such that $P = (A, A, B)$ (where $A, B \in \{0,1\}^n$ denote arbitrary blocks of n bits). The three blocks of the corresponding ciphertexts are denoted C_1, C_2, and C_3.

2 Using the notations of Figure 2.5, find a relation between A'', k_3, IV, and C_1. Similarly, find a relation between A'', IV, C_1, and C_2. Deduce a relation between k_3, IV, C_1, and C_2.

3 Deduce an attack which recovers k_3. Once k_3 is found, how do you recover k_1 and k_2? What is the complexity of the whole attack?

We now consider the OFB|CBC|ECB mode (see Figure 2.6). This time, we are going to mount a *chosen-ciphertext* attack. The ciphertext C we choose, is the concatenation of four n-bit blocks such that $C = (A, A, B, B)$ (where A, B denote arbitrary blocks of n bits). The four blocks of the corresponding plaintext are denoted P_1 to P_4.

4 Find a relation between k_1, k_3, IV$_1$, IV$_2$, P_1, P_2 and A. Similarly, find a relation between k_1, k_3, IV$_1$, P_3, P_4, A, and B.

5 Deduce a (smart) attack that recovers k_1 and k_3. Once this is done, how can k_2 be recovered? Compute the complexity of the attack.

▷ Solution on page 45

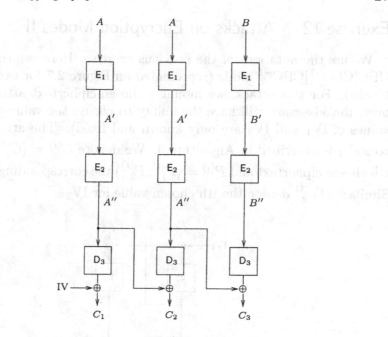

Figure 2.5. Attacking the ECB|ECB|CBC^{-1} mode of operation

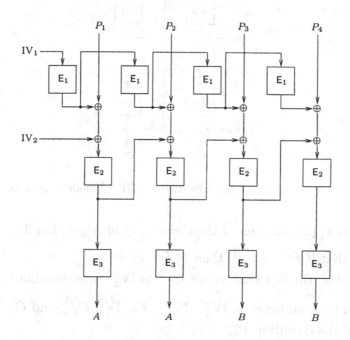

Figure 2.6. Attacking the OFB|CBC|ECB mode of operation

Exercise 12   Attacks on Encryption Modes II

We use the notations of the previous exercise. Here, we consider the $\text{CBC}|\text{CBC}^{-1}|\text{CBC}^{-1}$ mode (represented on Figure 2.7 for two plaintext blocks). For this attack, we mount a chosen-ciphertext attack. Moreover, the adversary will have the ability to *choose* the value of IV_2 (the values of IV_1 and IV_3 are only known and fixed). The attack we will consider is described in Algorithm 3. We denote $C^{(i)} = (C_1^{(i)}, C_2^{(i)})$ the ith chosen ciphertext and $P^{(i)} = (P_1^{(i)}, P_2^{(i)})$ the corresponding plaintext. Similarly, $\text{IV}_2^{(i)}$ denote the ith chosen value for IV_2.

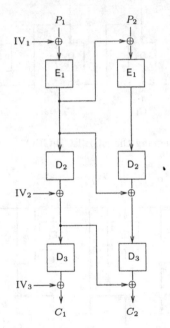

Figure 2.7. Attacking the $\text{CBC}|\text{CBC}^{-1}|\text{CBC}^{-1}$ mode of operation

1 Give an approximation of the complexity of Algorithm 3.

2 Show that if $P_1^{(i)} = P_1^{(j)}$, then $P_2^{(i)} = P_2^{(j)}$
  Hint: Use the fact that we set $C_2^{(i)}$ to $\text{IV}_2^{(i)}$ in Algorithm 3.

3 Find a relation between $\text{IV}_2^{(i)}$, $\text{IV}_2^{(j)}$, K_3, IV_3, $C_1^{(i)}$, and $C_1^{(j)}$ equivalent to the condition $P_1^{(i)} = P_1^{(j)}$.

4 Deduce an attack that recovers the value of K_3. Once K_3 is found, how can K_1 and K_2 be recovered? What is the overall complexity of the attack?

Algorithm 3 Looking for collisions in $\text{CBC}|\text{CBC}^{-1}|\text{CBC}^{-1}$

Output: $P^{(i)}$, $P^{(j)}$, $C^{(i)}$, and $C^{(j)}$, such that $P_1^{(i)} = P_1^{(j)}$
Processing:
  1: $i \leftarrow 1$
  2: **repeat**
  3:    Choose $C_1^{(i)}$ and $\text{IV}_2^{(i)}$ at random
  4:    $C_2^{(i)} \leftarrow \text{IV}_2^{(i)}$
  5:    Obtain and store $P_1^{(i)}$ and $P_2^{(i)}$
  6:    $i \leftarrow i + 1$
  7: **until** $P_1^{(i)} = P_1^{(j)}$ for some $j < i$
  8: Display $P^{(i)}$, $P^{(j)}$, $C^{(i)}$, and $C^{(j)}$

▷ Solution on page 47

Exercise 13   ⋆A Variant of A5/1 I

In stream ciphers, the prevailing encryption is a bitwise XOR operation between the m-bit plaintext and the m-bit keystream which is the output of a so-called keystream generator fed by the ℓ-bit secret key, where m is much larger than ℓ. An ideal assumption for good stream ciphers is that any ℓ-bit window of the m-bit keystream is eventually modified when the ℓ-bit key is modified. This exercise aims at doing a small test of the above assumption, taking as an example the A5/1 keystream generator. A5/1 consists of three Linear Feedback Shift Registers (LFSRs) denoted by R_1, R_2, and R_3, with respective length of 19, 22, and 23 bits. The total content of all three LFSRs is $19 + 22 + 23 = 64$ bits. Hereafter we call the 64-bit initial content (also called initial state) of the three LFSRs as the key of A5/1. We denote by $R_i[n]$ the content of the nth cell of R_i, for $i = 1, 2, 3$, where n starts at 0. Each LFSR has one clocking tap: $R_1[8]$, $R_2[10]$, and $R_3[10]$. At each clock cycle, one keystream bit is generated according to the following procedures (see Figure 2.8):

- The three LFSRs make a clocking vote according to the majority of the current three clocking taps.

- Each R_i compares the voting result with its own clocking tap. If they are equal, R_i is shifted:

    − a feedback bit is computed by XORing the content of the fixed subset of cells of R_i, i.e., the feedback for R_1, R_2, and R_3 is

$R_1[18] \oplus R_1[17] \oplus R_1[16] \oplus R_1[13]$, $R_2[21] \oplus R_2[20]$, and $R_3[22] \oplus R_3[21] \oplus R_3[20] \oplus R_3[7]$ respectively;

- the content of all cells in R_i (except the leftmost) are shifted to the left by one position simultaneously;

- $R_i[0]$ is updated by the precomputed feedback;

■ Output the bit $R_1[18] \oplus R_2[21] \oplus R_3[22]$.

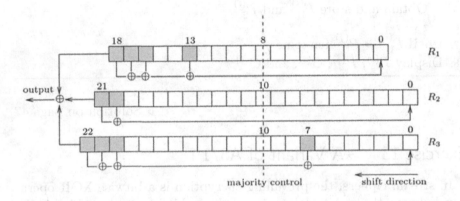

Figure 2.8.   A5/1 keystream generator

1 Show that when R_1 is loaded with a special initial state, then, regardless of its movement in the future, its state never changes. Is it possible to extend your solution to R_2 and R_3?

2 Use the previous answer to disprove the aforementioned assumption in the following special case of A5/1: show that the all-zero 64-bit keystream can be generated by different 64-bit keys.

3 Compute a tight lower bound on the number of different keys that generate such a keystream.

Let us now consider a variant of A5/1, by replacing the majority function with the minority function for the clocking vote, where the minority function of three binary bits a, b, c is defined by

$$\text{minority}(a, b, c) = \begin{cases} \overline{a} & \text{if } a = b = c \\ a \oplus b \oplus c & \text{otherwise.} \end{cases}$$

4 Similarly to Question 2, show that several keys will produce the all-zero 64-bit keystream for this variant.

5 Recompute Question 3 under the constraint that initially two clocking taps out of three are both one.

6 Check whether the assumption is true or false now for this variant of A5/1.

7 Compare the lower bounds obtained in questions 3 and 5, and briefly discuss the security strength of A5/1 and its variant.

▷ Solution on page 49

Exercise 14   ⋆A Variant of A5/1 II

We consider the A5/1 keystream generator described in Exercise 13 and shown on Figure 2.8. We assume that the three initial values of the LFSRs are chosen independently and uniformly at random.

1 For $i = 1, 2, 3$, what is the probability that R_i is shifted at the first clock? What is the probability that it is not shifted?

2 What is the probability that exactly two LFSRs are shifted at the first clock?

3 What is the probability mass function for the movement of three LFSRs at the first clock?

4 What is the conditional probability mass function of the first clocking given the initial clocking?

We define the minority function between three binary bits a, b, c by

$$\text{minority}(a, b, c) = \begin{cases} \overline{a} & \text{if } a = b = c \\ a \oplus b \oplus c & \text{otherwise.} \end{cases}$$

We consider a variant of A5/1 where we replace the majority function with the minority function for the clocking vote.

5 Recompute the previous questions for this variant of A5/1.

6 What conclusion can you draw about the security strength of using majority and minority function for the clocking vote?

▷ Solution on page 51

Exercise 15   ⋆Memoryless Exhaustive Search

A cryptanalyst would like to break a keyed cryptographic system. Assume he has access to an oracle which, for each queried key, answers whether it is the correct one or not. We use the following notations.

- The total number of possible keys is denoted N. The list of all possible keys is denoted $\{k_1, k_2, \ldots, k_N\}$.

- The random variable corresponding to the key known by the oracle is denoted K, i.e., the correct key known by the oracle is k_i ($i \in \{1, \ldots, N\}$) with probability $\Pr[K = k_i]$. Unless specified, K is *not* assumed to be uniformly distributed.

- The random variable corresponding to the key chosen by the cryptanalyst is denoted $\widetilde{K}$, i.e., the probability that the cryptanalyst sends k_i ($i \in \{1, \ldots, N\}$) to the oracle is $\Pr[\widetilde{K} = k_i]$.

The cryptanalyst iteratively queries the oracle with randomly selected keys, in an independent way, until he finds the right one. Note that, as the queries are independent, the complexity could in principle be infinite (we say that the algorithm is memoryless). The strategy of the cryptanalyst is to select a distribution for his queries.

1 Compute the expected complexity $\mathrm{E}[C]$ (in terms of oracle queries) in general, and when the key distribution is uniform (i.e., when K is uniformly distributed). How do you improve the attack?

2 If the *a priori* distribution of the keys is not uniform (but known by the adversary), what is the best memoryless algorithm for finding the key with the oracle? Prove that its complexity relates to the Rényi entropy of coefficient $\frac{1}{2}$ defined by

$$
H_{\frac{1}{2}}(K) = \left(\sum_{i=1}^{N} \sqrt{\Pr[K = k_i]} \right)^2 .
$$

Reminder: Lagrange multipliers can be used to find the extremum of a function

$$
f : \quad \begin{array}{ccc} \mathbf{R}^n & \longrightarrow & \mathbf{R} \\ (x_1, x_2, \ldots, x_n) & \longmapsto & f(x_1, x_2, \ldots, x_n), \end{array}
$$

subject to the $k < n$ constraints

$$
\begin{cases}
g_1(x_1, x_2, ..., x_n) &= 0, \\
g_2(x_1, x_2, ..., x_n) &= 0, \\
\quad \vdots \\
g_k(x_1, x_2, ..., x_n) &= 0,
\end{cases}
\tag{2.2}
$$

where $f, g_1, \ldots, g_k$ are functions with continuous first partial derivatives. Consider the function $\Phi : \mathbf{R}^n \to \mathbf{R}$ defined by

$$
\Phi(x_1, x_2, \ldots, x_n) = f(x_1, x_2, \ldots, x_n) + \sum_{i=1}^{k} \lambda_i g_i(x_1, x_2, \ldots, x_n).
$$

The λ_i's are the Lagrange multipliers. If a point $\mathbf{a} = (a_1, \ldots, a_n) \in \mathbf{R}^n$ is an extremum of f under the conditions (2.2), it must satisfy

$$
\begin{cases}
g_1(\mathbf{a}) = g_2(\mathbf{a}) = \cdots = g_k(\mathbf{a}) = 0, \\[2mm]
\dfrac{\partial \Phi}{\partial x_1}(\mathbf{a}) = \dfrac{\partial \Phi}{\partial x_2}(\mathbf{a}) = \cdots = \dfrac{\partial \Phi}{\partial x_n}(\mathbf{a}) = 0.
\end{cases}
\tag{2.3}
$$

Therefore, in order to find an extremum of f under the conditions given by (2.2), one should solve (2.3) with respect to the variables $a_1, a_2, \ldots, a_n, \lambda_1, \ldots, \lambda_k$.

▷ Solution on page 53

Solutions

Solution 1   Weak Keys of DES

If the subkeys k_1 to k_{16} are equal, then the reversed and original key schedules are identical. In that case, DES_k clearly is an involution. The sixteen subkeys will be equal when the registers C and D are all-zero or all-one bit vectors, as the rotation of such bitstrings has no effect on them. Therefore, the four weak keys of DES can easily be computed by applying $\mathrm{PC1}^{-1}$ to the four possible combinations of these C and D values. We have represented the weak keys of DES on Table 2.1, where $\{b\}^n$ denotes a sequence of n bits all equal to b. The existence of weak keys is known at least since the publication of [14].

Table 2.1.   Weak keys of DES

C	D	k
$\{0\}^{28}$	$\{0\}^{28}$	$\mathrm{PC1}^{-1}(\{0\}^{28}\|\{0\}^{28})$
$\{0\}^{28}$	$\{1\}^{28}$	$\mathrm{PC1}^{-1}(\{0\}^{28}\|\{1\}^{28})$
$\{1\}^{28}$	$\{0\}^{28}$	$\mathrm{PC1}^{-1}(\{1\}^{28}\|\{0\}^{28})$
$\{1\}^{28}$	$\{1\}^{28}$	$\mathrm{PC1}^{-1}(\{1\}^{28}\|\{1\}^{28})$

Solution 2   Semi-Weak Keys of DES

First, note that it is possible to generate a DES *decryption* schedule on-the-fly. After k_{16} is generated, the values of C and D are equal to the original ones, since they both have been submitted to a 28-bit rotation. Thus, provided that one exchanges the left rotations with right rotations and the amount of the *first* rotation to 0 (instead of 1), the same algorithm used to generate k_1 up to k_{16} can also generate the subkeys k_{16} down to k_1.

A pair of semi-weak keys occurs when the subkeys k_1 through k_{16} of the first key are respectively equal to the subkeys k'_{16} through k'_1 of the second one. This requires that the following system of equations is verified.

$$\begin{cases} \text{ROL}_{r_1}(C) & = \text{ROL}_{r_1+\cdots+r_{16}}(C') \\ \text{ROL}_{r_1+r_2}(C) & = \text{ROL}_{r_1+\cdots+r_{15}}(C') \\ \quad \vdots \\ \text{ROL}_{r_1+\cdots+r_{16}}(C) & = \text{ROL}_{r_1}(C') \end{cases}$$

Of course, a similar system should also hold between D and D'. Replacing the r_i's by their values, it is easy to see that the systems imply that $C = \text{ROL}_{2i+1}(C')$ and $D = \text{ROL}_{2i+1}(D')$ for any integer i. From this, we deduce the possible shapes of subkeys registers. They are represented on Table 2.2, where $\{b\}^n$ denotes a sequence of n bits all equal to b and where $\{b_1 b_2\}^n$ denotes a sequence of $2n$ bits having the following shape: $b_1 b_2 b_1 b_2 \cdots b_1 b_2$. The final semi-weak keys are obtained by applying PC1^{-1} on (C, D) and on (C', D'). The existence of semi-weak keys is known at least since the publication of [14].

Table 2.2. Semi-weak key pairs of DES

C	D	C'	D'
$\{01\}^{14}$	$\{01\}^{14}$	$\{10\}^{14}$	$\{10\}^{14}$
$\{01\}^{14}$	$\{10\}^{14}$	$\{10\}^{14}$	$\{01\}^{14}$
$\{01\}^{14}$	$\{0\}^{28}$	$\{10\}^{14}$	$\{0\}^{28}$
$\{01\}^{14}$	$\{1\}^{28}$	$\{10\}^{14}$	$\{1\}^{28}$
$\{0\}^{28}$	$\{01\}^{14}$	$\{0\}^{28}$	$\{10\}^{14}$
$\{1\}^{28}$	$\{01\}^{14}$	$\{1\}^{28}$	$\{10\}^{14}$

Solution 3 Complementation Property of DES

1 First note that $\bar{x} \oplus y = \overline{x \oplus y}$ and that $\bar{x} \oplus \bar{y} = x \oplus y$. The initial and final permutations (IP and IP^{-1}) do not have any influence on our computations, so we will not consider them. We can write one round of DES as

$$(C_L, C_R) \leftarrow (P_R, P_L \oplus F(P_R, K))$$

where P_L and P_R denote the left and right half of the plaintext, respectively, where C_L and C_R denote the left and right half of the ciphertext and where K denotes the key. From the definition of the key schedule algorithm, we see that if we take the bitwise complement of the key, then each subkey will turn into its bitwise complement as well. Furthermore, from DES F-function definition, we can see that if we complement its input and the subkey, then the input of the

S-boxes and thus the output will remain the same. We can thus write

$$(C_L, C_R) \leftarrow (\overline{P_R}, \overline{P_L} \oplus F(P_R, K)) = \overline{(P_R, P_L \oplus F(P_R, K))}$$

If we extend this to the whole Feistel scheme, then we can conclude that $\text{DES}_{\overline{K}}(\overline{x}) = \overline{\text{DES}_K(x)}$.

2 Algorithm 4 describes a brute force attack that exploits the complementation property of DES. Note that in this algorithm, $\overline{c}$ corresponds to $\overline{\text{DES}_k(x)} = \text{DES}_{\overline{k}}(\overline{x})$. Therefore, if the condition of line 6 is true, we almost surely have $K = \overline{k}$. In the loop, the only *heavy* computation is the computation of $\text{DES}_k(x)$, and we expect to perform 2^{54} such computations.

Algorithm 4 Brute force attack using the complementation property

Input: a plaintext x and two ciphertexts $\text{DES}_K(x)$ and $\text{DES}_K(\overline{x})$
Output: the key candidate for K
Processing:
1: **for all** non-tested key k **do**
2:     $c \leftarrow \text{DES}_k(x)$
3:     **if** $c = \text{DES}_K(x)$ **then**
4:         output k and stop.
5:     **end if**
6:     **if** $\overline{c} = \text{DES}_K(\overline{x})$ **then**
7:         output $\overline{k}$ and stop.
8:     **end if**
9: **end for**

The complementation property of DES is known at least since the publication of [14].

Solution 4   3DES Exhaustive Search

1 As the total length of the key is 112 bits, the average complexity of an exhaustive search against two-key 3DES is $\frac{1}{2} \cdot 2^{112} = 2^{111}$.

2 It is easy to see that the complementation property of DES can be extended to 3DES:

$$\begin{aligned}
3DES_{\overline{K_1},\overline{K_2}}(\overline{P}) &= DES_{\overline{K_1}}\left(DES_{\overline{K_2}}^{-1}\left(DES_{\overline{K_1}}(\overline{P})\right)\right) \\
&= DES_{\overline{K_1}}\left(DES_{\overline{K_2}}^{-1}\left(\overline{DES_{K_1}(P)}\right)\right) \\
&= DES_{\overline{K_1}}\left(\overline{DES_{K_2}^{-1}(DES_{K_1}(P))}\right) \\
&= \overline{3DES_{K_1,K_2}(P)}.
\end{aligned}$$

Using an algorithm very similar to Algorithm 4 (where we just replace DES_K by $3DES_{K_1,K_2}$), we can reduce the complexity by a factor 2. The average complexity becomes 2^{110}.

Solution 5   2DES and Two-Key 3DES

1 (a) A naive exhaustive search has a worst-case complexity of 2^{112} DES evaluations and an average complexity of 2^{111} DES evaluations.

(b) A meet-in-the-middle attack has a memory complexity of 2^{56} 64-bit blocks and a computational complexity of approximately $2 \cdot 2^{56}$ DES evaluations.

2 (a) A naive exhaustive search for a two-key 3DES has a worst-case complexity of $3 \cdot 2^{112}$ DES evaluations and an average complexity of $3 \cdot 2^{111}$ DES evaluations.

(b) The attack is given in Algorithm 5. It focuses on the case where the result after the first encryption stage is the all-zero vector, denoted by 0. Note that in the algorithm,

$$C_{K_1} = DES_{K_1}(DES_{K_2}^{-1}(0)),$$

and thus,

$$B_{K_1} = DES_{K_2}^{-1}(0) = P_{K_2}.$$

Consequently, the two keys k_1, k_2 found in line 10 in the algorithm (such that $B_{k_1} = P_{k_2}$) are indeed a candidate solution pair. The number of DES encryptions in Algorithm 5 is $2^{56} \cdot 5 < 2^{60}$. Both tables store 2^{56} entries of $56 + 64 = 120 < 2^7$ bits each. The memory requirements is thus $2 \cdot 2^{56} \cdot 2^7 \cdot 2^{-3} = 2^{61}$ bytes.

Solution 6   ⋆Exhaustive Search on 3DES

1 The algorithm successively tries each possible key. It does not stop until the last possible key is tried. Therefore, the number of iterations

---

Algorithm 5 Attacking two-key 3DES

Input: a box $3DES_{K_1,K_2}(\cdot)$ encrypting 64-bit plaintexts according to (2.1), under the keys K_1 and K_2

Output: K_1 and K_2

Processing:

1: **for all** $k \in \{0,1\}^{56}$ **do**
2:     $P_k \leftarrow DES_k^{-1}(0)$
3:     store (P_k, k) in a table T_1 (sorted according to P_k)
4:     $C_k \leftarrow 3DES_{K_1,K_2}(P_k)$
5:     $B_k \leftarrow DES_k^{-1}(C_k)$
6:     store (B_k, k) in a table T_2 (sorted according to B_k)
7: **end for**
8: sort the table T_1 according to the P_k's values
9: sort the table T_2 according to the B_k's values
10: Store the keys $k_1, k_2 \in \{0,1\}^{56}$ such that $B_{k_1} = P_{k_2}$ in another table T. This table contains candidate solution pairs $K_1 = k_1$ and $K_2 = k_2$.
11: If there are more than one candidate in T, test each key pair on a small number of plaintext/ciphertext pairs until only one remains. Display this solution.

---

is exactly equal to the number of possible keys times the number of DES encryptions for each (which is 3). Therefore, the number of DES encryptions/decryptions of the algorithm is $3 \cdot 2^{3 \cdot 56} = 3 \cdot 2^{168}$.

2 The random permutation C^* is uniformly distributed among all possible permutations, and there are $(2^{64})!$ of them. Consequently, if $c : \{0,1\}^{64} \rightarrow \{0,1\}^{64}$ is a given permutation, we have $\Pr[C^* = c] = \frac{1}{(2^{64})!}$ (see Exercise 1 in Chapter 1). Now, we are given two (fixed) values $P, C \in \{0,1\}^{64}$. We have

$$\Pr[C^*(P) = C] = \sum_c \mathbf{1}_{C^*(P)=C} \Pr[C^* = c]$$

$$= \frac{1}{(2^{64})!} \sum_c \mathbf{1}_{C^*(P)=C},$$

where the last sum simply is the number of permutations mapping P on C, which is the number of permutations of a set of cardinality $2^{64} - 1$. Finally,

$$\Pr[C^*(P) = C] = \frac{(2^{64} - 1)!}{(2^{64})!} = 2^{-64}.$$

3 We assume that $\Pr_K[3DES_K(P) = C] = \Pr_{C^*}[C^*(P) = C] = 2^{-64}$. Multiplying this probability by the number of tried keys, we obtain the number of keys that are displayed:

$$N = 2^{-64} \cdot 2^{168} = 2^{104}.$$

All the displayed keys (except one) are wrong keys!

4 We consider Algorithm 6. The algorithm clearly displays k as we do

---

Algorithm 6 Exhaustive key search algorithm on 3DES, using t plaintext/ciphertext pairs

---

Input: t plaintext/ciphertext pairs (P_i, C_i), for $i = 1, \ldots, t$, all encrypted under the same key k
Output: key candidate(s) for $k = (k_1, k_2, k_3)$
Processing:
1: **for** each possible key $K = (K_1, K_2, K_3)$ **do**
2:    **if** $C_i = 3DES_K(P_i)$ for $i = 1, \ldots, t$ **then**
3:       display $K = (K_1, K_2, K_3)$
4:    **end if**
5: **end for**

---

have $C_i = 3DES_k(P_i)$ for all $i = 1, \ldots, t$. It reduces the number of wrong keys that are displayed because it is clearly more difficult to find a wrong key $\tilde{k}$ satisfying $C_i = 3DES_{\tilde{k}}(P_i)$ for $i = 1, \ldots, t$ (with $t > 1$) than to find a wrong key such that $C = 3DES_{\tilde{k}}(P)$ (for only one pair). The total number of encryption/decryption steps that have to be performed is simply t times the number found in the first question (we assume that we always perform t times 3DES in the **if** statement of the algorithm). Therefore, this algorithm needs $3 \cdot 2^{168} \cdot t$ encryptions/decryptions.

5 Still assuming that $\Pr_K[3DES_K(P) = C] = \Pr_{C^*}[C^*(P) = C] = 2^{-64}$, the mean value N of wrong keys displayed by Algorithm 6 is

$$N = \text{number of tried keys} \times \prod_{i=1}^{t} \Pr_K[3DES_K(P_i) = C_i]$$

$$= 2^{168} \cdot (2^{-64})^t.$$

Table 2.3 gives the approximate number N of wrong keys that are displayed, in terms of the number t of available plaintext/ciphertext pairs. According to this table, only 3 pairs are necessary to make almost sure that only the good key will be displayed.

Table 2.3. Average value N of wrong keys that are displayed by Algorithm 6, in terms of the number t of plaintext/ciphertext pairs

t	1	2	3
N	2^{104}	2^{40}	2^{-24}

Solution 7   An Extension of DES to 128-bit Blocks

1 The exhaustive search complexity is 2^{56} in the worst case. It is 2^{55} in average and can be reduced by a factor of 2 by using the complementation property (see Exercise 3 in this chapter).

2 A key for 3DES consists of two keys for DES, so the key length is 112. The exhaustive search complexity is thus 2^{112} in the worst case for 3DES. It is 2^{111} in average and can be further reduced by a factor of 2 by using the complementation property (see Exercise 4 in Chapter 2).

3 In CBC mode of operation, the ith ciphertext block y_i is

$$y_i = \mathsf{DES}_K(y_{i-1} \oplus x_i), \quad \text{with } i \neq j,$$

where x_i is the ith plaintext block. If it happens that $y_i = y_j$ (which is a collision), we deduce that $y_{i-1} \oplus x_i = y_{j-1} \oplus x_j$ which leads to

$$y_{i-1} \oplus y_{j-1} = x_i \oplus x_j.$$

Hence, we can thus deduce some plaintext information from the value $y_{i-1} \oplus y_{j-1}$. The complexity corresponds to the expected number of blocks after which we can expect a collision (see Exercise 1, Chapter 3). According to the Birthday Paradox, we know that we need a number of blocks within the order of magnitude of the square root of the cardinality of the output domain, i.e., $\sqrt{2^{64}} = 2^{32}$. We note that the complexity of this attack is not increased by using 3DES instead of DES as the block size remains the same. In order to thwart this attack, we thus need to enlarge the block size.

4 See Figure 2.9.

5 With $x_L = x_R$, we obtain $y_L = y_R = \mathsf{3DES}_{K_1,K_2}(x_L)$. So a circuit which computes this new scheme can be used to compute 3DES.

Similarly, with $K_1 = K_2$, we obtain compatibility with DES.

6 The previous question leads to the intuition that this new scheme is at least as strong as DES and 3DES. It seems more secure than DES

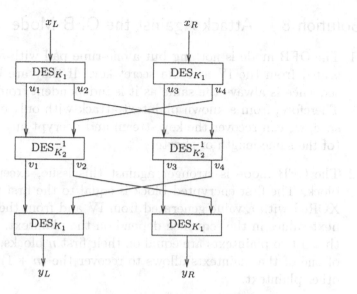

Figure 2.9. A 128 bit extention of DES

as the key size is increased and at least as secure as 3DES as the key size is the same. The advantage of this scheme is that it is protected against the collision attack in CBC mode.

7 If we choose x and x' such that $x_L = x'_L$, then

$$u_4 = u'_4 \text{ and } v_4 = v'_4 \quad \Leftrightarrow \quad y_L = y'_L.$$

8 We take an arbitrary (fixed) 64-bit string α. For many 64-bit strings β we encrypt $x = \alpha \| \beta$. With non-negligible probability, we will get a collision on the y_L's after a number of encryption within the order of magnitude of 2^{32}. We will thus get $x = \alpha \| \beta$ and $x' = \alpha \| \beta'$ such that $u_4 = u'_4$ and $v_4 = v'_4$. The complexity is within the order of magnitude of 2^{32}.

9 After the previous attack, the equation $u_4 = u'_4$ can be written as the equality between the 32 rightmost bits of $\mathsf{DES}_{K_1}(\beta)$ and $\mathsf{DES}_{K_1}(\beta')$. The equation $v_4 = v'_4$ can be written as the equality between the 32 rightmost bits of $\mathsf{DES}_{K_1}^{-1}(y_L)$ and $\mathsf{DES}_{K_1}^{-1}(y'_L)$. We can thus perform an exhaustive search in order to recover K_1, by testing both equalities. This attack requires 2^{56} operations. Note that with high probability, only the right key is raised. Once K_1 is found, 2^{56} additional operations are required in order to recover K_2.

We now see that this new scheme can be broken within about 2^{56} operations. Consequently, it is not more secure than DES and definitely less secure than 3DES.

Solution 8   Attack Against the OFB Mode

1 The OFB mode is nothing but a one-time pad with a sequence generated from the IV and the secret key. If they are both fixed, the sequence is always the same as it is independent from the plaintext. Therefore, from a known plaintext attack with only one known message, we can recover the key stream and decrypt any new ciphertext (of the same length or shorter).

2 The CFB mode is stronger against this issue, except for the first block. The first encrypted block is equal to the first plaintext block XORed with a value generated from IV and from the key only. The next values in the sequence depend on the plaintext. Similarly, note that if two plaintexts are equal on their first n blocks, the knowledge of one of the plaintexts allows to recover the $(n + 1)$th block of the other plaintext.

3 The CBC mode is not vulnerable to this kind of attack.

Solution 9   ⋆Linear Feedback Shift Registers

1 The first eight elements of the sequence are given in Table 2.4, from which it is clear that the period is equal to 7.

Table 2.4.   The first values of the simple LFSR sequence

i	$s_i(X)$	i	$s_i(X)$
0	1	4	$X^2 + X$
1	X	5	$X^2 + X + 1$
2	X^2	6	$X^2 + 1$
3	$X + 1$	7	1

2 We use a LSL (Logical Shift Left) instruction which shifts an integer one bit to the left. Furthermore, we suppose that we can test the bit in position d (the leftmost one being in the carry flag after a shift). If it is equal to 1, then one subtracts $P(X)$ in order to get the remainder. Note that subtracting $P(X)$ simply corresponds to XORing $P(X)$ as we work modulo 2 here.

3 We let $P(X) = P_0 + P_1 X + \cdots + P_{d-1} X^{d-1} + X^d$. Let $Q(X) = Q_0 + \cdots + Q_{d-1} X^{d-1}$ be a polynomial of **K**. It can be represented by a row

vector $\overline{Q} = (Q_0, \ldots, Q_{d-1}) \in \mathbf{Z}_2^d$. Consequently, the multiplication by X in $\mathbf{K}$ can be represented by a matrix multiplication. Indeed, if we denote by $R(X) = R_0 + \cdots + R_{d-1}X^{d-1} = X * Q(X)$, we have

$$R(X) = Q_{d-1} \cdot P_0 + (Q_0 \oplus Q_{d-1} \cdot P_1)X + \cdots + (Q_{d-2} \oplus Q_{d-1} \cdot P_{d-1})X^{d-1}$$

or equivalently

$$\overline{R} = (Q_{d-1} \cdot P_0, Q_0 \oplus Q_{d-1} \cdot P_1, \ldots, Q_{d-2} \oplus Q_{d-1} \cdot P_{d-1}).$$

From the previous equation, it is clear that the multiplication by X can be represented by

$$\overline{R} = \overline{Q} \times B \quad \text{where} \quad B = \begin{pmatrix} 0 & 1 & 0 & \cdots & 0 \\ 0 & 0 & 1 & \cdots & 0 \\ \vdots & \vdots & \vdots & \ddots & \vdots \\ 0 & 0 & 0 & \cdots & 1 \\ P_0 & P_1 & P_2 & \cdots & P_{d-1} \end{pmatrix}.$$

By definition of the sequence, we thus have $\overline{s}_{i+t} = \overline{s}_{i+t-1} \times B$ for all $i \geq 1$ and $t \geq 0$. Noting that the ith row of M_t corresponds to $\overline{s}_{i+t-1}$ and that the ith of M_{t+1} corresponds to $\overline{s}_{i+t}$, we deduce that

$$M_{t+1} = M_t \times B.$$

Noting that M_0 is the identity matrix, we can see that $M_t = B^t$ for all $t \geq 0$. Consequently M_t and B commute, so that $M_{t+1} = B \times M_t$. The linear recurrence is now given by

$$\begin{aligned} c_{t+d,j} &= (M_{t+1})_{d,j+1} \\ &= (B \times M_t)_{d,j+1} \\ &= P_0 \cdot c_{t,j} \oplus P_1 \cdot c_{t+1,j} \oplus \cdots \oplus P_{d-1} \cdot c_{t+d-1,j}. \end{aligned}$$

If we take the irreducible polynomial of degree 3 of the first question as an example, we obtain

$$c_{t+3,j} = c_{t,j} \oplus c_{t+1,j}$$

which can be computed by the circuit shown on Figure 2.10.

4 The natural subgroup $\mathbf{K}^*$ of the field $\mathbf{K}$ is of cardinality $(2^d - 1)$. The set $\{X^t \bmod P(X), \; t \geq 0\}$ being a subgroup of $\mathbf{K}^*$, its order must divide $(2^d - 1)$. Thus, the period of the sequence must be a divisor of $(2^d - 1)$. The period is maximal if X is a primitive element of $\mathbf{K}$, i.e., a generator of $\mathbf{K}^*$.

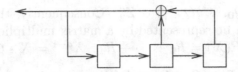

Figure 2.10. A circuit implementing the recurrence formula of the LFSR

Solution 10   ⋆Attacks on Cascade Ciphers

1 The time complexity is 2^ℓ. A cascade of L block ciphers can be viewed as a block cipher of key length $L \cdot \ell$ (as the L keys are independent), so that the time complexity would be $2^{L \cdot \ell}$.

When $L = 2$ the *meet-in-the-middle* attack reduces the time complexity from $2^{2\ell}$ down to $2 \cdot 2^\ell = 2^{\ell+1}$. In that case, the storage complexity is 2^ℓ.

2 As in Solution 6, we can prove that $\Pr[\mathsf{C}^*(x) = y] = 2^{-n}$. Assuming that E_K roughly behaves like a random permutation when K is randomly chosen among all possible wrong keys, we estimate $\Pr[\mathsf{E}_K(P) = C] \approx 2^{-n}$. Thus, the number of wrong keys displayed by the algorithm is approximately $2^\ell \cdot 2^{-n}$, that is $\mathcal{O}(2^{\ell-n})$. For a cascade cipher, a total of $\mathcal{O}(2^{L \cdot \ell - n})$ wrong keys are displayed.

3 Algorithm 7 exploits the t pairs at disposal. Considering that E_K

Algorithm 7 Exhaustive key search algorithm with t plaintext/ciphertext pairs

---

Input: t plaintext/ciphertext pairs (P_i, C_i), such that $C_i = \mathsf{E}_k(P_i)$, with $i = 1, \ldots, t$

Output: key candidate(s) for k

Processing:

1: **for** each possible key K **do**
2:     **if** $C_i = \mathsf{E}_K(P_i)$ for all $i = 1, \ldots, t$ **then**
3:         display K
4:     **end if**
5: **end for**

---

roughly behaves like a random permutation when K is chosen among all possible wrong keys, we obtain

$$\Pr[\mathsf{E}_K(P_i) = C_i \quad \text{for all } i = 1, \ldots, t] \approx \prod_{i=1}^{t} \Pr[\mathsf{E}_K(P_i) = C_i] \approx 2^{-tn} \ .$$

Table 2.5. Exhaustive key search on 3DES

t	1	2	3	4
Approx. number of wrong keys	$2 \cdot 10^{31}$	10^{12}	$6 \cdot 10^{-8}$	$3 \cdot 10^{-27}$

The number of wrong keys displayed by Algorithm 7 is thus $\mathcal{O}(2^{\ell-tn})$.

4 The number of wrong keys in this case is $\mathcal{O}(2^{L \cdot \ell - tn})$. For 3DES, $L = 3$, $\ell = 56$, and $n = 64$. The number of wrong keys displayed are given in Table 2.5 for different values of t. With 3 pairs, the adversary makes almost sure that only the good key is displayed.

More details about cascade ciphers and their security can be found in [29].

Solution 11   Attacks on Encryption Modes I

1 The inverse of the CBC|CFB mode is represented on Figure 2.11.

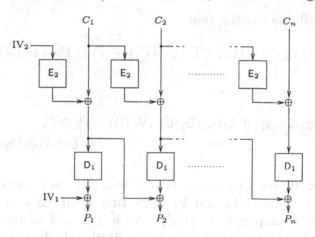

Figure 2.11. The inverse of the CBC|CFB mode

2 It can easily be checked that $D_3(A'') \oplus IV = C_1$ and that $IV \oplus C_1 = A'' \oplus C_2$, so that

$$D_3(IV \oplus C_1 \oplus C_2) = C_1 \oplus IV . \qquad (2.4)$$

3 Algorithm 8 recovers k_3 with a time complexity of $\mathcal{O}(2^\ell)$. As $n > \ell$,

---

Algorithm 8 Recovering k_3 in $\text{ECB}|\text{ECB}|\text{CBC}^{-1}$ mode

---

Input: the initial vector IV and two ciphertext blocks C_1 and C_2
Output: key candidate(s) for k_3
Processing:
1: **for** each possible key K_3 **do**
2:    **if** Equation (2.4) holds **then**
3:       display K_3
4:    **end if**
5: **end for**

---

it does not yield any wrong key (with high probability). Once k_3 is found, the adversary can peel the third layer off, and do a meet-in-the-middle attack on the last two layers. Note that we typically need both plaintext blocks A and B in order to eliminate wrong key candidates during the meet-in-the-middle. The complexity of this part of the attack is $\mathcal{O}(2^\ell)$ in time and $\mathcal{O}(2^\ell)$ in storage. The complexity of the whole attack is $\mathcal{O}(2^\ell)$ in time, $\mathcal{O}(2^\ell)$ in storage, and we need 3 chosen plaintext blocks.

4 It can easily be checked that

$$\text{IV}_2 \oplus \mathsf{E}_1(\text{IV}_1) \oplus \mathsf{E}_1(\mathsf{E}_1(\text{IV}_1)) \oplus P_1 \oplus P_2 = \mathsf{D}_3(A) \qquad (2.5)$$

and that

$$\mathsf{E}_1(\mathsf{E}_1(\mathsf{E}_1(\text{IV}_1))) \oplus \mathsf{E}_1(\mathsf{E}_1(\mathsf{E}_1(\mathsf{E}_1(\text{IV}_1)))) \oplus P_3 \oplus P_4 \\ = \mathsf{D}_3(A) \oplus \mathsf{D}_3(B). \quad (2.6)$$

5 Algorithm 9 uses a technique similar to a meet-in-the-middle attack in order to recover k_1 and k_3. The time complexity is $\mathcal{O}(2^\ell)$ and the storage complexity is $\mathcal{O}(2^\ell)$. As $n > \ell$ and as two equations have to hold before a key pair can be displayed, the algorithm does not yield any wrong key pair (with high probability). Once k_1 and k_3 are found, the adversary can peel off the first and third layers and perform a simple exhaustive search on k_2 in $\mathcal{O}(2^\ell)$. The overall complexity of the attack is $\mathcal{O}(2^\ell)$ in time, $\mathcal{O}(2^\ell)$ in storage, using four chosen ciphertext blocks.

A detailed study of cryptanalysis of multiple modes of operation can be found in [3, 4]. More recently, known-IV attacks against triple modes of operation were proposed in [20].

Algorithm 9 Recovering k_1 and k_3 in OFB|CBC|ECB mode with a meet-in-the-middle attack

Input: the initial vectors IV_1 and IV_2, the plaintext blocks P_1, P_2, P_3, and P_4, the two ciphertext blocks A and B

Output: key candidate(s) for k_1 and k_3

Processing:

1: **for** each possible key K_3 **do**
2:    insert $(D_3(A), D_3(A) \oplus D_3(B), K_3)$ in a table (keyed with the first entries)
3: **end for**
4: **for** each possible key K_1 **do**
5:    **if** equations (2.5) and (2.6) hold **then**
6:      display (K_1, K_3)
7:    **end if**
8: **end for**

Solution 12   Attacks on Encryption Modes II

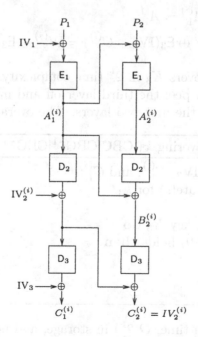

Figure 2.12. Collisions in CBC|CBC^{-1}|CBC^{-1} mode

1 The algorithm stops when a collision between two strings of n bits occurs. Therefore, its time complexity is $\mathcal{O}(2^{n/2})$.

2 We use the notations of Figure 2.12. We assume that $P_1^{(i)} = P_1^{(j)}$ for some $i \neq j$. As IV_1 is a constant, this implies that

$$A_1^{(i)} = A_1^{(j)}. \tag{2.7}$$

We also have

$$\begin{aligned}
B_2^{(i)} &= \mathsf{E}_3\left(C_2^{(i)} \oplus IV_2^{(i)} \oplus \mathsf{D}_2(A_1^{(i)})\right) \\
&= \mathsf{E}_3\left(\mathsf{D}_2(A_1^{(i)})\right) \qquad\qquad (\text{as } C_2^{(i)} = IV_2^{(i)})
\end{aligned}$$

so that $B_2^{(i)} = B_2^{(j)}$ because of (2.7). Thus, by using (2.7) again, we obtain

$$A_2^{(i)} = A_2^{(j)}. \tag{2.8}$$

From (2.7) and from (2.8) we conclude that

$$P_2^{(i)} = P_2^{(j)}.$$

3 As IV_1 is constant,

$$P_1^{(i)} = P_1^{(j)} \Leftrightarrow A_1^{(i)} = A_1^{(j)}$$
$$\Leftrightarrow IV_2^{(i)} \oplus \mathsf{E}_3(IV_3 \oplus C_1^{(i)}) = IV_2^{(j)} \oplus \mathsf{E}_3(IV_3 \oplus C_1^{(j)}). \tag{2.9}$$

4 Algorithm 10 recovers K_3 in 2^k time complexity. Once K_3 is found, the adversary can peel the third layer off and mount a meet-in-the-middle attack on the first two layers. The overall complexity of the

---

Algorithm 10 Recovering k_3 CBC$|$CBC$^{-1}|$CBC^{-1} mode

Input: $IV_2^{(i)}$, $IV_2^{(j)}$, IV_3, $C_1^{(i)}$, and $C_1^{(j)}$
Output: key candidate(s) for k_3
Processing:
1: **for** each possible key K_3 **do**
2:     **if** Equation (2.9) holds **then**
3:         display K_3
4:     **end if**
5: **end for**

---

attack is $\mathcal{O}(2^k)$ in time, $\mathcal{O}(2^k)$ in storage, and needs $\mathcal{O}(2^{n/2})$ chosen ciphertexts.

A detailed study of cryptanalysis of multiple modes of operation can be found in [3, 4]. More recently known-IV attacks against triple modes of operation were proposed in [20].

Solution 13   ⋆A Variant of A5/1 I

1 When R_1 is loaded with all zeros, no matter which subset of cells is chosen to compute the feedback, the feedback is always zero, hence, the next state of all zeros does not change. Of course, this also applies to R_2 and R_3.

2 When two LFSRs out of three are initialized by all zeros, we can view A5/1 equivalently as consisting of the remaining single LFSR, which outputs the leftmost bit at each clock pulse and is shifted if and only if its clocking tap is zero. Note that the clocking tap of a non-zero LFSR cannot always be zero. Thus, after a limited number of clock pulses, the clocking tap of the equivalent LFSR would be equal to 1 so that the LFSR will stop forever and output the same bit. So, as long as the non-zero LFSR outputs zero before (and when) its clocking tap turns to 1, A5/1 generates the all-zero keystream (including the special case of three all-zero LFSRs initially).

3 We consider the following four different cases:

- For $R_1 = R_2 = R_3 = 0$: There is only one (trivial) possibility.

- For $R_1 \neq 0$ and $R_2 = R_3 = 0$: If $R_1[8] = 1$, R_1 is never shifted. In that case, it is sufficient to also have $R_1[18] = 0$ to obtain a keystream with only zeros. This leaves $2^{19-2} = 2^{17}$ different initialization states. We can also consider the case where $R_1[8] = 0$ and $R_1[7] = 1$, so that R_1 will be shifted exactly once. Here, it is sufficient to have $R_1[18] = R_1[17] = 0$ to obtain a keystream with only zeros. This leaves $2^{19-4} = 2^{15}$ different initialization states. Following the same reasoning, we deduce the following lower bound on the number of possible initializations states in this case:

$$2^{17} + 2^{15} + 2^{13} + 2^{11} + 2^9 + 2^7 + 2^5 + 2^3 + 2 = \frac{2^{19} - 2}{3}.$$

- For $R_2 \neq 0$ and $R_1 = R_3 = 0$: We similarly obtain a lower bound equal to

$$2^{20} + 2^{18} + \cdots + 2^0 = \frac{2^{22} - 1}{3}.$$

- For $R_3 \neq 0$ and $R_1 = R_2 = 0$: We similarly obtain a lower bound equal to

$$2^{21} + 2^{19} + \cdots + 2^1 = \frac{2^{23} - 2}{3}.$$

Summing these values, we conclude that there are at least 2^{22} such initialization states.

4 When the initial clocking taps of the three LFSRs are all equal, none of the three LFSRs will ever be shifted. Hence, provided that the XOR of the three LFSRs output bits is zero at some time, we will obtain the all-zero keystream.

Alternatively, when one LFSR out of three is all-zero initially and the initial clocking taps of the other two LFSRs are both one, then only the all-zero LFSR is shifted (without changing its state however). It is actually shifted forever, while the remaining two LFSRs would stop forever. So, as long as the leftmost bits of two non-zero LFSRs are equal and the clocking taps are both one, the variant A5/1 generates the all-zero keystream.

5 We consider the following four different cases:

- Case where the three LFSRs all stop forever: we have $2^{64-2-1} = 2^{61}$ different initial states that satisfy two linear relations: one clocking constraint and one output constraint.

- For $R_1 = 0$: In this case, if $R_2[10] = R_3[10] = 1$ and $R_2[21] = R_3[22]$ we know that we obtain the all-zero keystream. There are $2^{22+23-3} = 2^{42}$ different initial states that satisfy these constraints.

- For $R_2 = 0$: Similarly, we find $2^{19+23-3} = 2^{39}$ different initial states that produce the all-zero keystream.

- For $R_3 = 0$: Similarly, we find $2^{19+22-3} = 2^{38}$ different initial states that produce the all-zero keystream.

Summing up these values, we obtain a lower bound between 2^{62} and 2^{63} on the number of possible initial states that produce the all-zero keystream.

6 Obviously, the assumption does not hold for this variant of A5/1.

7 A keystream generator should avoid generating the same keystream under several keys. These kind of keys are called *"weak* keys". Although we only computed lower bounds on the number of weak keys for both A5/1 and its variant, the huge difference between the two bounds (2^{22} for the real A5/1 against 2^{62} for its variant) suggests that the variant is much weaker.

Solution 14 ⋆A Variant of A5/1 II

1 Let T_i denote the value of the clocking tap of R_i just before it is clocked, for $i = 1, 2, 3$. We denote by $\mathrm{P}_i^{\text{shifted}}$ the probability that R_i is shifted at the next clock, and $\mathrm{P}_i^{\text{fixed}}$ the probability that it is not. By symmetry, it is sufficient to compute this probability for R_1. As R_1 is *not* shifted if and only if $T_1 \neq T_2 = T_3$, we have

$$\mathrm{P}_1^{\text{fixed}} = \frac{1}{2^3} \sum_{T_1, T_2, T_3} 1_{T_1 \neq T_2 = T_3} = \frac{1}{4}.$$

So that the probability that it is shifted is $\mathrm{P}_1^{\text{shifted}} = 1 - \mathrm{P}_1^{\text{fixed}} = \frac{3}{4}$. By symmetry, we obtain the same probabilities for R_2 and R_3, i.e.,

$$\mathrm{P}_i^{\text{shifted}} = \frac{3}{4} \quad \text{and} \quad \mathrm{P}_i^{\text{fixed}} = \frac{1}{4} \quad \text{for } i = 1, 2, 3.$$

2 Clearly, either 2 or 3 LFSRs are shifted at each clock. In other words, when one LFSR is fixed, the two others are shifted. The probability that exactly two LFSRs are shifted is thus equal to the probability that exactly one is fixed. This probability is simply equal to $P_1^{\text{fixed}} + P_2^{\text{fixed}} + P_3^{\text{fixed}} = \frac{3}{4}$ as the three events are disjoint.

3 We denote by $c^t \in \{0, 1, 2, 3\}$ the way the LFSRs are shifted at time t. More precisely, we denote by $c^t = 0$ the case where all three LFSRs are shifted, and by $c^t = i$ the case where R_i is fixed (the two others being necessarily shifted). From the previous questions, we immediately obtain

$$\Pr[c^0 = i] = \frac{1}{4} \quad \text{for } i = 0, 1, 2, 3.$$

4 If all LFSRs are shifted at time 0, we know that all three taps had the same value. But as we assumed that the cells of the LFSRs were drawn independently, this tells us nothing about c^1, and thus

$$\Pr[c^1 = c | c^0 = 0] = \Pr[c^1 = c] = \frac{1}{4}, \quad \text{for all } c \in \{0, 1, 2, 3\}.$$

When $c^0 \neq 0$, exactly two LFSRs are shifted. As the two new values of the clocking taps are uniformly distributed and independent random values, then we have no information whatsoever about the next majority value and hence, neither about c^1. Therefore,

$$\Pr[c^1 = c | c^0 \neq 0] = \Pr[c^1 = c] = \frac{1}{4}, \quad \text{for all } c \in \{0, 1, 2, 3\}.$$

We conclude that, for all $c, c' \in \{0, 1, 2, 3\}$,

$$\Pr[c^1 = c | c^0 = c'] = \frac{1}{4},$$

which corresponds to a uniform distribution.

5 We consider the variant of A5/1. We first note that in this case, either exactly one LFSR is clocked (when its clocking tap is different from the two others) or no LFSR is clocked at all (when all three clocking taps are equal). Using the notations of Question 1, we have

$$\mathrm{P}_1^{\text{fixed}} = \Pr[T_2 \neq T_3] + \Pr[T_1 = T_2 = T_3] = \frac{1}{2} + \frac{1}{4} = \frac{3}{4}.$$

Consequently, by symmetry,

$$\mathrm{P}_i^{\text{fixed}} = \frac{3}{4} \quad \text{and}$$

$$\mathrm{P}_i^{\text{shifted}} = 1 - \mathrm{P}_i^{\text{fixed}} = \frac{1}{4} \quad \text{for all } i = 1, 2, 3.$$

The probability that all three LFSRs stay still during next clock is $\Pr[T_1 = T_2 = T_3] = \frac{1}{4}$, and the probability that exactly one LFSR is shifted is $P_1^{\text{shifted}} + P_2^{\text{shifted}} + P_3^{\text{shifted}} = \frac{3}{4}$.

We denote $c^t \in \{0, 1, 2, 3\}$ the way the LFSRs are shifted at time t. This time, we denote by $c^t = 0$ the case where all three LFSRs stay still at time t, and by $c^t = i$ the case where R_i is clocked (the remaining two LFSRs staying necessarily still). We verify that $\Pr[c^0 = 0] = \frac{1}{4}$ and that $\Pr[c^0 = i] = P_i^{\text{shifted}} = \frac{1}{4}$. Therefore, the distribution of c^0 is uniform.

Obviously, if no LFSR is shifted at time t, no LFSR will ever be shifted. Therefore $\Pr[c^1 = 0 | c^0 = 0] = 1$ and $\Pr[c^1 \neq 0 | c^0 = 0] = 0$. Moreover, if two taps have the same value at time t, the corresponding LFSRs will never be clocked (as they will never be in a minority). Therefore, letting $c \neq 0$, $\Pr[c^1 \notin \{0, c\} | c^0 = c] = 0$ and, by independence of the LFSRs cells,

$$\Pr[c^1 = c | c^0 = c] = \Pr[c^1 = 0 | c^0 = c] = \frac{1}{2}.$$

6 For the majority control, the conditional mass function is identical to the mass function, which means the next clocking and the current clocking are independent. We notice that this is definitely not the case for the minority control. In terms of entropy, we can see that

$H(c^1|c^0) = \frac{3}{4}$ (resp. 2), and $H(c^0) = 2$ (resp. 2) under minority (resp. majority) control. In other words, in the case of minority control, if we try to recover the initial state of the LFSRs by guessing the clocking sequence, then after guessing two bits for the first clocking, we only need to guess 3/4 bit every clock afterwards on average. In the case of majority control, the knowledge of the previous clocking tells us nothing about the next one. We conclude that the majority control (the actual one used in A5/1) is a better choice from the security point of view.

Solution 15 ★Memoryless Exhaustive Search

1 We first compute the expected complexity E[C] in the general case, i.e., without making any assumption about the distribution of K. As the queries are independent, the worst case complexity is infinite (e.g., the case where the algorithm always tries the same wrong key). We have by definition

$$E[C] = \sum_{c=1}^{+\infty} c \Pr[C = c]. \tag{2.10}$$

Using the Total Probability Theorem, we have

$$\Pr[C = c] = \sum_{i=1}^{N} \Pr[C = c \mid K = k_i] \Pr[K = k_i]. \tag{2.11}$$

We can easily compute $\Pr[C = c \mid K = k_i]$ as it is the probability that the cryptanalyst chooses the right key after $(c-1)$ wrong guesses

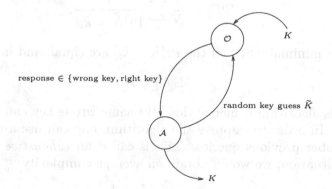

Figure 2.13. Adversary modeling a memoryless exhaustive search

(this is a geometrical distribution)

$$\Pr[C = c \mid K = k_i] = \left(1 - \Pr[\widetilde{K} = k_i]\right)^{c-1} \Pr[\widetilde{K} = k_i], \qquad (2.12)$$

where $\widetilde{K}$ denotes the key chosen by the cryptanalyst. From (2.10), (2.11), and (2.12) we deduce

$$
\begin{aligned}
\mathrm{E}[C] &= \sum_{c=1}^{+\infty} c \sum_{i=1}^{N} \left(1 - \Pr[\widetilde{K} = k_i]\right)^{c-1} \Pr[\widetilde{K} = k_i] \Pr[K = k_i] \\
&= \sum_{i=1}^{N} \Pr[\widetilde{K} = k_i] \Pr[K = k_i] \underbrace{\sum_{c=1}^{+\infty} c \left(1 - \Pr[\widetilde{K} = k_i]\right)^{c-1}}_{=\Pr[\widetilde{K}=k_i]^{-2} \text{ as shown below}} \\
&= \sum_{i=1}^{N} \frac{\Pr[K = k_i]}{\Pr[\widetilde{K} = k_i]}.
\end{aligned}
$$

Note that we needed a classical result, namely that we have

$$\sum_{c=1}^{+\infty} c x^{c-1} = \frac{d}{dx}\left(\sum_{c=0}^{+\infty} x^c\right) = \frac{d}{dx}\frac{1}{1-x} = \frac{1}{(1-x)^2},$$

when x is a real value such that $|x| < 1$. In the particular case where the key distribution is uniform, we have

$$\Pr[K = k_i] = \frac{1}{N} \quad \text{for all } i \in \{1, \ldots, N\},$$

so that

$$\mathrm{E}[C] = \frac{1}{N} \sum_{i=1}^{N} \frac{1}{\Pr[\widetilde{K} = k_i]}.$$

This is minimal when all the $\Pr[\widetilde{K} = k_i]$ are equal, and in this case

$$\mathrm{E}[C] = N.$$

As this algorithm is memoryless, the same wrong key can be queried twice. In order to improve the algorithm, one can use a memory to remember previous queries. This is called an *exhaustive search*. In that situation, we would obtain an average complexity

$$\mathrm{E}[C] = \frac{N-1}{2}.$$

2 We go back to the general case where K does not necessarily follow the uniform distribution. The cryptanalyst wants to minimize

$$E[C] = \sum_{i=1}^{N} \frac{\Pr[K = k_i]}{\Pr[\widetilde{K} = k_i]}.$$

We set $p_i = \Pr[K = k_i]$ (which are considered to be a fixed values, as they cannot be chosen by the cryptanalyst, but are only known to him) and $Q_i = \Pr[\widetilde{K} = k_i]$ (which are N real variables). The Q_i's can be chosen by the adversary, but still have to sum to 1 (as they correspond to a probability distribution). Therefore, we must compute

$$\begin{cases} \min_{\{Q_1,\ldots,Q_N\}} E[C] = \sum_{i=1}^{N} \frac{p_i}{Q_i} \\ \text{s.t.} \quad \sum_{i=1}^{N} Q_i = 1. \end{cases}$$

In order to compute this, we use the theory of the Lagrange Multipliers. Let Φ be defined by

$$\Phi(Q_1, Q_2, \ldots, Q_N) = \sum_{i=1}^{N} \frac{p_i}{Q_i} + \lambda \left(\sum_{i=1}^{N} Q_i - 1 \right),$$

where λ is the Lagrange multiplier. If $(q_1, \ldots, q_N)$ is an extremum, it must satisfy

$$\begin{cases} \sum_{i=1}^{N} q_i = 1 \\ \\ \dfrac{\partial \Phi}{\partial Q_j}(q_1, \ldots, q_N) = 0 \quad \text{for all } j \in \{1, \ldots, N\}, \end{cases} \tag{2.13}$$

that is

$$(2.13) \quad \Leftrightarrow \quad \begin{cases} \displaystyle\sum_{i=1}^{N} q_i = 1 \\[2mm] \lambda = \dfrac{p_j}{q_j^2} \quad \text{for all} \quad j \in \{1, \ldots, N\} \end{cases}$$

$$\Leftrightarrow \quad \begin{cases} \displaystyle\sum_{i=1}^{N} q_i = 1 \\[2mm] q_j = q_d \sqrt{\dfrac{p_j}{p_d}} \quad \text{for all} \quad d, j \in \{1, \ldots, N\} \end{cases}$$

so we obtain, for all $d \in \{1, \ldots, N\}$,

$$q_d = \frac{1}{\sum_{j=1}^{N} \sqrt{p_j/p_d}} = \sqrt{\frac{p_d}{H_{\frac{1}{2}}(K)}}. \qquad (2.14)$$

The best strategy for the cryptanalyst is therefore to draw the queries according to the distribution defined by (2.14). In that case, the average complexity is

$$\begin{aligned} \mathrm{E}[C] &= \sum_{i=1}^{N} p_i \sqrt{\frac{H_{\frac{1}{2}}(K)}{p_i}} \\ &= H_{\frac{1}{2}}(K). \end{aligned}$$

Chapter 3

DEDICATED CONVENTIONAL CRYPTOGRAPHIC PRIMITIVES

Exercises

Exercise 1   Collisions in CBC Mode

We consider the encryption of an n-block message $x = x_1 \| \cdots \| x_n$ by a block cipher E in CBC mode. We denote by $y = y_1 \| \cdots \| y_n$ the n-block ciphertext produced by the CBC encryption mode.

1 Show that one can extract information about the plaintext if we get a collision, i.e., if $y_i = y_j$ with $i \neq j$.

2 What is the probability of getting a collision when the block size of E is 64 bits?

3 For which n does this attack become useful?

▷ Solution on page 66

Exercise 2   Collisions

We iteratively pick random elements in $\{1, 2, \ldots, n\}$ in an independent and uniformly distributed way until we obtain a collision. Denoting T the random variable corresponding to the number of trials, show that

$$\mathrm{E}(T) \underset{n \to +\infty}{\sim} \sqrt{\frac{n\pi}{2}}.$$

Hint: Letting

$$\Psi_n = \sum_{k=0}^{n} \frac{n^k}{k!},$$

it can be shown that $\Psi_n e^{-n} \xrightarrow[n \to \infty]{} \frac{1}{2}$.

▷ Solution on page 66

Exercise 3   Expected Number of Collisions

We let $F : \{1, 2, \ldots, m\} \to \{1, 2, \ldots, n\}$ be a uniformly distributed random function.

1 Let N_2 be the number of pairs $\{i, j\}$ such that $i \neq j$ and $F(i) = F(j)$. N_2 is considered as a random variable defined by the distribution of F. Compute the expected value $\mathrm{E}(N_2)$ of N_2 (note that $\{i, j\} = \{j, i\}$, so that we should not count it twice). Compute the variance $\mathrm{V}(N_2)$ of N_2.

2 We recall Chebyshev Inequality for a random variable X

$$\Pr\left[|X - \mathrm{E}(X)| \geq t\right] \leq \frac{\mathrm{V}(X)}{t^2} \quad \text{for all } t > 0.$$

By using the previous question, give a lower bound on the probability that $N_2 > 0$ for $m = \theta \sqrt{n}$. You can assume that $n, m \gg 1$.

3 Let us assume that we have a uniformly distributed random function F whose output domain has a cardinality of n. In order to find a collision on F, we take m distinct points $x_1, \ldots, x_m$ at random and store $F(x_1), \ldots, F(x_m)$ in a hash table. Give a lower bound of the success probability when $m = \theta \sqrt{n}$ using the previous results.

▷ Solution on page 69

Exercise 4   Multicollisions on Hash Functions

Preliminaries

In this problem, we consider a cryptographic hash function $h : \mathcal{M} \to \mathcal{H}$, where $\mathcal{M} = \{0, 1\}^N$ and $\mathcal{H} = \{0, 1\}^n$. We generalize the notion of collision to the one of r-collision. A r-collision on the cryptographic hash function $h : \mathcal{M} \to \mathcal{H}$ is a set of r distinct messages $m_1, m_2, \ldots, m_r \in \mathcal{M}$ such that $h(m_1) = h(m_2) = \cdots = h(m_r)$. The aim of this problem is to study r-collisions first in the realistic case of iterated hash functions (for example hash functions based on the Merkle-Damgård construction), then in a more idealistic model, called the *Random Oracle Model* (where hash functions are replaced by random functions).

1 How many messages do we need to find a 2-collision with a non-negligible probability by using the Birthday Paradox?

Multicollisions in Iterated Hash Functions

We consider a hash function $h : \mathcal{M} \rightarrow \mathcal{H}$ based on the Merkle-Damgård scheme (see Figure 3.1). We denote by $f : \{0,1\}^n \times \{0,1\}^\ell \rightarrow \{0,1\}^n$ the compression function. Recall that in this construction the padding is mandatory and only depends on the length of the message. We will

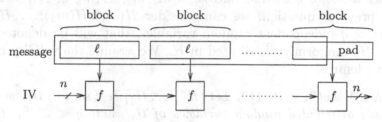

Figure 3.1. The Merkle-Damgård scheme

assume that $\ell \gg n$ (e.g., $\ell = 512$ and $n = 128$), i.e., the size of the message blocks is larger than the size of the hash.

2 Let x be an arbitrary value in $\{0,1\}^n$. Using the Birthday Paradox, evaluate the number of necessary blocks in order to find two distinct blocks B and B' in $\{0,1\}^\ell$ such that $f(x, B) = f(x, B')$, and give the probability of success.

Let $h_0 : \{0,1\}^{c \times \ell} \rightarrow \mathcal{H}$ be a hash function similar to h, but without padding, for which the messages we consider have a fixed length $c \times \ell$.

3 Using the previous question, show how to find a 4-collision on h_0 with $c = 2$. Estimate the success probability.
   Hint: Use two (well chosen) 2-collision search on the compression function.

4 Explain how the 4-collision found on h_0 in the previous question leads to a 4-collision on h.

5 Explain how the previous idea can be generalized in order to find a 2^t-collision on h with only t (well chosen) 2-collision searches on the compression function f.

6 Deduce from the previous questions the complexity (i.e., the total number of calls to f) of finding a 2^t-collision on h together with the probability of success.

Multicollisions in the Random Oracle Model

In the *Random Oracle Model*, a hash function $H : M \to \mathcal{H}$ is considered as a random function, uniformly distributed over all possible functions from M onto $\mathcal{H}$.

7 Let m_1 and m_2 be two *distinct* fixed elements of M and let h_1 and h_2 be two fixed elements of $\mathcal{H}$. Show that the events $H(m_1) = h_1$ and $H(m_2) = h_2$ are independent.

Consider a set of q distinct messages $m_1, m_2, \ldots, m_q$ of M. Thanks to the previous question, we can consider $H(m_1), H(m_2), \ldots, H(m_q)$ as a set of q independent random variables, that will be denoted H_1, $H_2, \ldots, H_q$, uniformly distributed in $\mathcal{H}$. We assume the validity of the following lemma.

LEMMA 3.1 *Let* $\mathcal{H} = \{0, 1\}^n$. *Let* $\{H_1, \ldots, H_q\}$ *be a set of q independent uniformly distributed random variables of* $\mathcal{H}$, *where* $q < 2^{n-8}$. *Let us call r-coincidence an element of* $\mathcal{H}$ *which occurs exactly r times in the sequence* $H_1, \ldots, H_q$. *Let* λ *be such that* $q = (\lambda r!)^{1/r} 2^{n(r-1)/r}$. *If* $\lambda \leq 1$, *then the probability that there is* no *s-coincidence for any* $s \geq r$ *is close to* $e^{-\lambda}$.

8 Using Lemma 3.1, for any $s \geq 2$ compute the probability that there is no s-coincidence in the sequence $H_1, \ldots, H_q$ and use it to prove the Birthday Paradox (when n is large enough).

9 Compute the number q of distinct messages that are necessary to obtain an r-collision with probability $1 - e^{-1/2}$.

10 Show that q is lower-bounded by 2^{96} when $r = 4$ and $n = 128$. For a similar probability of success, show that the complexity of finding a 4-collision when h is an iterated hash function is much smaller.

11 Compare the results of questions 6 and 9. Conclude.

▷ Solution on page 71

Exercise 5 Weak Hash Function Designs

In this problem we will see that if a hash function preserves some algebraic relation, then its security is likely to be compromised. We will consider two different hash functions, each one satisfying a particular relation.

1 In this question, we consider a hash function $H : \mathcal{X} \to \mathcal{Y}$ as a random function from $\mathcal{X}$ to $\mathcal{Y}$. This is called the random oracle model. Given $y \in \mathcal{Y}$, explain how to find a preimage x of y, i.e., a value $x \in \mathcal{X}$ such that $H(x) = y$. Compute an approximation of the expected complexity of the corresponding algorithm when $|\mathcal{X}| \gg |\mathcal{Y}|$.

We consider a hash function $h : \{0, 1\}^{1024} \longrightarrow \{0, 1\}^{128}$ that satisfies the following property

$$\mathrm{Par}(x) = \mathrm{Par}(h(x)) \quad \text{for all } x \in \{0, 1\}^{1024}, \tag{3.1}$$

where the parity Par of a string of n bits $a_1 a_2 \cdots a_n$ is defined by

$$\mathrm{Par}(a_1 a_2 \cdots a_n) = a_1 \oplus a_2 \oplus \cdots \oplus a_n.$$

For example $\mathrm{Par}(010100011111) = 1$.

2 Explain how one can take advantage of the property (3.1) in order to mount a preimage attack. Compute an approximation of the complexity of the attack.

3 Show how one can use (3.1) to find a collision on h. Compute the number of elements of $\{0, 1\}^{1024}$ that are needed by this method for a success probability equal to $1 - e^{-2} \approx 0.86$.

Let $h : \{0, 1, \ldots, 2^{2048} - 1\} \longrightarrow \{0, 1, \ldots 2^{256} - 1\}$ be a hash function satisfying

$$x_1 \equiv x_2 \pmod{2^{32}} \Rightarrow h(x_1) = h(x_2). \tag{3.2}$$

4 Let Y be a uniformly distributed random element of $\{0, 1, \ldots 2^{256} - 1\}$. Compute an upper bound on the probability that Y has a preimage.

5 Given a value $y = h(x)$, show how to take advantage of the property (3.2) in order to find a preimage of y. Compute the worst case complexity of this algorithm.

6 Is (3.2) useful for performing a second preimage attack? Explain your answer.

7 Is (3.2) useful for finding a collision? Explain your answer.

▷ Solution on page 74

Exercise 6   Collisions on a Modified MD5

We modify MD5 by replacing the original padding scheme by a mandatory padding only made of zeros. The padded length should be a multiple of 512 bits. Exhibit a collision.

▷ Solution on page 75

Exercise 7   First Preimage on a Modified MD5

The compression function of MD5 follows a Davies-Meyer scheme: from an "encryption function" $C_0 : \{0,1\}^{128} \times \{0,1\}^{512} \longrightarrow \{0,1\}^{128}$, the scheme defines the compression function C of MD5. Here, we consider a modified MD5 where the compression function is C_0 itself. Prove that one can mount a first preimage attack within a time complexity of 2^{64} and a space complexity of 2^{64}, by performing a meet-in-the-middle attack: for any target digest h, we can find a message m for which $\text{MD5}(m) = h$.

Hint: You may note that, for a given $m \in \{0,1\}^{512}$, we can consider $C_0(\cdot, m)$ as a permutation of $\{0,1\}^{128}$.

▷ Solution on page 76

Exercise 8   ⋆Attacks on Yi-Lam Hash Function

In this exercise, we denote by ℓ the constant equal to 64, by $+$ the addition modulo 2^ℓ, and by E_K a secure block cipher of block length ℓ and key size 2ℓ.

The Yi-Lam hash function can be described as follows: let h_i^1 and h_i^2 be m-bit blocks for $i = 0, 1, \ldots, n$. Assume for simplicity that each message m can be divided into blocks of ℓ bits before it is hashed. Given an n-block message $m = m_1 \| m_2 \| \cdots \| m_n$, where m_i is the ith block of m, and an initial value $\text{IV} = (h_0^1, h_0^2)$, we compute

$$\begin{cases} h_i^1 = \left(\mathsf{E}_{h_{i-1}^2 \| m_i}(h_{i-1}^1) \oplus m_i \right) + h_{i-1}^2 \\ h_i^2 = \mathsf{E}_{h_{i-1}^2 \| m_i}(h_{i-1}^1) \oplus h_{i-1}^1 \end{cases} \tag{3.3}$$

for $i = 1, 2, \ldots, n$. The final hash of m is the 2ℓ-bit string (h_n^1, h_n^2).

1 Give the complexity of a preimage attack (IV is fixed) on the Yi-Lam hash function in terms of ℓ, supposing that it is an ideal hash function.

2 A faster preimage attack on Yi-Lam hash function is shown in Algorithm 11. Read it carefully and find a necessary and sufficient termination condition of the loop in line 6.

Algorithm 11 A preimage attack on Yi-Lam hash

Input: IV, h_n^1, h_n^2 (n is unknown)
Output: m such that the Yi-Lam hash of m equals (h_n^1, h_n^2)
Processing:

1: **repeat**
2:     choose a random n
3:     choose $m_1, m_2, \ldots, m_{n-1}$ at random
4:     compute h_{n-1}^1, h_{n-1}^2
5:     Find m_n such that $h_n^1 = (h_n^2 \oplus h_{n-1}^1 \oplus m_n) + h_{n-1}^2$
6: **until** *a certain condition is met*
7: output $m = m_1 \| m_2 \| \ldots \| m_n$

---

3 Compute the average number of rounds for the loop in Algorithm 11.

A *free start collision attack* on a hash function $\mathsf{hash}(\mathsf{IV}, M)$ consists in finding IV, IV′, m, and m' with $m \neq m'$ such that

$$\mathsf{hash}(\mathsf{IV}, m) = \mathsf{hash}(\mathsf{IV}', m'),$$

where IV, IV′ can be freely and independently chosen.

4 Give the complexity of a free start collision attack on the Yi-Lam hash in terms of ℓ, supposing that it is an ideal hash scheme.

5 Find a sufficient condition on h_0^1, h_0^2, and a *one-block* message $m = m_1$, such that $h_1^1 = h_1^2$ always holds.

6 Using the solution of the previous question, deduce a free start collision attack on Yi-Lam hash function. Estimate the attack complexity.

▷ Solution on page 77

Exercise 9   MAC from Block Ciphers

The CBC-MAC construction builds a MAC function from a block cipher by taking the last encrypted block of the CBC-mode encryption. Can we similarly invent an ECB-MAC or an OFB-MAC and obtain secure constructions?

▷ Solution on page 78

Exercise 10   CFB-MAC

In this problem, we study a MAC scheme based on the CFB encryption mode. We consider a block cipher $E : \{0,1\}^{64} \times \{0,1\}^{64} \to \{0,1\}^{64}$, where $E_k(x) = E(k,x)$ denotes the encryption of the plaintext x under the key k. The CFB-MAC of a given message $m \in \{0,1\}^*$ with the key k is obtained by first encrypting m with E_k using the CFB encryption mode and then combining the output blocks by XORing them together. More precisely, for a message $m = x_1\|x_2\| \cdots \|x_n$, $\text{CFB-MAC}_k(m) = y_1 \oplus y_2 \oplus \cdots \oplus y_n$, where $y_i = E_k(y_{i-1}) \oplus x_i$ for $i = 2, \ldots, n$ and $y_1 = E_k(\text{IV}) \oplus x_1$, IV being an initialization vector. For the sake of simplicity, we assume that all messages have a length that is a multiple of 64 bits. We also assume in all the questions of this problem that IV is constant and known.

1 Assume we have access to an oracle $\mathcal{O}$ that computes the CFB-MAC under a given secret key k and a fixed known IV. Show that you can recover $E_k(\text{IV})$ by querying *only one* message to the oracle.

2 Assume that an adversary has access to an oracle $\mathcal{O}$ that computes the CFB-MAC under a given secret key k and a fixed known IV. The adversary would like to find a CFB-MAC collision on two different messages of 192 bits. How many messages of 192 bits does the adversary need to query to $\mathcal{O}$ in order to get a collision with probability close to $0.9996 \approx 1 - e^{-8}$?

3 Given a message m of n blocks and $h = \text{CFB-MAC}_k(m)$. Show how it is possible to generate a new message m' of n blocks and a $h' \in \{0,1\}^{64}$ such that $m' \neq m$ and $\text{CFB-MAC}_k(m') = h'$.

4 Assume we are given IV, $E_k(\text{IV})$, and a $h \in \{0,1\}^{64}$. Show how it is possible to generate a message m of two blocks, such that $\text{CFB-MAC}_k(m) = h$.

5 Can we extend the attack of the previous question to messages m of more than two blocks? Explain your answer.

▷ Solution on page 78

Exercise 11   ⋆Universal Hashing

A traditional way to study regular hash functions in computer science consists in considering them as a random variables: we do not have a fixed hash function, but a *family* of hash functions[1], one being picked at random. Hence we must consider the probability that $H(x) = H(y)$ for any different x and y over the distribution of H.

We say that a random hash function H is *ε-universal* if for any $x \neq y$, we have

$$\Pr_H [H(x) = H(y)] \leq \varepsilon.$$

We say that it is *strongly ε-universal* if for any $x \neq y$ and any a and b,

$$\Pr_H [H(x) = a, H(y) = b] \leq \frac{\varepsilon}{|\mathcal{H}|}$$

where $\mathcal{H}$ is the codomain of H. Finally, we say that H is *ε-XOR-universal* if for any $x \neq y$ and any a, we have

$$\Pr_H [H(x) \oplus H(y) = a] \leq \varepsilon.$$

Let $\mathbf{K}$ be a finite field of order k. We define

$$\begin{aligned} H : \quad \mathbf{K} &\longrightarrow \mathbf{K} \\ x &\longmapsto Ax, \end{aligned}$$

for a random variable A uniformly distributed in $\mathbf{K}$.

1 Show that H is $\frac{1}{k}$-universal. Is it strongly $\frac{1}{k}$-universal? How is it possible to modify H to be so?

2 We consider now $\mathbf{K} = \{0,1\}^\ell$ as a finite field of order 2^ℓ. Show that H is $2^{-\ell}$-XOR-universal.

▷ Solution on page 79

---

[1]This approach was motivated by the theory of MACs.

Solutions

Solution 1   Collisions in CBC Mode

1 If $y_i = y_j$ for $i \neq j$, then $y_{i-1} \oplus x_i = y_{j-1} \oplus x_j$. As y_{i-1} and y_{j-1} are known, we can deduce the value $x_i \oplus x_j = y_{i-1} \oplus y_{j-1}$.

2 Using the Birthday Paradox, we know that the probability of getting a collision when we have $n = \theta\sqrt{2^{64}}$ blocks at disposal is approximately equal to $1 - e^{-\frac{\theta^2}{2}}$.

3 Table 3.1 gives the success probabilities for different amounts of available blocks.

Table 3.1.   Collision probability in CBC mode

n	Size of data	Success probability
2^{17}	1 MB	$4.66 \cdot 10^{-10}$
2^{21}	16 MB	$1.19 \cdot 10^{-7}$
2^{24}	128 MB	$7.63 \cdot 10^{-6}$
2^{26}	512 MB	$1.22 \cdot 10^{-4}$
2^{27}	1 GB	$4.88 \cdot 10^{-4}$
2^{32}	32 GB	0.393
2^{33}	64 GB	0.865
2^{34}	128 GB	0.9997

Solution 2   Collisions

We first note that the possible number t of necessary trials follows the condition $2 \leq t \leq n + 1$. Table 3.2 summarizes the different possibilities. This suggests the following expression for the expected number of trials

$$\mathrm{E}\left[T\right] = \sum_{t=2}^{n+1} t \cdot \frac{(n-1)!}{(n-t+1)!} \cdot \frac{t-1}{n^{t-1}}.$$

This last expression can be approximated when n is large. We have

$$
\begin{aligned}
\mathrm{E}(T) &= \sum_{t=2}^{n+1} t \cdot \frac{(n-1)!}{(n-t+1)!} \cdot \frac{t-1}{n^{t-1}} \\
&= \sum_{i=1}^{n} i(i+1) \cdot \frac{(n-1)!}{(n-i)!} \cdot \frac{1}{n^i} \qquad (i = t-1) \\
&= \sum_{k=1}^{n} (n-k)(n-k+1) \cdot \frac{(n-1)!}{k!} \cdot \frac{1}{n^{n-k}} \qquad (k = n-i) \\
&= \frac{(n-1)!}{n^n} \sum_{k=1}^{n} (n^2 + n - 2kn + k(k-1)) \frac{n^k}{k!}.
\end{aligned}
$$

Letting

$$
\Psi_n = \sum_{k=0}^{n} \frac{n^k}{k!}
$$

we obtain

$$
\begin{aligned}
\mathrm{E}(T) &= \frac{(n-1)!}{n^n} \left((n^2 + n)(\Psi_n - 1) - 2n^2 \left(\Psi_n - \frac{n^n}{n!} \right) \right. \\
&\left. \quad + n^2 \left(\Psi_n - \frac{n^n}{n!} - \frac{n^{n-1}}{(n-1)!} \right) \right) \\
&= \frac{n!}{n^n} \Psi_n - \frac{n!(n+1)}{n^n}.
\end{aligned}
$$

Using the Stirling Approximation, we have

$$
\frac{n!(n+1)}{n^n} \underset{n \to +\infty}{\sim} \frac{\sqrt{2\pi} n^{3/2}}{e^n} \underset{n \to +\infty}{\longrightarrow} 0 \quad \text{and} \quad \frac{n!}{n^n} \Psi_n \underset{n \to +\infty}{\sim} \sqrt{2\pi n} \Psi_n e^{-n},
$$

so that

$$
\mathrm{E}(T) \underset{n \to +\infty}{\sim} \sqrt{2\pi n} \Psi_n e^{-n}.
$$

Table 3.2. Number of trials before a collision occurs

t	$\Pr[T = t]$
$t = 2$	$\frac{1}{n}$
$t = 3$	$\frac{n-1}{n} \cdot \frac{2}{n}$
$t = 4$	$\frac{n-1}{n} \cdot \frac{n-2}{n} \cdot \frac{3}{n}$
$\ldots$	$\ldots$
$t = n$	$\frac{n-1}{n} \cdot \frac{n-2}{n} \cdot \ldots \cdot \frac{2}{n} \cdot \frac{n-1}{n}$
$t = n+1$	$\frac{n-1}{n} \cdot \frac{n-2}{n} \cdot \ldots \cdot \frac{1}{n} \cdot 1$

If we use the hint, we are done. In what follows, we provide a proof of the hint.

The Taylor development of e^n with Lagrange remainder tells us that

$$\Psi_n = e^n - \frac{1}{n!} \int_0^n e^t (n-t)^n dt.$$

Hence, we obtain

$$
\begin{aligned}
\Psi_n e^{-n} &= 1 - \frac{e^{-n}}{n!} \int_0^n e^t (n-t)^n dt \\
&= 1 - \frac{e^{-n} n^n}{n!} \int_0^n e^t \left(1 - \frac{t}{n}\right)^n dt \\
&= 1 - n \frac{e^{-n} n^n}{n!} \int_0^1 e^{nu} (1-u)^n \, du \\
&= 1 - n \frac{e^{-n} n^n}{n!} \int_0^1 e^{n(u+\log(1-u))} \, du.
\end{aligned}
$$

Using the Stirling Approximation again,

$$\frac{e^{-n} n^n}{n!} = \frac{1}{\sqrt{2\pi n}} (1 + o(1)),$$

and thus

$$\Psi_n e^{-n} = 1 - (1 + o(1)) \sqrt{\frac{n}{2\pi}} \int_0^1 e^{n(u+\log(1-u))} \, du.$$

The function in the integral is close to $e^{-\frac{1}{2}nu^2}$ when u is close to 0 and we have

$$\sqrt{\frac{n}{2\pi}} \int_0^1 e^{-\frac{1}{2}nu^2} \, du = \frac{1}{\sqrt{2\pi}} \int_0^{\sqrt{n}} e^{-\frac{1}{2}v^2} \, dv \xrightarrow[n\to\infty]{} \frac{1}{2},$$

by using the normal distribution law. Hence,

$$\Psi_n e^{-n} - \frac{1}{2} = o(1) + (1 + o(1)) \sqrt{\frac{n}{2\pi}} \int_0^1 \left(e^{-\frac{1}{2}nu^2} - e^{n(u+\log(1-u))}\right) du.$$

In what follows, we show that the integral is indeed $o(n^{-1/2})$, which completes the proof. Let

$$\Delta = \int_0^1 \left(e^{-\frac{1}{2}nu^2} - e^{n(u+\log(1-u))}\right) du.$$

Since $u + \log(1-u) \leq -\frac{1}{2}u^2$ for any $u \geq 0$, Δ is positive. We split the sum over $[0, \varepsilon]$ and $[\varepsilon, 1]$, for some $\varepsilon > 0$ to be chosen later. We have

$$
\int_{\varepsilon}^{1} \left(e^{-\frac{1}{2}nu^2} - e^{n(u+\log(1-u))} \right) du \;\leq\; \int_{\varepsilon}^{1} e^{-\frac{1}{2}nu^2} du
$$
$$
= \frac{1}{\sqrt{n}} \int_{\varepsilon\sqrt{n}}^{\sqrt{n}} e^{-\frac{1}{2}v^2} dv
$$
$$
= o(n^{-1/2}),
$$

as, provided that $\lim_{n\to\infty} \varepsilon\sqrt{n} = \infty$,

$$
0 \leq \int_{\varepsilon\sqrt{n}}^{\sqrt{n}} e^{-\frac{1}{2}v^2} dv \leq \int_{\varepsilon\sqrt{n}}^{\infty} e^{-\frac{1}{2}v^2} dv \xrightarrow[n\to\infty]{} 0.
$$

On the other hand, since $u + \log(1-u) + u^2/2 \geq -(1+\varepsilon)u^3/3$ for $0 \leq u \leq \varepsilon$ (provided that ε is small enough), we have

$$
\int_{0}^{\varepsilon} \left(e^{-\frac{1}{2}nu^2} - e^{n(u+\log(1-u))} \right) du \;\leq\; \int_{0}^{\varepsilon} e^{-\frac{1}{2}nu^2} \left(1 - e^{-\frac{1}{3}n(1+\varepsilon)u^3} \right) du
$$
$$
\leq \int_{0}^{\varepsilon} \left(1 - e^{-\frac{1}{3}n(1+\varepsilon)u^3} \right) du
$$
$$
\leq \frac{1}{3}n(1+\varepsilon) \int_{0}^{\varepsilon} u^3 du
$$
$$
\leq n\varepsilon^4
$$
$$
= o(n^{-1/2}),
$$

for $\varepsilon = n^{-7/16}$, which is not in contradiction with the previous condition on ε. Finally, $\Delta = o(n^{-1/2})$ and thus,

$$
\Psi_n e^{-n} \xrightarrow[n\to\infty]{} \frac{1}{2} \quad \text{and} \quad E(T) \underset{n\to+\infty}{\sim} \sqrt{\frac{n\pi}{2}}.
$$

Solution 3   Expected Number of Collisions

1 We have

$$
N_2 = \sum_{i<j} 1_{F(i)=F(j)}.
$$

Hence

$$
E(N_2) = \sum_{i<j} E\left(1_{F(i)=F(j)} \right) = \sum_{i<j} \Pr_F[F(i) = F(j)].
$$

As $\Pr[F(i) = F(j)] = \frac{1}{n}$ (see Exercise 1, Chapter 1), we obtain

$$E(N_2) = \frac{m(m-1)}{2} \times \frac{1}{n}.$$

We have $V(N_2) = E(N_2^2) - E(N_2)^2$. As

$$E(N_2^2) = \sum_{i<j} \sum_{i'<j'} E\left(\mathbf{1}_{F(i)=F(j)} \cdot \mathbf{1}_{F(i')=F(j')}\right),$$

we deduce

$$V(N_2) = \sum_{\substack{i<j \\ i'<j'}} \left(E\left(\mathbf{1}_{\substack{F(i)=F(j) \\ F(i')=F(j')}}\right) - E\left(\mathbf{1}_{F(i)=F(j)}\right) \cdot E\left(\mathbf{1}_{F(i')=F(j')}\right)\right)$$

$$= \sum_{\substack{i<j \\ i'<j'}} \left(\Pr\left[\begin{matrix}F(i)=F(j) \\ F(i')=F(j')\end{matrix}\right] - \Pr[F(i) = F(j)]\Pr[F(i') = F(j')]\right).$$

When $\{i, j\} \neq \{i', j'\}$, the difference in the parenthesis is zero because the events $F(i) = F(j)$ and $F(i') = F(j')$ are independent. Thus, we have

$$V(N_2) = \sum_{i<j} \left(\Pr[F(i) = F(j)] - (\Pr[F(i) = F(j)])^2\right)$$

$$= \sum_{i<j} \left(\frac{1}{n} - \frac{1}{n^2}\right)$$

$$= \frac{m(m-1)}{2} \times \frac{1}{n}\left(1 - \frac{1}{n}\right).$$

2 For all $t > 0$,

$$\Pr[|N_2 - E(N_2)| \geq t] = 1 - \Pr[|N_2 - E(N_2)| < t]$$
$$= 1 - \Pr[-t < N_2 - E(N_2) < t].$$

For $t = E(N_2)$, this gives

$$\Pr[|N_2 - E(N_2)| \geq E(N_2)] = 1 - \Pr[0 < N_2 < 2 \cdot E(N_2)]$$
$$\geq 1 - \Pr[N_2 > 0],$$

and thus

$$\Pr[N_2 > 0] \geq 1 - \Pr[|N_2 - E(N_2)| \geq E(N_2)].$$

Using the Chebyshev Inequality, and using both results of the previous question, we get

$$\Pr[N_2 > 0] \geq 1 - \frac{V(N_2)}{(E(N_2))^2} = 1 - \frac{2(n-1)}{m(m-1)}.$$

Assuming that $n, m \gg 1$, we finally obtain

$$\Pr[N_2 > 0] \geq 1 - \frac{2}{\theta^2},$$

as $m = \theta \sqrt{n}$.

3 This problem is completely equivalent to the previous one, so that the probability of success is equal to $\Pr[N_2 > 0]$. It is thus lower bounded by $1 - \frac{2}{\theta^2}$. Note that this bound is not as tight as the one provided by the Birthday Paradox: $1 - e^{-\frac{\theta^2}{2}}$. See the textbook [56] for more details.

Solution 4   Multicollisions on Hash Functions

Preliminaries

1 According to the Birthday Paradox, we need approximately $2^{n/2}$ messages to find a collision on h (i.e., a 2-collision on h) with a probability of success of $1 - e^{-1/2} \approx 0.393$.

Multicollisions in Iterated Hash Functions

2 Using the Birthday Paradox once again, we need $\theta \cdot 2^{n/2}$ blocks in order to find a collision on the compression function, with a probability of success of $1 - e^{-\frac{\theta^2}{2}}$. As the blocks are chosen in a set of cardinality $2^\ell \gg 2^{n/2}$, there are enough of them to be sure to find a collision.

3 The idea is to look for two distinct blocks B_1 and B_1' such that $f(IV, B_1) = f(IV, B_1')$. Calling x_1 this output of the compression function, we search for B_2 and B_2' such that $f(x_1, B_2) = f(x_1, B_2')$. We call x_2 this last value. This is represented on Figure 3.2. We now consider the four following messages: $B_1\|B_2$, $B_1\|B_2'$, $B_1'\|B_2$, and $B_1'\|B_2'$. Clearly, the all produce the same hash value y when they are hashed with h_0. Therefore, we have found a 4-collision on h_0. In order to do this, we had to find two 2-collisions on the compression function f, so that the overall complexity is $2 \cdot \theta \cdot 2^{n/2}$, for a probability of success of $(1 - e^{-\theta^2/2})^2$ (as we need both collision searches to be successful).

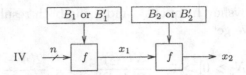

Figure 3.2. How to find a 4-collision on h_0

4 Assume we hash the four messages of the previous question with h instead of h_0. The only difference is that a padding has to be concatenated to the messages. But as this padding only depends on the length of the message to be hashed, all four messages will have the same padding (that we denote PAD). We represent this situation on Figure 3.3.

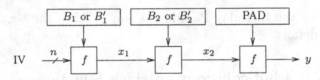

Figure 3.3. How to find a 4-collision on h, based on a 4-collision on h_0

5 We denote IV $= x_0$ and construct the sequence x_i, for $i = 1, \ldots, t$ as follows. Given x_{i-1}, find two distinct blocks B_i and B_i' such that $f(x_{i-1}, B_i) = f(x_{i-1}, B_i')$. This corresponds to a 2-collision search on f. Call x_i this value. This construction is represented on Figure 3.4. Clearly, the 2^t messages $\{B_1, B_1'\} \| \{B_2, B_2'\} \| \cdots \| \{B_t, B_t'\}$ all

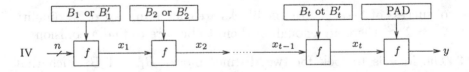

Figure 3.4. Finding a 2^t-collision on h

produce the same h_0 hash value. As they all are of the same length (t blocks) this implies that they also produce the same h value. We have obtained a 2^t-collision on h.

6 According to the previous question, we need t successful collision searches on f. If we make $\theta \cdot 2^{n/2}$ calls to f each time we look for a collision on f, this makes a total of $t \cdot \theta \cdot 2^{n/2}$ calls to f. We need the

t collision searches to be successful, so that the overall probability of success is $(1 - e^{-\theta^2/2})^t$.

Multicollisions in the Random Oracle Model

7 The number of functions from $\mathcal{M}$ to $\mathcal{H}$ is $|\mathcal{H}|^{|\mathcal{M}|}$. We have

$$\Pr[H(m_1) = h_1] = \sum_h 1_{h(m_1)=h_1} \Pr[H = h]$$

$$= \frac{1}{|\mathcal{H}|^{|\mathcal{M}|}} \sum_h 1_{h(m_1)=h_1},$$

where the last sum is the number of functions mapping m_1 on h_1, which is the number of functions of a set of cardinality $|\mathcal{M}| - 1$ to a set of cardinality $|\mathcal{H}|$. Therefore

$$\Pr[H(m_1) = h_1] = \frac{|\mathcal{H}|^{|\mathcal{M}|-1}}{|\mathcal{H}|^{|\mathcal{M}|}}$$

$$= \frac{1}{|\mathcal{H}|}.$$

Similarly,

$$\Pr[H(m_1) = h_1, H(m_2) = h_2] = \sum_h 1_{h(m_1)=h_1, h(m_2)=h_2} \Pr[H = h]$$

$$= \frac{1}{|\mathcal{H}|^{|\mathcal{M}|}} \sum_h 1_{h(m_1)=h_1, h(m_2)=h_2},$$

where the last sum is the number of functions mapping m_1 on h_1 and m_2 on h_2, which is the number of functions of a set of cardinality $|\mathcal{M}| - 2$ to a set of cardinality $|\mathcal{H}|$. Therefore

$$\Pr[H(m_1) = h_1, H(m_2) = h_2] = \frac{1}{|\mathcal{H}|^2}.$$

This proves that

$$\Pr[H(m_1) = h_1, H(m_2) = h_2] = \Pr[H(m_1) = h_1] \Pr[H(m_2) = h_2].$$

Therefore, the two events are independent.

8 Using the lemma with $r = 2$, we see that there is not s-coincidence for any $s \geq 2$ in $\{H_1, \ldots, H_q\}$ with a probability e^λ, where λ is such that $q = \sqrt{2\lambda} \cdot 2^{n/2}$. Let $\theta = \sqrt{2\lambda}$. In other words, we have at least a 2-coincidence (a collision) with probability $1 - e^{-\theta^2/2}$ in $\{H_1, \ldots, H_q\}$, when $q = \theta \cdot 2^{n/2}$.

9 An r-collision in $\{m_1, \ldots, m_q\}$ corresponds to an r-coincidence in $\{H_1, \ldots, H_q\}$. We obtain (at least) an r-coincidence with probability $1 - e^{-1/2}$ (i.e., $\lambda = \frac{1}{2}$) when $q = (\frac{r!}{2})^{1/r} 2^{n(r-1)/r}$.

10 With $r = 4$ and $n = 128$, the previous relation gives $q = 12^{1/4} 2^{96} > 2^{96}$. For iterated hash function, we showed that a 4-collision can be found with probability $(1 - e^{-\theta^2/2})^2 \approx 1 - 2 \cdot e^{-\theta^2/2}$ when $q = 2 \cdot \theta \cdot 2^{n/2}$. This shows that we roughly need 2^{64} hash computations for similar probabilities of success. This is indeed much smaller than 2^{96}.

11 We can see that the values found in the random oracle model are way larger than the realistic ones. The random oracle model is definitively of no help for studying this problem!

This exercise is based on a very recent article [23] of A. Joux, published at Crypto'04. A discussion about preimage and second-preimage resistance is also proposed, together with some other extensions, like the security of the concatenation of two independent hash functions.

Solution 5   Weak Hash Function Designs

1 In order to find a preimage, one can exhaustively search through all possible $x \in \mathcal{X}$ and test whether $H(x) = y$. Note that we do not test the same message twice. For $|\mathcal{X}| \gg |\mathcal{Y}|$ (which is typically the case) this succeeds with very high probability as H is likely to be surjective. Considering H as a random function, we have $\Pr_H[H(x) = y] = 1/|\mathcal{Y}|$ for any $x \in \mathcal{X}$ and $y \in \mathcal{Y}$. We denote $p = 1/|\mathcal{Y}|$. Denoting x_i the ith message hashed and C the random variable corresponding to the total number of tests in the algorithm, we have

$$\Pr[C = c] = \Pr[H(x_1) \neq y, \ldots, H(x_{c-1}) \neq y, H(x_c) = y].$$

As the x_i's are different from each other, the c events in the previous probability are independent, and thus $\Pr[C = c] = (1 - p)^{c-1} p$. Therefore

$$E(C) = \sum_{c=1}^{|\mathcal{X}|} c(1 - p)^{c-1} p \approx \sum_{c=1}^{\infty} c(1 - p)^{c-1} p = \frac{1}{p},$$

where the approximation comes from the fact that $|\mathcal{X}| \gg 1$. Finally,

$$E(C) = |\mathcal{Y}|.$$

2 By using property (3.1), we can restrict the exhaustive search to the elements x satisfying $\text{Par}(x) = \text{Par}(y)$. According to the previous

question, the complexity of the algorithm is approximately equal to 2^{127}, since these elements are mapped onto a set of cardinality 2^{127}.

3 We first note that two elements of different parities cannot be mapped onto the same hashes. For finding a collision, we pick n distinct values $x_1, \ldots, x_n \in \{0,1\}^{1024}$ with the same parity and test whether there is a collision. The Birthday Paradox applies here. Since the $h(x_i)$'s are lying in a set of cardinality 2^{127}, one needs approximately $2 \cdot \sqrt{2^{127}} = 2^{64.5}$ distinct messages to reach a success probability equal to $0.86 \approx 1 - e^{-2}$.

4 Property (3.1) implies that h can produce at most 2^{32} different values. Hence,

$$\Pr_Y[\exists x \mid h(x) = Y] \leq \frac{2^{32}}{2^{256}} = 2^{-224}.$$

5 The search for the preimage can be restricted to $\{0, 1, \ldots, 2^{32} - 1\}$, as its elements are mapped onto all possible values of $h(x)$. Note that the result of Question 1 does not apply here as we are not in the situation where $|\mathcal{X}| \gg |\mathcal{Y}|$. In the worst case, we have a complexity equal to 2^{32}. We could also compute the average complexity, the average being taken over the random initial permutation of the 2^{32} values that have to be hashed. This problem is completely equivalent to an exhaustive key search for a block cipher. The average complexity is $(2^{32} - 1)/2 \approx 2^{31}$.

6 Yes, it is useful! For a given $x \in \{0, 1, \ldots 2^{2048} - 1\}$ we know that any $x' = x \pmod{2^{32}}$ is hashed onto the same value. We can thus choose $x' = x + k \cdot 2^{32} \bmod 2^{2048}$ for any integer k (taking care not to have $x' = x$).

7 Yes, it is also useful! Picking $x \in \{0, 1, \ldots 2^{2048} - 1\}$ at random and taking a $x' = x + k \cdot 2^{32} \bmod 2^{2048}$ for some integer k (such that $x' \neq x$) does the trick, as $h(x) = h(x')$.

Solution 6   Collisions on a Modified MD5

One just has to find two different messages x and x' which will be identical after the zero-padding operation. For example, one can take $x = m$ and $x' = m \| 0$ for any message m, provided that its length $|m|$ satisfies $|m| - 1 \not\equiv 0 \pmod{512}$.

Solution 7   First Preimage on a Modified MD5

We denote by MD5$'$ the modified MD5. The attack is described in Algorithm 12. The objective of the algorithm is to build a message made of two blocks $m = m_1 \| m_2$ such that MD5$'(m) = h$. As the

---

Algorithm 12 A first preimage attack on a modified MD5

Input: a target value $h \in \{0,1\}^{128}$, an initial vector IV $\in \{0,1\}^{128}$, and a 65-bit string **pad** equal to 1 followed by 64 bits encoding the length of a message of $2 \cdot 512 - 65 = 959$ bits

Output: a preimage m of h for MD5$'$

Processing:

1: **for** 2^{64} different $m_1 \in \{0,1\}^{512}$ **do**
2:     $h_1 \leftarrow C_0(\text{IV}, m_1)$
3:     store (h_1, m_1) in a table T, sorted according to h_1
4: **end for**
5: **loop**
6:     choose $x \in \{0,1\}^{512-65}$ at random
7:     $m_2 \leftarrow x \| \text{pad}$
8:     $h_2 \leftarrow C_0^{-1}(h, m_2)$
9:     **if** there exists $(h_1, m_1) \in T$ such that $h_1 = h_2$ **then**
10:         output $m = m_1 \| m_2$
11:     **end if**
12: **end loop**

---

message must be valid, the trailing part of m_2 must contain a valid padding, i.e., a padding following the specifications of Merkle-Damgård scheme. This is ensured by line 7 of the algorithm.

The reason why the algorithm works comes from the Birthday Paradox. Considering the h_1's and the h_2's as random values, we can consider that we are actually building two sequences of random elements of $\{0,1\}^{128}$ (the first sequence is of length 2^{64}, the second grows until a collision is found). When the growing sequence reaches a size equal to $\theta \cdot \sqrt{2^{128}} = \theta \cdot 2^{64}$, a special version of the Birthday Paradox (see the textbook [56]) states that the probability that there is at least one common number in the two sequences (i.e., that the condition on line 9 is true) is

$$1 - e^{-\theta}.$$

Obviously, after 2^{64} iterations of the loop, the algorithm succeeds with a non-negligible probability.

We should note that this attack does not apply to MD5, as the compression function is not invertible in this case, and thus, it is not possible to perform the computation made on line 7.

Solution 8   ⋆Attacks on Yi-Lam Hash Function

1 The output of the hash function being of size 2ℓ bits, the complexity of a first preimage attack if the scheme is considered to be ideal is $\mathcal{O}(2^{2\ell})$.

2 As

$$(3.3) \Leftrightarrow \begin{cases} h_i^1 &= (h_i^2 \oplus h_{i-1}^1 \oplus m_i) + h_{i-1}^2 \\ h_i^2 &= \mathsf{E}_{h_{i-1}^2 \| m_i}(h_{i-1}^1) \oplus h_{i-1}^1 \end{cases},$$

the necessary and sufficient termination condition of the loop is

$$h_n^2 = \mathsf{E}_{h_{n-1}^2 \| m_n}(h_{n-1}^1) \oplus h_{n-1}^1.$$

3 At each iteration, we can consider that the condition of the previous question is true with probability $p = 2^{-\ell}$. Denoting C the random variable corresponding to the number of iterations of the loop, we have

$$\mathrm{E}(C) = \sum_{c=1}^{\infty} c \Pr[C = c] = \sum_{c=1}^{\infty} c(1 - p)^{c-1} p.$$

This corresponds to the mean of a geometric distribution, so that the expected number of iterations in the loop is

$$\mathrm{E}(C) = \frac{1}{p} = 2^{\ell}.$$

4 According to the Birthday Paradox, the complexity of a collision attack on a 2ℓ-bit hash is $\mathcal{O}(2^{2\ell/2}) = \mathcal{O}(2^{\ell})$.

5 If we set

$$\begin{cases} h_0^2 &= \mathbf{0} \\ m_1 &= h_0^1 \end{cases}$$

then, we always have

$$h_1^1 = h_1^2 = m_1 \oplus \mathsf{E}_{0\|m_1}(m_1).$$

6 The attack is described in Algorithm 13. In the algorithm, the messages are such that their Yi-Lam hash is of the form (h_1^1, h_1^1), as the

---

Algorithm 13 A collision search on Yi-Lam hash

Output: two one-block messages that produce a collision on the Yi-Lam hash function

Processing:

1: **repeat**
2:     choose m_1 at random
3:     $h_1^1 \leftarrow m_1 \oplus E_{0\|m_1}(m_1)$
4:     store (h_1^1, m_1) in a table sorted according to h_1^1
5: **until** there exists two entries (h, m) and (h', m') such that $h = h'$ and $m \neq m'$
6: output m and m'

---

parameters are chosen according to the result of the previous question. To obtain a collision, it is sufficient to get a collision on the first half of the hash, i.e., on h_1^1. The complexity of the algorithm (the number of repetitions of the loop) is thus $\mathcal{O}(2^{\ell/2})$.

See [46, 57] for more details about these attacks.

Solution 9   MAC from Block Ciphers

- ECB-MAC: We consider the last block of the ECB encryption of a message as the MAC of this message. Obviously, this scheme is highly insecure since the MAC of the message $m = m_1\| \cdots \|m_n\|m_{n+1}$ is equal to the MAC of $m' = m_1'\| \cdots \|m_n'\|m_{n+1}$ for any blocks $m_1, \ldots, m_n$.

- OFB-MAC: We consider the last block of the OFB encryption of a message as the MAC of this message. Once again, the scheme is insecure. Given the MAC c of a one-block message m, i.e., $c = m \oplus E(IV)$, it is easy to forge the MAC of the message $m' = m \oplus \alpha$ as it simply is $c' = m' \oplus E(IV) = c \oplus \alpha$.

Solution 10   CFB-MAC

1 We can simply query a message x of one block to the oracle $\mathcal{O}$. The oracle returns the value $y = x \oplus E_k(IV)$. Hence, $E_k(IV)$ is found by computing $x \oplus y$.

2 After querying n different messages to $\mathcal{O}$, we receive n MAC values for which we would like to get a collision. The probability to have at least one collision is given by the Birthday Paradox. Let $N = 2^{64}$.

We know that the probability is approximated by $1 - e^{-\frac{\theta^2}{2}}$, where $n = \theta\sqrt{N}$. In our case, $\theta = 4$ since $\frac{\theta^2}{2} = 8$. Thus, n must at least be equal to $4 \cdot 2^{32} = 2^{34}$.

3 Let $m = x_1\|x_2\|\cdots\|x_n$ and $h = \text{CFB-MAC}_k(m)$. We take another message $m' = x_1\|x_2\|\cdots\|x_{n-1}\|x'_n$ where x'_n is any block of 64 bits. Since CFB mode is used with a fixed IV the output blocks of m' will be identical to those of m except the last one. Since $h' = \text{CFB-MAC}_k(m') = y_1 \oplus \cdots \oplus y_{n-1} \oplus y'_n$ and $h = y_1 \oplus \cdots \oplus y_n$, we have $h \oplus h' = y_n \oplus y'_n$. We also know that $y_n = E_k(y_{n-1}) \oplus x_n$ and $y'_n = E_k(y_{n-1}) \oplus x'_n$. Using these two relations, we finally deduce that $h' = h \oplus y_n \oplus y'_n = h \oplus x_n \oplus x'_n$.

4 Set $m = x_1\|x_2$ and $x_1 = E_k(\text{IV}) \oplus \text{IV}$. We then have $y_1 = \text{IV}$ and $y_2 = h \oplus \text{IV}$. Thus, $x_2 = E_k(y_1) \oplus y_2 = E_k(\text{IV}) \oplus \text{IV} \oplus h$.

5 Yes, this works in the same way! Set $m = x_1\|x_2\|\cdots\|x_n$ where $x_1 = x_2 = \cdots = x_{n-1} = E_k(\text{IV}) \oplus \text{IV}$. Hence, $y_1 = y_2 = \cdots = y_{n-1} = \text{IV}$. If n is even, setting $x_n = h \oplus \text{IV} \oplus E_k(\text{IV})$ gives $y_n = h \oplus \text{IV}$ and thus $y_1 \oplus \cdots \oplus y_n = h$. If n is odd, setting $x_n = h \oplus E_k(\text{IV})$ gives $y_n = h$ and thus $y_1 \oplus \cdots \oplus y_n = h$.

Solution 11 $\star$Universal Hashing

1 Let $x, y \in \mathbf{K}$ be two fixed elements such that $x \neq y$. By definition, $H(x) = Ax$ (where $A \in \mathbf{K}$) is $\frac{1}{k}$-universal if

$$\forall x \neq y \in \mathbf{K}: \quad \Pr[H(x) = H(y)] \leq \frac{1}{k}$$

over the distribution of H. We have

$$
\begin{aligned}
\Pr[H(x) = H(y)] &= \Pr[Ax = Ay] \\
&= \Pr[A(x - y) = 0] \\
&= \Pr[A = 0] \\
&= \frac{1}{k}
\end{aligned}
$$

where the second equality is a consequence of the field structure of $\mathbf{K}$ ($x - y \neq 0$ is invertible).

The random hash function is $\frac{1}{k}$-strongly universal if, for any $x \neq y \in \mathbf{K}$ and any $i, j \in \mathbf{K}$,

$$\Pr[Ax = i, Ay = j] \leq \frac{1}{k^2}.$$

This is clearly not the case for $i = j = 0$ as

$$\Pr[Ax = 0, Ay = 0] = \Pr[A = 0] = \frac{1}{k} > \frac{1}{k^2}.$$

The definition of H can be modified. We let $H(x) = Ax + B$, where $A, B \in \mathbf{K}$ are uniformly distributed. In this case, H becomes $\frac{1}{k}$-strongly universal. We have

$$\Pr_{A,B}[Ax + B = i, Ay + B = j] = \frac{|\{a, b \mid ax + b = i, ay + b = j\}|}{k^2},$$

so that the probability we are looking for is the number of solutions of the system of equation

$$\begin{pmatrix} x & 1 \\ y & 1 \end{pmatrix} \times \begin{pmatrix} a \\ b \end{pmatrix} = \begin{pmatrix} i \\ j \end{pmatrix}$$

divided by k^2. As the determinant of the matrix is $x - y \neq 0$, it is invertible and thus, the system has a unique solution. Therefore,

$$\Pr_{A,B}[Ax + B = i, Ay + B = j] = \frac{1}{k^2},$$

which proves that the modified H is $\frac{1}{k}$-strongly universal.

2 H is $2^{-\ell}$-XOR-universal. For all $x, y \in \mathbf{K}$ such that $x \neq y$,

$$\Pr[Ax \oplus Ay = b] = \Pr[A(x \oplus y) = b] = \Pr[A = b(x \oplus y)^{-1}] = 2^{-\ell}$$

where the second equality holds because, we have $x \oplus y \neq 0$, as $x \neq y$. Note that as the field is of characteristic 2, the addition and the subtraction of two elements is simply the XOR of these elements.

Chapter 4

CONVENTIONAL SECURITY ANALYSIS

Exercises

Exercise 1   The SAFER Permutation

Prove that

$$x \mapsto (45^x \bmod 257) \bmod 256$$

is a permutation over $\{0, \ldots, 255\}$.

▷ Solution on page 97

Exercise 2   ⋆Linear Cryptanalysis

Let m be an integer such that $2^m + 1$ is a prime number. Let g be a generator of $\mathbf{Z}^*_{2^m+1}$ and let E be defined over $\mathbf{Z}_{2^m}$ by

$$E(x) = (g^x \bmod (2^m + 1)) \bmod 2^m.$$

Prove that $\Pr[E(X) \equiv X \pmod 2] = \frac{1}{2}$ when X is uniformly distributed.

▷ Solution on page 97

Exercise 3   ⋆Differential and Linear Probabilities

We consider a block cipher using the following function f as a building block

$$f : \begin{array}{rcl} \{0,1\}^{32} \times \{0,1\}^{32} & \rightarrow & \{0,1\}^{32} \\ (x,y) & \mapsto & f(x,y) = x + y \bmod 2^{32}. \end{array}$$

1 Compute $\mathrm{DP}^f(\delta\|\delta, 0)$, where $\delta = \mathtt{0x80000000}$, where $\|$ denotes the concatenation operation and $(\delta\|\delta) \cdot (x,y) = \delta \cdot x \oplus \delta \cdot y$.

2 Compute $\mathrm{DP}^f(\delta\|\delta, 0)$, where $\delta = \mathtt{0xC0000000}$.

3 Compute $\mathrm{LP}^f(\delta\|\delta, \delta)$, where $\delta = \mathtt{0x00000001}$.

4 Compute $\mathrm{LP}^f(\delta\|\delta, \delta)$, where $\delta = \mathtt{0x00000003}$.

Reminder: The differential and linear probabilities of a function f are defined by

$$\begin{array}{rcl} \mathrm{DP}^f(a,b) & = & \Pr[f(X \oplus a) = f(X) \oplus b] \quad \text{and} \\ \mathrm{LP}^f(a,b) & = & (2\Pr[a \cdot X = b \cdot f(X)] - 1)^2, \end{array}$$

where X is a uniformly distributed random variable over the plaintext space.

▷ Solution on page 98

Exercise 4   ⋆Feistel Schemes

We consider a Feistel scheme of one round with 64-bit blocks (see Figure 4.1(a)).

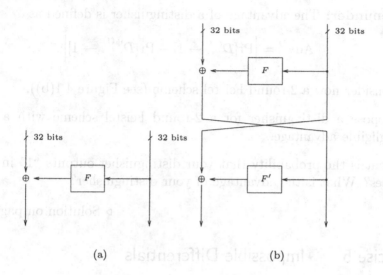

Figure 4.1. Feistel schemes with one or two rounds

Algorithm 14 is a distinguisher $\mathcal{D}$ which tries to predict whether an oracle $\mathcal{O}$ is a 1-round Feistel scheme or a uniformly random permutation.

Algorithm 14 1-round Feistel distinguisher $\mathcal{D}$

Input: an oracle $\mathcal{O}$ implementing either a 1-round Feistel scheme $\Psi^{(1)}$ or a random permutation C^*

Output: 0 (if the guess is that $\mathcal{O}$ implements C^*) or 1 (if the guess is that $\mathcal{O}$ implements $\Psi^{(1)}$)

Processing:
1: let $P = (x_\ell, x_r)$ be the input plaintext
2: submit P to $\mathcal{O}$ and get $C = (y_\ell, y_r)$
3: **if** $x_r = y_r$ **then**
4:     output 1
5: **else**
6:     output 0
7: **end if**

---

1 What is the probability that this distinguisher outputs "1" with a 1-round Feistel scheme, denoted $\Psi^{(1)}$?

2 Same question with the uniformly random permutation over $\{0,1\}^{64}$, denoted C^*. What is the advantage of $\mathcal{D}$?

Reminder: The advantage of a distinguisher is defined as

$$\mathrm{Adv}^{\mathcal{D}} = \left| \Pr[\mathcal{D}^{C^*} \to 1] - \Pr[\mathcal{D}^{\Psi^{(1)}} \to 1] \right|.$$

We consider now a 2-round Feistel scheme (see Figure 4.1(b)).

3 Propose a distinguisher for a 2-round Feistel scheme with a non-negligible advantage.

4 What is the probability that your distinguisher outputs "1" in both cases? What is the advantage of your distinguisher?

▷ Solution on page 100

Exercise 5   ⋆Impossible Differentials

We consider a classical Feistel scheme (with two balanced branches, with the usual $\oplus$ operation). Following standard notations, $\Psi(f_1, \ldots, f_r)$ denotes an r-round Feistel scheme in which the ith round function is f_i. Note that we omit the branch swap in the last round. Let $C = \Psi(f_1, f_2, f_3, f_4, f_5)$ where the f_i's are *permutations* (note that usually, the f_i's are simple functions) over $\{0,1\}^{\frac{m}{2}}$. Let $\Delta \in \{0,1\}^{\frac{m}{2}}$ such that $\Delta \neq 0$. We let $a = \Delta \| 0 \in \{0,1\}^m$ be the concatenation of Δ followed by $\frac{m}{2}$ zero bits. Show that $\mathrm{DP}^C(a, a) = 0$ for any choice of the permutations and any $\Delta \neq 0$.

▷ Solution on page 101

Exercise 6   ⋆Attacks Using Impossible Differential

We study classical Feistel schemes (with two balanced branches, with the usual $\oplus$ operation). Following standard notations, $\Psi(f_1, \ldots, f_r)$ denotes an r-round Feistel scheme in which the ith round function is f_i. Note that we omit the branch swap in the last round.

1 Draw a picture of $\Psi(f_1, f_2, f_3)$. Recall what is the inverse function.

2 Let c be a permutation of $\{0,1\}^m$. Given $a, b \in \{0,1\}^m$, recall the definition of the differential probability $\mathrm{DP}^c(a, b)$. Let C^* be a uniformly distributed random permutation over $\{0,1\}^m$. Assuming that $a \neq 0$ and $b \neq 0$, compute the *expected* value of $\mathrm{DP}^{C^*}(a, b)$.

3 Let C be a random permutation. Recall what is a distinguisher between C and C^*. What is the advantage of the distinguisher?

4 Let $C = \Psi(f_1, f_2)$ where f_1 and f_2 are functions on $\{0,1\}^{\frac{m}{2}}$. We want to construct a distinguisher between C and C^* which is limited to two queries to the oracle. Find two queries $x_1, x_2 \in \{0,1\}^m$ and a distinguisher which achieves an advantage close to 1.

5 In this question we let $C = \Psi(f_1, f_2, f_3, f_4, f_5)$ where the f_i's are *permutations* of $\{0,1\}^{\frac{m}{2}}$.

(a) Let $\Delta \in \{0,1\}^{\frac{m}{2}}$ such that $\Delta \neq 0$, and let $a = \Delta \| 0 \in \{0,1\}^m$ be the concatenation of Δ followed by $\frac{m}{2}$ zero bits. Show that $\mathrm{DP}^C(a, a) = 0$ for any choice of the permutations and any $\Delta \neq 0$.

(b) Let A be a pool of $2^{\frac{m}{2}}$ tuples $(t\|u, v\|w)$ with $t, u, v, w \in \{0,1\}^{\frac{m}{2}}$, $v\|w = C(t\|u)$, where u is a constant and where t goes through all values of $\{0,1\}^{m/2}$. Show that two tuples $(t\|u, v\|w)$ and $(t'\|u', v'\|w')$ define a pair of plaintext-ciphertext couples within the difference described in the previous question if and only if $(t \oplus v, w) = (t' \oplus v', w')$. In other words, show that for all $(t\|u, v\|w), (t'\|u', v'\|w') \in A$ we have

$$\exists \Delta \in \{0,1\}^{\frac{m}{2}} \text{ such that } \begin{cases} t \oplus t' = \Delta \\ u \oplus u' = 0 \\ v \oplus v' = \Delta \\ w \oplus w' = 0 \end{cases} \Leftrightarrow \begin{cases} t \oplus v = t' \oplus v' \\ w = w'. \end{cases}$$

Deduce that finding such two tuples reduces to a collision problem.

(c) Let u be an arbitrary constant and let A be the corresponding pool of $2^{\frac{m}{2}}$ tuples, but computed with the uniformly distributed random permutation C^* instead of C. Compute the expected number of $(t\|u, v\|w), (t'\|u', v'\|w') \in A$ pairs such that $(t\|u, v\|w) \neq (t'\|u', v'\|w')$ and

$$\exists \Delta \in \{0,1\}^{\frac{m}{2}} \text{ such that } \begin{cases} t \oplus t' = \Delta \\ u \oplus u' = 0 \\ v \oplus v' = \Delta \\ w \oplus w' = 0. \end{cases}$$

By using the Birthday Paradox, estimate the probability that we have at least one such a pair.

(d) We now consider the f_i's as *random* permutations. Deduce a distinguisher between C and C^* with $2^{\frac{m}{2}}$ queries and a non-negligible advantage.

6 We want to instantiate a 6-round Feistel schem using "random" permutations as round functions. To do so, we let $f_i = \text{DES}_{K_i}$ where K_i is a random 56-bit key. We consider $C = \Psi(f_1, f_2, f_3, f_4, f_5, f_6)$. Using the previous distinguisher, describe an attack against C which recovers K_6 by using $n \cdot 2^{64}$ chosen plaintexts and $n \cdot 2^{120}$ DES computations for a small constant n.

▷ Solution on page 101

Exercise 7   ⋆Multipermutations

Let $\mathcal{X}$ be a finite set. A function $f : \mathcal{X}^p \rightarrow \mathcal{X}^q$ is said to be a (p, q)-*multipermutation on* $\mathcal{X}$ if for any two different tuples $(x_1, \ldots, x_{p+q}) \in \mathcal{X}^p \times \mathcal{X}^q$ such that $(x_{p+1}, \ldots, x_{p+q}) = f(x_1, \ldots, x_p)$, at least $q + 1$ coordinates take different values. The hash function MD4 uses the following three Boolean functions

$$
\begin{aligned}
f_1(a, b, c) &= \text{ if } a \text{ then } b \text{ else } c \\
f_2(a, b, c) &= \text{ if } c \text{ then } a \text{ else } b \\
f_3(a, b, c) &= a \oplus b \oplus c.
\end{aligned}
$$

1 Show that f_1 and f_2 are *not* $(3, 1)$-multipermutations.

2 Show that f_3 is a $(3, 1)$-multipermutation.

The block cipher SAFER involves a transformation called 2-PHT defined by

$$2\text{-PHT}(a, b) = (2a + b \bmod 256, a + b \bmod 256),$$

where a and b are 8-bit values.

3 Show that the 2-PHT transform is *not* a $(2, 2)$-multipermutation.

The block cipher CS-CIPHER uses a mixing box M defined as follows

$$
\begin{aligned}
M : \quad &\{0,1\}^8 \times \{0,1\}^8 &\longrightarrow \quad &\{0,1\}^8 \times \{0,1\}^8 \\
&(x_\ell, x_r) &\longmapsto \quad &(y_\ell, y_r),
\end{aligned}
$$

with

$$
\begin{cases}
y_\ell &= P(\varphi(x_\ell) \oplus x_r) \\
y_r &= P(\text{ROTL}(x_\ell) \oplus x_r)
\end{cases}
$$

where P is a nonlinear permutation and φ is a linear permutation and ROTL is a rotation of one bit to the left. This mixing box is actually a permutation itself.

4 Show that the M-function is a $(2, 2)$-multipermutation.

▷ Solution on page 107

Exercise 8   ⋆Orthomorphisms

A XOR-orthomorphism is a permutation

$$\sigma: \ S \ \to \ S$$
$$a \ \mapsto \ \sigma(a)$$

defined on a set $S = \{0,1\}^n$, such that

$$\sigma': \ S \ \to \ S$$
$$a \ \mapsto \ a \oplus \sigma(a)$$

is also a permutation. We restrict to $S = \{0,1\}^8$ in this exercise. We consider the permutation

$$\omega: \ S \ \to \ S$$
$$x \ \mapsto \ \mathrm{ROT}^4(x \oplus (x \gg 4))$$

where $x \gg 4$ denotes a shift of 4 bits to the right of x and $\mathrm{ROT}^i(x)$ denotes a rotation of x of i bits to the right. For example, the shift of an 8-bit string $b_7 b_6 b_5 b_4 b_3 b_2 b_1 b_0$ is

$$b_7 b_6 b_5 b_4 b_3 b_2 b_1 b_0 \gg 4 = 0000 b_7 b_6 b_5 b_4$$

and the rotation of 1 bit is

$$\mathrm{ROT}^1(b_7 b_6 b_5 b_4 b_3 b_2 b_1 b_0) = b_0 b_7 b_6 b_5 b_4 b_3 b_2 b_1.$$

1 Prove that ω is a XOR-orthomorphism.

2 Draw a diagram representing ω. What is the inverse of ω?

We now consider

$$\pi: \ S \ \to \ S$$
$$x \ \mapsto \ (x \ \mathrm{AND} \ c) \oplus \mathrm{ROT}^1(x)$$

with $c = \mathtt{0xAA}$.

3 Prove that π is a XOR-orthomorphism. What is the inverse of π?

4 We consider the same permutation π as before, but with $c = \mathtt{0x01}$. Prove that it is a XOR-orthomorphism. What is the inverse of this new permutation?

5 Prove that the function

$$(a,b) \mapsto (a \oplus b, a \oplus \sigma(b))$$

is a $(2,2)$-multipermutation if and only if σ is a XOR-orthomorphism.

Reminder: A function $f : (x_1, x_2) \mapsto (f_1(x_1, x_2), f_2(x_1, x_2))$ is a $(2,2)$-multipermutation if and only if two 4-tuples of the form $(x_1, x_2, f_1(x_1, x_2), f_2(x_1, x_2))$ and $(x_1', x_2', f_1(x_1', x_2'), f_2(x_1', x_2'))$ are either identical or differ at least on 3 positions.

▷ Solution on page 108

Exercise 9   ⋆Decorrelation

In this exercise we consider a random permutation $C : \{0, 1\}^m \to \{0, 1\}^m$ and compare it to the uniformly distributed random permutation $C^* : \{0, 1\}^m \to \{0, 1\}^m$.

1 Prove that $\||[C]^{d-1} - [C^*]^{d-1}\||_\infty \leq \||[C]^d - [C^*]^d\||_\infty$.

2 Prove that $0 \leq \||[C]^d - [C^*]^d\||_\infty \leq 2$.

Hint: Use the interpretation of $\||[C]^d - [C^*]^d\||_\infty$ in term of best non-adaptive distinguisher.

3 Show that the property $\mathrm{Dec}^d(C) = 0$ does not depend on the choice of the distance on the matrix space.

4 Show that if $\mathrm{Dec}^1(C) = 0$, then the cipher C provides perfect secrecy for any distribution of the plaintext.

5 Show that if $\mathrm{Dec}^2(C) = 0$, then C is a Markov cipher.

In a typical situation, C is a block cipher and the randomness actually comes from the randomness of the secret key. Let $f_K : \{0, 1\}^m \to \{0, 1\}^m$ be a function parametered by a uniformly distributed random key K in a key space $\mathcal{K} = \{0, 1\}^m$. We compare f_K to a uniformly distributed random function F^*.

6 Prove that if $\mathrm{Dec}^d(f_K) = 0$, then $|\mathcal{K}| \geq 2^{md}$.

7 Show that for $f_K(x) = x \oplus K$, we obtain $\mathrm{Dec}^1(f_K) = 0$.

8 Propose a construction for f_K such that $\mathrm{Dec}^d(f_K) = 0$ and $|\mathcal{K}| = 2^{md}$.

▷ Solution on page 110

Exercise 10   ⋆Decorrelation and Differential Cryptanalysis

A typical measure in the differential cryptanalysis of a random permutation C is the maximum value of the expected differential probability defined by

$$\text{EDP}^C_{\max} = \max_{a \neq 0, b} \text{E}_C(\Pr_X[C(X \oplus a) = C(X) \oplus b]).$$

Prove that

$$\text{EDP}^C_{\max} \leq \frac{1}{2^m - 1} + \text{BestAdv}_{\text{Cl}^2_a}(C, C^*).$$

▷ Solution on page 113

Exercise 11   ⋆Decorrelation of a Feistel Cipher

Prove that for any independent random function $F_1, \ldots, F_r$ on $\{0,1\}^{\frac{m}{2}}$ such that

$$\text{BestAdv}_{\text{Cl}^d_a}(F_i, F^*) \leq \varepsilon$$

we have

$$\text{BestAdv}_{\text{Cl}^d_a}(\Psi(F_1, \ldots, F_r), C^*) \leq \frac{1}{2}(2d^2 \cdot 2^{-\frac{m}{2}} + 6\varepsilon)^{\lfloor \frac{r}{3} \rfloor}$$

▷ Solution on page 114

Exercise 12   ⋆A Saturation Attack against IDEA

The International Data Encryption Algorithm (IDEA) is a block cipher that was originally proposed by Xuejia Lai and James Massey at ETH Zürich. It is based on a Lai-Massey scheme (Figure 4.2). IDEA encrypts 64-bit blocks, uses 128-bit keys, and is made of 8 identical rounds (Figure 4.3) followed by one last shorter round (that we do not need to detail). We use the following notations

- The input of round r is denoted $X^{(r)} = \left(X_1^{(r)}, X_2^{(r)}, X_3^{(r)}, X_4^{(r)}\right)$, where $X_i^{(r)} \in \{0,1\}^{16}$.

- Similarly, the output of round r is denoted

$$Y^{(r)} = \left(Y_1^{(r)}, Y_2^{(r)}, Y_3^{(r)}, Y_4^{(r)}\right),$$

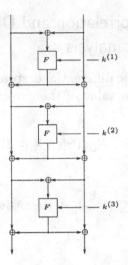

Figure 4.2. A three-round Lai-Massey scheme

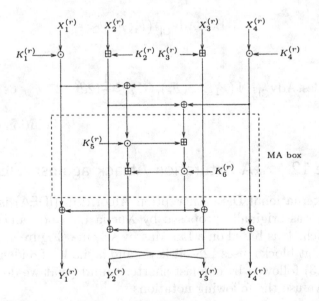

Figure 4.3. One round of IDEA

where $Y_i^{(r)} \in \{0,1\}^{16}$. Obviously, the output of round r is the input of round $r + 1$.

- The subkey of round r is denoted $K^{(r)} = \left(K_1^{(r)}, K_2^{(r)}, \ldots, K_6^{(r)}\right)$, where $K_i^{(r)} \in \{0,1\}^{16}$. A key-schedule (that we will not detail here) is used to compute each subkey $K^{(r)}$ from a secret key $K \in \{0,1\}^{128}$.

- The internal operations of IDEA are $\oplus$ (which is the bitwise XOR operation), $\odot$ (which is the multiplication modulo $2^{16}+1$ of two 16-bit integers where the block of 16 zeros corresponds to 2^{16}), and $\boxplus$ (which is the addition modulo 2^{16} of two 16-bit integers). These three operations are *group operations*.

Preliminaries

1 What is the worst case complexity of an exhaustive key search against IDEA? What is the average complexity? Is such an attack practical?

2 Consider the three-round Lai-Massey scheme represented on Figure 4.2. Using the same notations, draw a three-round decryption scheme. Is there any particular condition on F in order for the Lai-Massey scheme to be a permutation? Justify your answer.

Properties of internal operations of IDEA

From now on, we focus our attention on a reduced version of IDEA made of only two rounds (see Figure 4.4). The objective of this exercise is to develop an attack which shall be faster than exhaustive key search. In this section c denotes a 16-bit constant.

3 Prove that

$$f : \{0,1\}^{16} \longrightarrow \{0,1\}^{16} \qquad g : \{0,1\}^{16} \longrightarrow \{0,1\}^{16}$$
$$x \longmapsto x \oplus c, \qquad\qquad x \longmapsto x \odot c,$$

and

$$h : \{0,1\}^{16} \longrightarrow \{0,1\}^{16}$$
$$x \longmapsto x \boxplus c,$$

are permutations (recall that $\oplus$, $\odot$, and $\boxplus$ are three group laws).

In the light of the preceeding question, we can now see the keystone of the *saturation attack* against IDEA. Consider the following portion of IDEA:

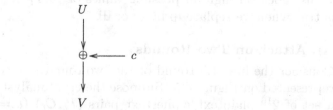

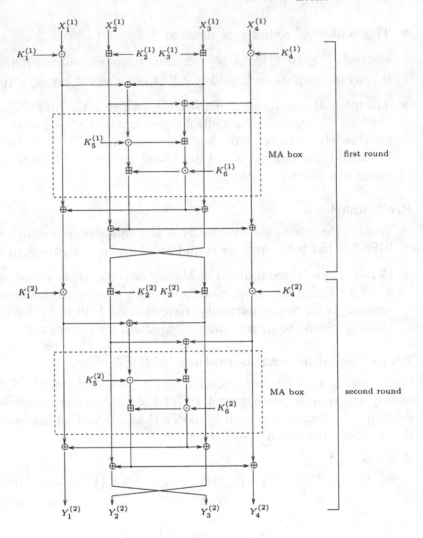

Figure 4.4.   IDEA reduced to two rounds

If the input U of the transformation goes through all possible values, i.e., if U successively takes the 2^{16} values of the set $\{0,1\}^{16}$, we know that V also goes through all possible values of $\{0,1\}^{16}$. The same property is true when we replace $\oplus$ by $\odot$ or $\boxplus$.

An Attack on Two Rounds

Consider the first 1.5 round of the two-round reduced version of IDEA, represented on Figure 4.5. Suppose the cryptanalyst has at his disposal a set of 2^{16} plaintext/ciphertext pairs (P_ℓ, C_ℓ) $(\ell = 1, \ldots, 2^{16})$, where

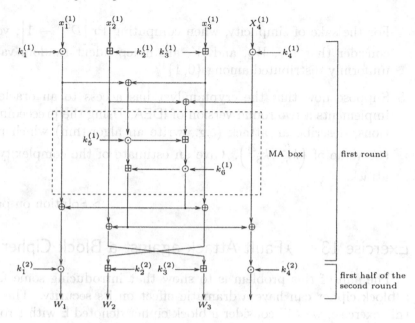

Figure 4.5. 1.5 round of IDEA

each ciphertext C_ℓ was obtained by encrypting P_ℓ with a fixed (but unknown) secret key $k \in \{0,1\}^{128}$ and using the two-round version of IDEA. Suppose moreover that any plaintext $P \in \{P_1, \ldots, P_{2^{16}}\}$ has the following shape

$$P = \left(x_1^{(1)}, x_2^{(1)}, x_3^{(1)}, X_4^{(1)} \right),$$

where $x_1^{(1)}, x_2^{(1)}, x_3^{(1)}$ are constant values and where $X_4^{(1)}$ goes through all possible values of $\{0,1\}^{16}$ when P goes through $\{P_1, \ldots, P_{2^{16}}\}$.

4 What is the shape of the set described by W_1 (see Figure 4.5) when P goes through $\{P_1, \ldots, P_{2^{16}}\}$? Justify your answer.

5 Same question for W_2 and W_3.

6 Deduce a distinguisher $\mathcal{D}$ which tries to predict whether an oracle $\mathcal{O}$ is the 1.5 round version of IDEA or a permutation C^* chosen uniformly at random among all possible permutations on $\{0,1\}^{64}$.

7 Compute the advantage of the distinguisher.
   Hint: If your distinguisher outputs 1 when its predicts that the oracle implements 1.5 round IDEA and 0 if it predicts that the oracle implements C^*, its advantage is defined by

$$\mathrm{Adv}^{\mathcal{D}} = \left| \Pr\left[\mathcal{D}^{C^*} \to 1 \right] - \Pr\left[\mathcal{D}^{\mathsf{IDEA}} \to 1 \right] \right|.$$

For the sake of simplicity, when computing $\Pr\left[\mathcal{D}^{C^*} \to 1\right]$, you may consider that W_1, W_2, and W_3 are independent random variables, uniformly distributed among $\{0,1\}^{16}$.

8 Suppose now that the cryptanalyst has access to an oracle which implements a two round version of IDEA. Using the preceeding questions, describe an attack (e.g., write an algorithm) which recovers the value of $\left(k_5^{(2)}, k_6^{(2)}\right)$. Give an estimate of the complexity of the attack.

▷ Solution on page 115

Exercise 13   ⋆Fault Attack against a Block Cipher

The aim of this problem is to show that introducing some faults in a block cipher can have a dramatic effect on its security. Throughout this exercise, we will consider a block cipher denoted E with ℓ rounds, a block size and a key size of n bits. This block cipher simply consists of an iteration of functions T_i and subkey additions (see Figure 4.6). The subkeys k_i, $0 \leq i \leq \ell$, are all derived from the secret key k associated to E. The ith round is denoted as R_i and the intermediate state of the plaintext p after the ith round is denoted p_i. So, we have $R_0(p) = k_0 \oplus p = p_0$, $R_i(p_{i-1}) = T_i(p_{i-1}) \oplus k_i = p_i$ for $1 \leq i \leq \ell$, and the ciphertext $c = p_\ell$.

1 Show how the decryption algorithm works. Under which conditions can we decrypt the ciphertexts encrypted by E?

From now on, we will assume we have a device at our disposal which allows to produce some faults in a given implementation of E (in a smart-card, for example). Usually, one fault will correspond to flipping one chosen bit of an intermediate state p_i. We will also assume that k_ℓ is uniformly distributed in $\{0,1\}^n$ and that $T_1 = T_2 = \cdots = T_\ell = T$.

2 Here, we will produce some faults on $p_{\ell-1}$, i.e., we modify $p_{\ell-1}$ to $p'_{\ell-1} = p_{\ell-1} \oplus \delta$, where δ is a bitstring of length n with a 1 at the position of the bits we aim at modifying in the ciphertext, and 0's everywhere else. Let c' be the ciphertext obtained when introducing the faults δ. Find a relation between δ, $p_{\ell-1}$, c, and c'.

3 Assume here that our device only allows us to produce some faults in the subkeys. How can we get the same c' as above with such a device?

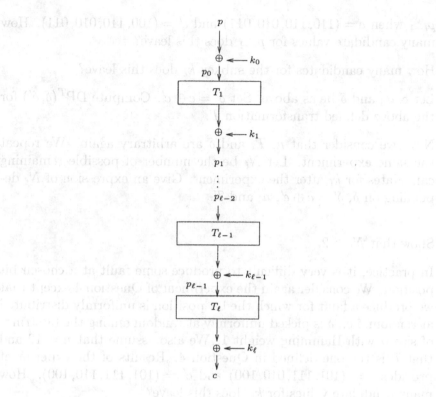

Figure 4.6. The block cipher E

Table 4.1. Definition of the function f

x	000	001	010	011	100	101	110	111
$f(x)$	101	100	010	111	110	000	001	011

4 Assume here that $n = 12$ and that T is defined as follows

$$T : (x_1, x_2, x_3, x_4) \mapsto (f(x_1), f(x_2), f(x_3), f(x_4)),$$

where the function $f : \{0,1\}^3 \to \{0,1\}^3$ is defined by Table 4.1. Now, we will try to obtain some information about one subkey. For this, we first encrypt a plaintext p chosen uniformly at random, using the target implementation of E. Then, we encrypt the same plaintext again, but we introduce some faults in $p_{\ell-1}$ such that it is transformed into $p_{\ell-1} \oplus \delta$, with $\delta = (001, 000, 000, 000)$, i.e., we flip the last bit of x_1. Let c be the ciphertext $\mathsf{E}(p)$ and c' be the ciphertext obtained with the introduced fault. Show that we can deduce some information on

$p_{\ell-1}$ when $c = (110, 110, 010, 011)$ and $c' = (100, 110, 010, 011)$. How many candidate values for $p_{\ell-1}$ does this leave?

5 How many candidates for the subkey k_ℓ does this leave?

6 Let c, c', and δ be as above. Set $\delta' = c \oplus c'$. Compute $\mathrm{DP}^T(\delta, \delta')$ for the above defined transformation T.

7 Now, we consider that n, T, and δ are arbitrary again. We repeat the same experiment. Let N_ℓ be the number of possible remaining candidates for k_ℓ after the experiment. Give an expression of N_ℓ depending on δ, $\delta' = c \oplus c'$, n, and T.

8 Show that $N_\ell \geq 2$.

9 In practice, it is very difficult to produce some fault at a chosen bit position. We consider again the experiment of Question 4 except that we produce a fault for which the bit position is uniformly distributed at random, i.e., δ is picked uniformly at random among the bitstrings of size n with Hamming weight 1. We also assume that $n = 12$ and that T is the one defined in Question 4. Results of the experiment provides $c = (101, 111, 010, 100)$ and $c' = (101, 111, 110, 100)$. How many candidate values for k_ℓ does this leave?

▷ Solution on page 122

Solutions

Solution 1   The SAFER Permutation

$\mathbf{Z}_{257}^*$ is a multiplicative group of order $\varphi(257) = 256$, since 257 is a prime number, where φ is the Euler Totient Function and $\varphi(n)$ is equal to the number of integers in the interval $[1, n]$ which are relatively prime to n. The order of an element $a \in \mathbf{Z}_n^*$ is the least positive integer t such that $a^t \equiv 1 \pmod{n}$. By Fermat's Little Theorem, we know that, if $\gcd(a, p) = 1$ and p is a prime number, then $a^{p-1} \equiv 1 \pmod{p}$. Thus, $45^{256} \equiv 1 \pmod{257}$. By Lagrange's Theorem, we also know that the order of 45 divides the group order, i.e., 256 and thus the order of 45 must be a power of 2. We observe that $45^{128} \equiv 256 \pmod{257}$, so that the smallest integer t (being a power of 2) such that $45^t \equiv 1 \pmod{257}$ is 256. Therefore, the order of 45 is equal to the group order, which proves that 45 is a *generator* of the group $\mathbf{Z}_{257}^*$. The group $\mathbf{Z}_{257}^*$ is thus cyclic and we can write

$$\mathbf{Z}_{257}^* = \{45^i \bmod 257 \quad \text{where} \quad 0 \le i \le 255\}.$$

Thus, the function $x \mapsto 45^x \pmod{257}$ is a bijection from $\{0, \ldots, 255\}$ to $\{1, \ldots, 256\}$. Reducing the former set modulo 256 transforms this bijection into a permutation over $\{0, \ldots, 255\}$.

The reference paper on SAFER-K is [26].

Solution 2   ⋆Linear Cryptanalysis

The idea is to build pairs of elements $(a, 2^{m-1} + a)$ such that $a < 2^{m-1}$ with identical parity bits and to show that they have different parity bits after the application of $E(\cdot)$. We have

$$E(a) = (g^a \bmod (2^m + 1)) \bmod 2^m$$

and

$$E(2^{m-1} + a) = (g^{2^{m-1}} \cdot g^a \bmod (2^m + 1)) \bmod 2^m.$$

It can be shown that $g^{2^{m-1}} \equiv -1 \pmod{2^m + 1}$. Indeed, if p is a prime, then $x^2 \equiv 1 \pmod{p}$ if and only if $p \mid (x-1)(x+1)$. As p is prime, this means that $p \mid x - 1$ or $p \mid x + 1$, i.e., that $x \equiv \pm 1 \pmod{p}$. Conversely, if either of those two congruences holds, then $x^2 \equiv 1 \pmod{p}$. In our case, we know that $g^{2^{m-1}}$ cannot be congruent to 1, as g is a generator. Therefore, $g^{2^{m-1}}$ must be congruent to -1. We obtain

$$E(2^{m-1} + a) = (-g^a \bmod (2^m + 1)) \bmod 2^m.$$

Note that the two images have different parity bits, since $2^m + 1$ is an odd number. Let $n = 2^m$. $\mathbf{Z}_n$ can be partitioned into 4 *disjoint* sets:

$$
\begin{aligned}
A &= \{x \in \mathbf{Z}_n \mid x \equiv 0 \pmod 2 \quad \text{and} \quad E(x) \equiv 0 \pmod 2\} \\
B &= \{x \in \mathbf{Z}_n \mid x \equiv 0 \pmod 2 \quad \text{and} \quad E(x) \equiv 1 \pmod 2\} \\
C &= \{x \in \mathbf{Z}_n \mid x \equiv 1 \pmod 2 \quad \text{and} \quad E(x) \equiv 0 \pmod 2\} \\
D &= \{x \in \mathbf{Z}_n \mid x \equiv 1 \pmod 2 \quad \text{and} \quad E(x) \equiv 1 \pmod 2\}
\end{aligned}
$$

Clearly, $A \cup B = \{x \in \mathbf{Z}_n \mid x \equiv 0 \pmod 2\}$ and $C \cup D = \{x \in \mathbf{Z}_n \mid x \equiv 1 \pmod 2\}$ and thus, $|A \cup B| = |C \cup D| = 2^{m-1}$. We have shown that there is a bijection between A and B. Namely, any pair of the form $(x, x + 2^{m-1})$ with $x < 2^{m-1}$ contains one element of A and one element of B. Thus, we have $|A| = |B| = 2^{m-2}$. The same holds between C and D. Thus

$$
\Pr[x \equiv E(x) \pmod 2] = \Pr[x \in A \text{ or } x \in D] = \frac{1}{2}.
$$

More details about the linear cryptanalysis of SAFER can be found in [53].

Solution 3   ⋆Differential and Linear Probabilities

1 We denote by $+$ the addition modulo 32. We have

$$
\begin{aligned}
\mathrm{DP}^f(\delta \| \delta, 0) &= \Pr_{X,Y}[f(X \oplus \delta, Y \oplus \delta) = f(X, Y)] \\
&= \Pr_{X,Y}[(X \oplus \delta) + (Y \oplus \delta) = X + Y],
\end{aligned}
$$

where $X = X_{31}X_{30} \cdots X_0$ and $Y = Y_{31}Y_{30} \cdots Y_0$ are uniformly distributed random 32-bit strings. We introduce the following notations: we let S_i be the addition modulo 2^{32} of $X_i X_{i-1} \cdots X_0$ and $Y_i Y_{i-1} \cdots Y_0$ and let C_i be the carry bit resulting from this addition. Note that $S_{31} = X + Y$ and that the modular addition erases the last carry bit, so that $C_{31} = 0$.

We have $X' = X \oplus \delta = \overline{X_{31}}X_{30} \cdots X_0$ and $Y' = Y \oplus \delta = \overline{Y_{31}}Y_{30} \cdots Y_0$, therefore $S_{30} = S'_{30}$ and $C_{30} = C'_{30}$. Finally,

$$
X + Y = (X \oplus \delta) + (Y \oplus \delta) \Leftrightarrow X_{31} \oplus Y_{31} = \overline{X_{31}} \oplus \overline{Y_{31}},
$$

and as $\bar{a} \oplus \bar{b} = a \oplus b$ for any bitstrings a and b, we conclude that

$$
\mathrm{DP}^f(\delta \| \delta, 0) = 1.
$$

2 This time, $X' = X \oplus \delta = \overline{X_{31}X_{30}}X_{29} \cdots X_0$ and $Y' = Y \oplus \delta = \overline{Y_{31}Y_{30}}Y_{29} \cdots Y_0$. Similarly to the previous question, $S_{29} = S'_{29}$ and $C_{29} = C'_{29}$. Therefore,

$$X + Y = X' + Y' \quad \Leftrightarrow \quad \begin{cases} X_{30} \oplus Y_{30} = \overline{X_{30}} \oplus \overline{Y_{30}} \\ X_{31} \oplus Y_{31} \oplus C_{30} = \overline{X_{31}} \oplus \overline{Y_{31}} \oplus C'_{30} \end{cases}$$

$$\Leftrightarrow \quad C_{30} = C'_{30}.$$

Denoting $b = C_{29} = C'_{29}$, Table 4.2 shows the different values of the carry bits C_{30} and C'_{30} depending on the values of X_{30}, Y_{30}, and b. We deduce that $C_{30} = C'_{30}$ occurs with probability $\frac{1}{2}$. Finally,

$$\mathrm{DP}^f(\delta \| \delta, 0) = \frac{1}{2}.$$

3 We have

$$\begin{aligned} \mathrm{LP}^f(\delta \| \delta, \delta) &= (2\Pr[\delta \cdot X \oplus \delta \cdot Y = \delta \cdot f(X, Y)] - 1)^2 \\ &= (2\Pr[\delta \cdot X \oplus \delta \cdot Y = \delta \cdot (X + Y)] - 1)^2. \end{aligned}$$

As $\delta \cdot X = X_0$, $\delta \cdot Y = Y_0$, and as $\delta \cdot (X + Y) = X_0 \oplus Y_0$,

$$\mathrm{LP}^f(\delta \| \delta, \delta) = 1.$$

4 Here, we have $\delta \cdot X = X_1 \oplus X_0$ and $\delta \cdot Y = Y_1 \oplus Y_0$. As $\delta \cdot (X + Y) = X_0 \oplus Y_0 \oplus X_1 \oplus Y_1 \oplus C_0$ (using the notations of the previous questions), we have

$$\mathrm{LP}^f(\delta \| \delta, \delta) = (2\Pr[C_0 = 0] - 1)^2.$$

As $C_0 = 0$ with probability $\frac{3}{4}$, we conclude that

$$\mathrm{LP}^f(\delta \| \delta, \delta) = \frac{1}{4}.$$

The reference papers on differential and linear cryptanalysis are [5] and [28] respectively.

Table 4.2. Possible values of the carry bits C_{30} and C'_{30}, depending on X_{30}, Y_{30}, and on the previous carry bit $b = C_{29} = C'_{29}$

X_{30}	Y_{30}	$\overline{X_{30}}$	$\overline{Y_{30}}$	C_{30}	C'_{30}
0	0	1	1	0	1
0	1	1	0	b	b
1	0	0	1	b	b
1	1	0	0	1	0

Solution 4 ⋆Feistel Schemes

1 The probability is equal to 1 as we always have $x_r = y_r$ for $\Psi^{(1)}$.

2 We have
$$\Pr[\mathcal{D}^{\Psi^{(1)}} \to 1] = \Pr[C^*(x_r) = x_r].$$

We recall (from Exercise 1, Chapter 1) that for the random permutation C^* uniformly distributed over all possible permutations of $\{0,1\}^n$, we have for any $x, y \in \{0,1\}^n$

$$\Pr[C^*(x) = y] = \Pr_{Y \in \{0,1\}^n}[Y = y] = 2^{-n},$$

Therefore
$$\Pr[\mathcal{D}^{\Psi^{(1)}} \to 1] = 2^{-32}.$$

Finally, the advantage of the distinguisher $\mathcal{D}$ is $\mathrm{Adv}^{\mathcal{D}} = 1 - 2^{-32}$.

3 We consider the distinguisher described in Algorithm 15.

Algorithm 15 2-round Feistel distinguisher $\mathcal{D}$

Input: an oracle $\mathcal{O}$ implementing either a 2-round Feistel scheme $\Psi^{(2)}$ or a uniformly random permutation C^*

Output: 0 (if the guess is that $\mathcal{O}$ implements C^*) or 1 (if the guess is that $\mathcal{O}$ implements $\Psi^{(2)}$)

Processing:

1: let $P = (x_\ell, x_r)$ and $P' = (x'_\ell, x_r)$ with $x_\ell \neq x'_\ell$ be two input plaintexts
2: submit P and P' to the oracle and get $C = (y_\ell, y_r)$ and $C' = (y'_\ell, y'_r)$
3: if $x_\ell \oplus x'_\ell = y_r \oplus y'_r$, then output "1", otherwise, output "0"

---

4 If the oracle $\mathcal{O}$ implements a 2-round Feistel scheme $\Psi^{(2)}$, we always have $x_\ell \oplus x'_\ell = y_r \oplus y'_r$, so that

$$\Pr[\mathcal{D}^{\Psi^{(2)}} \to 1] = 1.$$

Consider now the case where $\mathcal{O}$ implements C^* and denote $x = (x_\ell, x_r)$, $x' = (x'_\ell, x_r)$, $y = (y_\ell, y_r)$, and $y' = (y'_\ell, y'_r)$ such that

$$C^*(x) = y \qquad C^*(x') = y'.$$

As already mentioned, one can consider $C^*(x)$ and $C^*(x')$ as two random variables, that we will respectively denote $Y = (Y_\ell, Y_r)$ and $Y' = (Y'_\ell, Y'_r)$, uniformly distributed over $\{0,1\}^{64}$. But as we know that $x \neq x'$ and as C^* is a permutation, Y and Y' are different (which are therefore not independent). Consequently, if we denote $\alpha = x_\ell \oplus x'_\ell \neq 0$, we obtain

$$
\begin{aligned}
\Pr[\mathcal{D}^{C^*} \to 1] &= \Pr[Y_r \oplus Y'_r = \alpha \mid Y \neq Y'] \\
&= \frac{\Pr[Y_r \oplus Y'_r = \alpha, Y \neq Y']}{\Pr[Y \neq Y']} \\
&= \frac{\Pr[Y \neq Y' \mid Y_r \oplus Y'_r = \alpha] \Pr[Y_r \oplus Y'_r = \alpha]}{\Pr[Y \neq Y']} \\
&= \frac{1 \times 2^{-32}}{1 - 2^{-64}} \\
&\approx 2^{-32}.
\end{aligned}
$$

Consequently, the distinguisher $\mathcal{D}$ defined by Algorithm 15 has the following advantage

$$
\mathrm{Adv}^{\mathcal{D}} \approx 1 - 2^{-32}.
$$

Solution 5   ⋆Impossible Differentials

The propagation of the $(\Delta\|0, \Delta\|0)$ differential characteristic is depicted in Figure 4.7. As we know that the functions f_1, f_2, f_3, f_4, and f_5 are in fact permutations, we must take into account that a non-zero difference in input will result in a (possibly identical) non-zero difference in output. Thus, we see that there is a contradiction at the output of f_3. A value Δ XORed with a non-zero β difference cannot give a Δ difference. Thus, the probability that such a differential characteristic occurs in a 5-round Feistel scheme is equal to 0, provided that the f_i's are permutations.

A complete security analysis of Feistel ciphers with 6 rounds or less is available in [24].

Solution 6   ⋆Attacks Using Impossible Differential

1 A three-round Feistel scheme is represented on Figure 4.8. The inverse of this scheme is $\Psi(f_3, f_2, f_1)$.

2 The differential probability of a permutation c is

$$
\mathrm{DP}^c(a, b) = \Pr_X[c(X \oplus a) = c(X) \oplus b],
$$

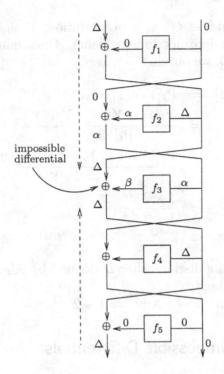

Figure 4.7. Propagation of a differential characteristic $(\Delta\|0, \Delta\|0)$ in a 5-round Feistel scheme

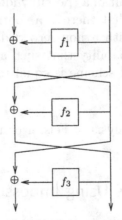

Figure 4.8. A three-round Feistel scheme $\Psi(f_1, f_2, f_3)$

where the probability is taken over the uniformly distributed random variable $X \in \{0,1\}^m$. We now consider a *random* permutation C^*, uniformly distributed. We have

$$\mathrm{E}_{C^*}\left[\mathrm{DP}^{C^*}(a,b)\right] = \sum_c \Pr[c(X \oplus a) = c(X) \oplus b]\Pr[C^* = c]$$

$$= \sum_c \sum_x 1_{c(x \oplus a) = c(x) \oplus b}\Pr[X = x]\Pr[C^* = c]$$

$$= \sum_x \Pr_{C^*}[C^*(x \oplus a) = C^*(x) \oplus b]\Pr[X = x].$$

Since $a \neq 0$, x and $x \oplus a$ are different and thus, so are $C^*(x)$ and $C^*(x \oplus a)$. The difference $C^*(x) \oplus C^*(x \oplus a)$ is thus uniformly distributed among all non-zero differences. Therefore

$$\Pr_{C^*}[C^*(x \oplus a) = C^*(x) \oplus b] = \frac{1}{2^m - 1},$$

and

$$\mathrm{E}_{C^*}\left[\mathrm{DP}^{C^*}(a,b)\right] = \frac{1}{2^m - 1}.$$

3 A distinguisher is a probabilistic Turing machine which can play with an oracle (The Turing machine sends queries to the oracle and receives answers.). At the end, the Turing machine outputs 0 or 1. The advantage for distinguishing C from C^* is the difference between the probability that the Turing machine outputs 1 when the oracle implements C^* and the probability that it outputs 1 when the oracle implements C.

4 The distinguisher is described by Algorithm 16. Obviously, when the oracle is $\Psi(f_1, f_2)$, the distinguisher outputs 1 with probability 1. When the oracle is a permutation chosen at random, y_1 and y_2 are different random elements. The probability that the distinguisher outputs 1 in this case is thus

$$\Pr[u \oplus w = a \oplus b | y_1 \neq y_2] = \frac{\Pr[u \oplus w = a \oplus b, y_1 \neq y_2]}{\Pr[y_1 \neq y_2]},$$

and as the numerator of the fraction is equal to

$$\Pr[y_1 \neq y_2 | u \oplus w = a \oplus b]\Pr[u \oplus w = a \oplus b] = 1 \cdot 2^{-m/2},$$

we obtain

$$\Pr[u \oplus w = a \oplus b | y_1 \neq y_2] = \frac{2^{-m/2}}{1 - 2^{-m}} \approx 2^{-m/2}.$$

Algorithm 16 A distinguisher of a two-round Feistel scheme

Input: an oracle $\mathcal{O}$ implementing either a two-round Feistel scheme $\Psi(f_1, f_2)$ (where f_1 and f_2 are random permutations) or the uniformly distributed random permutation C^*.

Output: 0 (if the guess is that $\mathcal{O}$ implements C^*) or 1 (if the guess is that $\mathcal{O}$ implements $\Psi(f_1, f_2)$)

Processing:

1: let $a, b, c \in \{0,1\}^{m/2}$ such that $a \neq b$
2: let $x_1 = a\|c$ and $x_2 = b\|c$, send the two queries x_1 and x_2 to the oracle
3: receive the two answers $y_1 = t\|u$ and $y_2 = v\|w$ from the oracle, where $t, u, v, w \in \{0,1\}^{m/2}$
4: **if** $a \oplus b = u \oplus w$ **then**
5:    output 1
6: **else**
7:    output 0
8: **end if**

Therefore the advantage for distinguishing $\Psi(f_1, f_2)$ from a random permutation is approximately $1 - 2^{-\frac{m}{2}}$.

5 (a) The solution of this question is given in Solution 5 of this chapter.

 (b) Let us assume there exists Δ such that

$$\begin{cases} t \oplus t' = \Delta \\ u \oplus u' = 0 \\ v \oplus v' = \Delta \\ w \oplus w' = 0. \end{cases}$$

By XORing the first and third equation, we obtain $t \oplus v = t' \oplus v'$. The fourth equation is equivalent to $w = w'$. This proves the "$\Rightarrow$" direction.

Let us now assume that $t \oplus v = t' \oplus v'$ and $w = w'$. Since the tuples are taken from the pool, we already have $u = u'$, therefore $u \oplus u' = 0$. Obviously we have $w \oplus w' = 0$. We let Δ be equal to $t \oplus t'$. We have now

$$v \oplus v' = t \oplus t' = \Delta$$

which proves the "$\Leftarrow$" direction.

We deduce that finding two such tuples in the pool is equivalent to finding collisions on the $(t \oplus v, w)$ pair: whenever we have $(t \oplus v, w) = (t' \oplus v', w')$, we have found two such tuples.

(c) We set u to a constant. We denote $(t_i\|u, v_i\|w_i)$ the ith tuple of A. To ensure that all the tuples are distinct one from each other, we increment the value of t_i for each tuple, starting from 0, where a binary string is implicitly considered as the binary representation of an integer. According to the previous question, the first computation is equivalent to finding the expected number of collisions of the type

$$(t_i \oplus v_i, w_i) = (t_j \oplus v_j, w_j) \quad \text{where } i \neq j, \qquad (4.1)$$

among the $2^{m/2}$ tuples of A. Let N be the random value corresponding to the number of such collisions. We have

$$N = \sum_{i<j} 1_{(t_i \oplus v_i, w_i) = (t_j \oplus v_j, w_j)},$$

and thus

$$E(N) = \sum_{i<j} \Pr[(t_i \oplus v_i, w_i) = (t_j \oplus v_j, w_j)].$$

As $v_i\|w_i = C^*(t_i\|u_i)$, we can consider v_i and w_i as uniformly distributed random values[1] of $\{0,1\}^{m/2}$, and thus the probability of the last sum is equal to 2^{-m}. We finally deduce that the expected number of tuples satisfying the condition is

$$E(N) = 2^{-m} \sum_{i<j} 1 = 2^{-m} \binom{2^{m/2}}{2} \approx \frac{1}{2}.$$

Using the Birthday Paradox, the probability that we get at least one collision such as (4.1) (which is a collision on m-bit binary strings) among the $2^{m/2}$ tuples is $1 - e^{-1/2}$.

(d) The distinguisher is described in Algorithm 17. When the oracle implements C (where the f_i's are random permutations), the probability that the distinguisher outputs 1 is 1 as, according to the previous questions, a collision such as (4.1) cannot occur. On the other hand, if the oracle implements C^*, we know from the previous question that no such collision occurs with a probability $e^{-1/2}$. Therefore, the advantage of the distinguisher is $1 - e^{-1/2}$.

6 The attack is described in Algorithm 18. The number of chosen plain-

---

[1]See Exercise 1 in Chapter 1

Algorithm 17 Distinguishing a 5-round Feistel scheme with random permutations from C^*

Input: an oracle $\mathcal{O}$ implementing either the 5-round Feistel scheme C or the uniformly distributed random permutation C^*

Output: 0 (if the guess is that $\mathcal{O}$ implements C^*) or 1 (if the guess is that $\mathcal{O}$ implements C)

Processing:

1: set u to some fixed value of $\{0,1\}^{m/2}$
2: **for** $i = 1$ to $2^{m/2}$ **do**
3:     let t_i be the binary representation of i
4:     send $t_i \| u$ to the oracle and receive $v_i \| w_i$
5: **end for**
6: sort the $(t_i \oplus v_i, w_i)$ tuples
7: **if** there is a collision such as Equation (4.1) **then**
8:     output 0
9: **else**
10:     output 1
11: **end if**

Algorithm 18 Attacking a 6-round Feistel scheme with random permutations

---

Input: an oracle which implements the 6-round Feistel scheme

Output: key candidate(s) for K_6

Processing:

1: set u to some fixed value of $\{0,1\}^{m/2}$
2: **for** $i = 1$ to $2^{m/2}$ **do**
3:     let t_i be the binary representation of i
4:     send $t_i \| u$ to the oracle and receive $r_i \| v_i$
5: **end for**
6: **for all** possible candidate value k_6 for K_6 **do**
7:     **for** $i = 1$ to $2^{m/2}$ **do**
8:         $w_i \leftarrow r_i \oplus \mathsf{DES}_{k_6}(v_i)$
9:     **end for**
10:     sort the $(t_i \oplus v_i, w_i)$ tuples
11:     **if** there is a collision such as equation (4.1) **then**
12:         reject k_6
13:     **else**
14:         accept k_6 as a candidate
15:     **end if**
16: **end for**

---

texts that are needed in the algorithm is 2^{64} as $m = 128$ here. The time complexity of this attack is $2^{64} \times 2^{56} = 2^{120}$ DES computations. For a wrong key, the probability that it is discarded is $1 - e^{-1/2}$, i.e., a fraction $\alpha = 1 - e^{-1/2}$ of wrong keys are rejected at each execution of the algorithm. If we iterate n times the algorithm, until $(1 - \alpha)^n < 2^{-56}$, only the good key remains. This is achieved for $n \approx 112 \log(2) \approx 78$. Finally, we can recover the right key with a time complexity close to $n \cdot 2^{120}$ DES computations and using $n \cdot 2^{64}$ chosen plaintexts.

A complete security analysis of Feistel ciphers with 6 rounds or less is available in [24].

Solution 7   ⋆Multipermutations

1 The two different tuples $(0, 1, 1, 1)$ and $(1, 1, 1, 1)$ are valid ones for f_1 and f_2. They differ only in 1 coordinate. If f_1 (resp. f_2) was a $(3, 1)$-multipermutation, two distinct tuples should differ in at least 2 coordinates.

2 Consider the following two tuples

$$(a, b, c, a \oplus b \oplus c) \quad \text{and} \quad (a', b', c', a' \oplus b' \oplus c'). \qquad (4.2)$$

We want to prove that if these tuples differ in some position, they differ in at least 2 positions. Note that it is only necessary to deal with the cases where the tuples a priori differ at only one position since the other cases already fulfill the desired property.

- Suppose that the two inputs (a, b, c) and (a', b', c') differ in one, and only one position. By symmetry, we can consider the case where $a \neq a'$, $b = b'$, and $c = c'$. As

$$a \neq a', \, b = b', \text{ and } c = c' \Rightarrow a \oplus b \oplus c \neq a' \oplus b' \oplus c',$$

the tuples defined in (4.2) differ in at least two positions.

- Suppose now that $a \oplus b \oplus c \neq a' \oplus b' \oplus c'$. By definition of a function, it cannot be the case that the tuples (a, b, c) and (a', b', c') are equal. Hence, the tuples also differ in at least 2 positions.

We showed that in any case, if the two tuples defined in (4.2) differ, they differ in at least two positions and thus f_3 is a $(3, 1)$-multipermutation.

3 The key observation is that the most significant bit of a is lost during the multiplication by two. Thus, we can easily build the following counterexample

$$(0,0) \longmapsto (0,0)$$
$$(128,0) \longmapsto (0,128).$$

We see that the two valid tuples $(0,0,0,0)$ and $(128,0,0,128)$ differ in only 2 positions, which is impossible when considering a $(2,2)$-multipermutation. Therefore 2-PHT is not a $(2,2)$-multipermutation.

4 We consider the two tuples

$$(x_\ell, x_r, y_\ell, y_r) \quad \text{and} \quad (x'_\ell, x'_r, y'_\ell, y'_r), \tag{4.3}$$

and we try to show that if they differ, they differ in at least 3 positions.

- If $x_\ell \neq x'_\ell$ and $x_r \neq x'_r$: As M is a permutation and as we clearly have $(x_\ell, x_r) \neq (x'_\ell, x'_r)$ then we know that $M(x_\ell, x_r) \neq M(x'_\ell, x'_r)$, i.e., that $(y_\ell, y_r) \neq (y'_\ell, y'_r)$. This means that $y_\ell \neq y'_\ell$ and/or $y_r \neq y'_r$. Therefore, the tuples defined by (4.3) differ in at least 3 positions.

- If $x_\ell \neq x'_\ell$ and $x_r = x'_r$: We have

$$x_\ell \neq x'_\ell$$
$$\Rightarrow \varphi(x_\ell) \neq \varphi(x'_\ell) \qquad\qquad \text{as } \varphi \text{ is a permutation}$$
$$\Rightarrow \varphi(x_\ell) \oplus x_r \neq \varphi(x'_\ell) \oplus x'_r \qquad \text{as } x_r = x'_r$$
$$\Rightarrow P\left(\varphi(x_\ell) \oplus x_r\right) \neq P\left(\varphi(x'_\ell) \oplus x'_r\right) \quad \text{as } P \text{ is a permutation}$$
$$\Rightarrow y_\ell \neq y'_\ell.$$

Similarly, we can show that $y_r \neq y'_r$, and thus that the tuples defined by (4.3) differ in exactly 3 positions.

- If $x_\ell = x'_\ell$ and $x_r \neq x'_r$: Just as in the previous case, it is possible to show that $y_\ell \neq y'_\ell$ and $y_r \neq y'_r$, so that the tuples defined by (4.3) differ in exactly 3 positions.

Finally, in any case, if the two tuples defined by (4.3) differ, they differ in at least 3 positions. Therefore, M is a $(2,2)$-multipermutation.

The reference papers on multipermutations are [47, 53].

Solution 8   ⋆Orthomorphisms

1 We observe that $\omega(x) \oplus x = \text{ROT}^4(x \oplus (x \ll 4)) = \omega^{-1}(x)$. As $\omega(x) \oplus x$ has an inverse (which is $\omega(x)$), it is a permutation, and thus ω is a XOR-orthomorphism.

2 The XOR-orthomorphism is represented in Figure 4.9. We can use this representation to find the inverse, which is

$$\omega^{-1}: \quad S \;\rightarrow\; S$$
$$x \;\mapsto\; x \oplus (x \ggg 4).$$

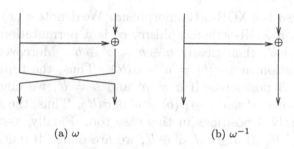

(a) ω (b) ω^{-1}

Figure 4.9. A XOR-orthomorphism

3 If we denote an input $x = x_7|x_6|x_5|x_4|x_3|x_2|x_1|x_0$ we get

$$\pi(x) = x_0 \oplus x_7|x_7|x_6 \oplus x_5|x_5|x_4 \oplus x_3|x_3|x_2 \oplus x_1|x_1$$

and

$$\pi(x) \oplus x = x_0|x_7 \oplus x_6|x_6|x_5 \oplus x_4|x_4|x_3 \oplus x_2|x_2|x_1 \oplus x_0,$$

which is invertible. Thus, $\pi(x) \oplus x$ is a permutation and $\pi(x)$ is a XOR-orthomorphism. $\pi^{-1}(y) = \mathrm{ROT}^7(\mathrm{ROT}^7(y \text{ AND } \text{0x55}) \oplus y)$.

4 We denote this new permutation by π'. We have

$$\pi'(x) = x_0|x_7|x_6|x_5|x_4|x_3|x_2|x_1 \oplus x_0$$

and

$$\pi'(x) \oplus x = x_0 \oplus x_7|x_7 \oplus x_6|x_6 \oplus x_5|x_5 \oplus x_4|x_4 \oplus x_3|x_3 \oplus x_2|x_2 \oplus x_1|x_1.$$

Obviously, it is easy to invert this last expression. Therefore, $\pi'(x) \oplus x$ is a permutation, thus $\pi'(x)$ is a XOR-orthomorphism. Furthermore, $\pi'^{-1}(y) = \mathrm{ROT}^7(\mathrm{ROT}^7(y \text{ AND } \text{0x80}) \oplus y)$.

5 In this proof, we consider two 4-tuples denoted by $(a, b, a \oplus b, a \oplus \sigma(b))$ and $(a', b', a' \oplus b', a' \oplus \sigma(b'))$.

- Assume that the function is a $(2,2)$-multipermutation. For any b and b' such that $b \neq b'$, we know that $\sigma(b) \neq \sigma(b')$ as the tuples $(0, b, b, \sigma(b))$ and $(0, b', b', \sigma(b'))$ must differ on 3 positions at least. Therefore, σ is a permutation. For any a and a' such that $a \neq a'$, we have $a \oplus \sigma(a) \neq a' \oplus \sigma(a')$, as the tuples $(a, a, 0, a \oplus \sigma(a))$ and $(a', a', 0, a' \oplus \sigma(a'))$ must differ on 3 positions at least. Therefore, σ is a XOR-orthomorphism.

- Assume σ is a XOR-orthomorphism. We denote $\sigma'(x) = x \oplus \sigma(x)$. As σ is a XOR-orthomorphism, σ' is a permutation. If $a = a'$ and $b \neq b'$, then clearly $a \oplus b \neq a' \oplus b'$. Moreover, as σ is a permutation, $a \oplus \sigma(b) \neq a' \oplus \sigma(b')$. Thus, the tuples differ on exactly 3 positions. If $a \neq a'$ and $b = b'$, we obviously have $a \oplus b \neq a' \oplus b'$ and $a \oplus \sigma(b) \neq a' \oplus \sigma(b')$. Thus, the tuples differ on exactly 3 positions in this case too. Finally, assume $a \neq a'$ and $b \neq b'$. If $a \oplus b \neq a' \oplus b'$, we are done. If $a \oplus b = a' \oplus b'$, and if we moreover assume that $a \oplus \sigma(b) = a' \oplus \sigma(b')$, we obtain $\sigma'(b) = \sigma'(b')$, which is a contradiction to the fact that σ' is a permutation. We have shown that the tuples differ on at least 3 positions in this case as well, which concludes the proof.

The reference papers on XOR-orthomorphisms and their applications to block ciphers construction are [52, 54].

Solution 9   ⋆Decorrelation

1 By definition,

$$\||[C]^d - [C^*]^d\|_\infty = 2 \cdot \text{BestAdv}_{\text{Cl}_{\text{na}}^d}.$$

As this "measure" represents the advantage of the best non-adaptive distinguisher using d queries, it is rather clear that

$$\||[C]^{d-1} - [C^*]^{d-1}\|_\infty \leq \||[C]^d - [C^*]^d\|_\infty$$

since the best non-adaptative distinguisher using $d-1$ queries can be considered as a non-adaptative distinguisher using d queries, including one which is not taken into account.

2 By definition, an advantage is given by

$$|\Pr[\mathcal{A}^C \to 1] - \Pr[\mathcal{A}^{C^*} \to 1]|.$$

As a probability measure returns always a result in the interval $[0, 1]$, we have

$$|\Pr[\mathcal{A}^C \to 1] - \Pr[\mathcal{A}^{C^*} \to 1]| \leq 1$$

which implies that

$$\left|\left|\left|[C]^d - [C^*]^d\right|\right|\right|_\infty \le 2.$$

Furthermore, as $\left|\left|\left|.\right|\right|\right|_\infty$ is a norm, we have

$$\left|\left|\left|[C]^d - [C^*]^d\right|\right|\right|_\infty \ge 0.$$

3 The property $\text{Dec}^d(C) = 0$ means that the distance between $[C]^d$ and $[C^*]^d$ is zero. By definition of a distance, this happens if and only if $[C]^d = [C^*]^d$. Obviously this does not depend on the choice of the distance.

4 The above property with $d = 1$ means that $[C]^1 = [C^*]^1$. The coefficient of these matrices are the probabilities $\Pr[C(x) = y]$. Therefore, this property means that for any x and y, we have

$$\Pr[C(x) = y] = \Pr[C^*(x) = y].$$

Since $\Pr[C^*(x) = y] = 2^{-m}$ (see Exercise 1, Chapter 1), the property means that for any x and y we have $\Pr[C(x) = y] = 2^{-m}$. In this case we can prove that we have perfect secrecy. For any x and y, we have

$$\Pr[X = x | C(X) = y] = \frac{\Pr[X = x]}{\Pr[C(X) = y]} \Pr[C(x) = y].$$

The probability $\Pr[C(X) = y]$ can be computed as follows

$$\Pr[C(X) = y] = \sum_{x'} \Pr[C(x') = y | X = x'] \Pr[X = x'].$$

Since C and X are independent, we have

$$\Pr[C(x') = y | X = x'] = \Pr[C(x') = y] = 2^{-m}.$$

Thus $\Pr[C(X) = y] = 2^{-m}$. Therefore we obtain that

$$\Pr[X = x | C(X) = y] = \Pr[X = x]$$

for any distribution of X.

5 The property of Question 3 with $d = 2$ means that for any x, x', y, y' we have

$$\Pr[C(x) = y, C(x') = y'] = \Pr[C^*(x) = y, C^*(x') = y'].$$

In particular, for $x \neq x'$ and $y \neq y'$, we obtain

$$\Pr[C(x) = y, C(x') = y'] = \frac{1}{2^m(2^m - 1)}.$$

In this case we can prove that we have a Markov cipher: let x, a, b be any m-bit strings such that $a \neq 0$ and $b \neq 0$. We have

$$\Pr[C(x + a) - C(x) = b] = \sum_y \Pr[C(x) = y, C(x + a) = y + b]$$

$$= \frac{1}{2^m - 1}.$$

Similarly, we have

$$\Pr[C(X + a) - C(X) = b] = \sum_x \Pr[X = x] \Pr[C(x + a) - C(x) = b]$$

$$= \frac{1}{2^m - 1}.$$

Therefore, as $\Pr[C(x+a) - C(x) = b] = \mathrm{E}(\Pr[C(X+a) - C(X) = b])$, we have a Markov cipher.

6 $\mathrm{Dec}^d(f_K) = 0$ means that for any pairwise different $x_1, \ldots, x_d$ and any $y_1, \ldots, y_d$, we have $\Pr[f_K(x_i) = y_i$ for $i = 1, \ldots, d] = 2^{-md}$.

Let us pick random pairwise different $x_1, \ldots, x_d$. We obtain that for any $y_1, \ldots, y_d$, the above probability is non-zero. This implies that there exists at least one key k such that $f_k(x_i) = y_i$ for all $i = 1, \ldots, d$. Therefore we must have at least 2^{md} keys, i.e., K must at least have a bit length of md. The purpose of the exercise is to show how to achieve this minimal key size.

7 For any $x, y \in \{0, 1\}^m$ we have

$$[f_K]^1_{x,y} = \Pr[f_K(x) = y] = \Pr[K = x \oplus y] = 2^{-m} = [C^*]^1_{x,y}.$$

Therefore $[f_K]^1 = [F^*]^1$ which clearly implies that f_K is at distance 0 from F^*, i.e.,

$$\mathrm{Dec}^1(f_K) = 0.$$

We notice that we achieve the minimal length for the key here.

8 We take $K = (K_1, \ldots, K_d) \in (\mathrm{GF}(2^m))^d$ (which achieves the minimal length). We define $f_K(x) = K_1 + K_2 x + K_3 x^2 + \ldots + K_d x^{d-1}$ in the sense of $\mathrm{GF}(2^m)$ operations. For pairwise different $x_1, \ldots, x_d$ and any $y_1, \ldots, y_d$, we can find a unique polynomial P such that $P(x_i) = y_i$

by interpolation. The coefficients of this polynomial define a unique key K such that the polynomial is actually f_K. This proves that $\Pr[f_K(x_i) = y_i \text{ for } i = 1, \ldots, d] = 2^{-md}$.

The reference paper on the Decorrelation theory is [55].

Solution 10 ⋆Decorrelation and Differential Cryptanalysis

Let $a \neq 0$ and b be such that

$$\text{EDP}^C_{\max} = E_C(\text{DP}^C(a, b)).$$

As $\text{DP}^C(a, b) \geq 0$ and as $\text{DP}^C(a, 0) = 0$, we can assume that $b \neq 0$. We consider the distinguisher described in Algorithm 19. This distin-

---

Algorithm 19 A differential distinguisher between C and C^*

Input: an oracle $\mathcal{O}$ implementing either C or C^*, two masks a and b such that $a \neq 0$ and $b \neq 0$

Output: 0 (if the guess is that $\mathcal{O}$ implements C^*) or 1 (if the guess is that $\mathcal{O}$ implements C)

Processing:
1: pick x uniformly at random
2: submit x and $x \oplus a$ to $\mathcal{O}$ and get y_1 and y_2
3: **if** $y_1 = y_2 \oplus b$ **then**
4:     output 1
5: **else**
6:     output 0
7: **end if**

---

guisher is limited to two queries. Its advantage must thus be less than $\text{BestAdv}_{\text{Cl}^2_a}(C, C^*)$.

We now look for an expression of this advantage. When the oracle implements C, the probability that the distinguisher outputs 1 is $E_C(\text{DP}^C(a, b))$. When it implements C^*, the probability that it outputs 1 is $1/(2^m - 1)$ since y_1 and y_2 are different random elements and $b \neq 0$ (see Exercise 1, Chapter 1 for a proof). Therefore, the advantage of the distinguisher is equal to

$$E_C(\text{DP}^C(a, b)) - \frac{1}{2^m - 1}.$$

This leads to the inequality.

The reference paper on the Decorrelation theory is [55].

Solution 11   ⋆Decorrelation of a Feistel Cipher

We let $r' = 3\lfloor\frac{r}{3}\rfloor$. Let $C = \Psi(F_1,\ldots,F_r)$ and $C' = \Psi(F_1,\ldots,F_{r'})$. Since C can be written $C'' \circ C'$ with C'' independent from C', we notice that any distinguisher between C and C^* can be transformed into a distinguisher between C' and C^* with the same advantage by simulating C'' (we simulate a C oracle by using a C' oracle and simulating the C'' function). Therefore

$$\text{BestAdv}_{\text{Cl}_a^d}(C, C^*) \leq \text{BestAdv}_{\text{Cl}_a^d}(C', C^*).$$

Assuming that we can prove the result with r' instead of r, this proves the inequality. So let us now focus on r' instead of r, which means that we concentrate on $r = r'$ multiple of 3.

We consider $C_i = \Psi(F_{3i-2}, F_{3i-1}, F_{3i})$ for $i = 1,\ldots,\frac{r}{3}$. We have $C = C_{\frac{r}{3}} \circ \cdots \circ C_1$. Since all C_i's are independent and the decorrelation is multiplicative, we have

$$\text{BestAdv}_{\text{Cl}_a^d}(C, C^*) = \frac{1}{2}\text{Dec}^d(C)$$

$$\leq \frac{1}{2}\prod_{i=1}^{\frac{r}{3}}\text{Dec}^d(C_i)$$

$$= \frac{1}{2}\prod_{i=1}^{\frac{r}{3}}2 \cdot \text{BestAdv}_{\text{Cl}_a^d}(C_i, C^*).$$

Assuming that we can prove the result with $r = 3$, we can use the inequality with all $\text{BestAdv}_{\text{Cl}_a^d}(C_i, C^*)$ and prove the result. So let us now focus on $r = 3$.

We consider $C_0 = C$, $C_1 = \Psi(F_1, F_2, F_3^*)$, $C_2 = \Psi(F_1, F_2^*, F_3^*)$, and $C_3 = \Psi(F_1^*, F_2^*, F_3^*)$ where F_1^*, F_2^*, F_3^* are truly random functions. We interpret again the best advantage in term of decorrelation. Since the decorrelation is a distance, we can use the triangular inequality. So the best advantage for distinguishing C from C^* is less than the sum of all best advantages for distinguishing C_i from C_{i+1} and the best advantage for distinguishing C_3 from C^*. By using the Luby-Rackoff Theorem we obtain that

$$\text{BestAdv}_{\text{Cl}_a^d}(C_3, C^*) \leq d^2 2^{-\frac{m}{2}}.$$

Now we can estimate $\text{BestAdv}_{\text{Cl}_a^d}(C_i, C_{i+1})$. We only have to show that it is less than ε.

If we take a distinguisher between C_i and C_{i+1}, we need to use an oracle which implements C_i or C_{i+1}. But only F_{3-i} has been replaced by

F^*_{3-i}. Thus, if we have an oracle which implements either F_{3-i} or F^*_{3-i}, by simulating the other F_j or F^*_j, we can simulate an oracle which implements either C_i or C^*_i. This means that we can transform a distinguisher between C_i and C^*_i into a distinguisher between F_{3-i} and F^*_{3-i} with the same advantage. We however know that $\text{BestAdv}_{\text{Cl}^d_a}(F_{3-i}, F^*_{3-i})$ is less than ε. Therefore we have $\text{BestAdv}_{\text{Cl}^d_a}(C_i, C_{i+1}) \leq \varepsilon$.

The reference paper on the Decorrelation theory is [55].

Solution 12   ⋆A Saturation Attack against IDEA

1 Algorithm 20 describes a generic exhaustive key search among the N keys of a cipher. The key of IDEA is 128-bit long, so that the worst case complexity of an exhaustive key search is 2^{128} (i.e., the right key is the last to be tested). The average complexity $\text{E}[C]$ of Algorithm 20 is

$$\text{E}[C] = \sum_{c=1}^{N} c \Pr[C = c] = \sum_{c=1}^{N} c \underbrace{\Pr[k_{\sigma(c)} \text{ is the right key}]}_{= \frac{1}{N}} = \frac{N+1}{2}.$$

Therefore the average complexity of an exhaustive key search against IDEA is approximately 2^{127}. The attack is not practical.

2 The three-round decryption scheme is given on Figure 4.10. The Lai-Massey scheme is a permutation on the simple condition that F is a function. If we respectively denote x_ℓ and x_r the left and right input of the first round, its left and right outputs are $x_\ell \oplus F_1(x_\ell \oplus x_r)$ and $x_r \oplus F_1(x_\ell \oplus x_r)$ respectively. Going through the first round with

---

Algorithm 20 Exhaustive key search algorithm

Input: a set $\mathcal{K} = \{k_1, \ldots, k_N\}$ of key candidates and an oracle $\mathcal{O}$ such that $\mathcal{O}(k_i)$ is true if k_i is the right key and false otherwise
Output: the right key
Processing:
1: pick a random permutation σ of $\{1, \ldots, N\}$
2: **for** $i = 1$ to N **do**
3:    **if** $\mathcal{O}(k_{\sigma(i)})$ **then**
4:       output $k_{\sigma(i)}$ and stop
5:    **end if**
6: **end for**

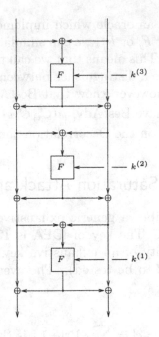

Figure 4.10.   Inverse of the three-round Lai-Massey scheme

these values, we obtain

$$x_\ell \oplus F_1(x_\ell \oplus x_r) \oplus F_1(x_\ell \oplus F_1(x_\ell \oplus x_r) \oplus x_r \oplus F_1(x_\ell \oplus x_r))$$
$$= x_\ell \oplus F_1(x_\ell \oplus x_r) \oplus F_1(x_\ell \oplus x_r) = x_\ell$$

on the left and

$$x_r \oplus F_1(x_\ell \oplus x_r) \oplus F_1(x_\ell \oplus F_1(x_\ell \oplus x_r) \oplus x_r \oplus F_1(x_\ell \oplus x_r))$$
$$= x_r \oplus F_1(x_\ell \oplus x_r) \oplus F_1(x_\ell \oplus x_r) = x_r$$

on the right.

3 All three functions are defined from $\{0,1\}^{16}$ over $\{0,1\}^{16}$. In order
to show that they are bijective, it is therefore sufficient to show that
they are injective. Let $\diamond \in \{\oplus, \odot, \boxplus\}$ be one of the three group laws.
Let $x, y \in \{0,1\}^{16}$ such that

$$x \diamond c = y \diamond c.$$

As $\diamond$ is a group law, c must be invertible. If we denote c^{-1} its inverse,
we have

$$x \diamond c \diamond c^{-1} = y \diamond c \diamond c^{-1} \Rightarrow x = y,$$

which proves that all three functions are injective and therefore bijective.

4 When P goes through $\{P_1, \ldots, P_{2^{16}}\}$, $X_4^{(1)}$ goes through all possible values of $\{0,1\}^{16}$. We will say that this *word* is *active* and denote a word verifying this property by Λ. Similarly, constant words will be denoted c. The conclusion of the preceeding question shows that Λ and c follow the propagation rules shown on Figure 4.11. The propagations of Λ and c through the first 1.5 round of IDEA are shown on Figure 4.12. We see on the figure that W_1 is an active word, i.e., W_1 goes through all possible values of $\{0,1\}^{16}$ when P goes through $\{P_1, \ldots, P_{2^{16}}\}$.

5 Figure 4.12 shows that W_2 and W_3 are active words.

6 From the previous results, we deduce a distinguisher $\mathcal{D}$ described by Algorithm 21. This distinguisher outputs 1 when it predicts that the oracle $\mathcal{O}$ implements 1.5 round IDEA and 0 otherwise.

7 If the oracle $\mathcal{O}$ implements 1.5 round IDEA, we showed in a previous question that W_1, W_2 and W_3 are always active words. Therefore

$$\Pr\left[\mathcal{D}^{\mathsf{IDEA}} \to 1\right] = 1.$$

Using the hint to compute $\Pr\left[\mathcal{D}^{C^*} \to 1\right]$.

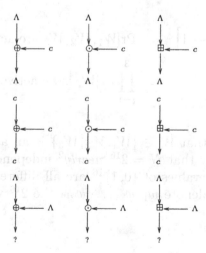

Figure 4.11. Active and constant words propagation rules

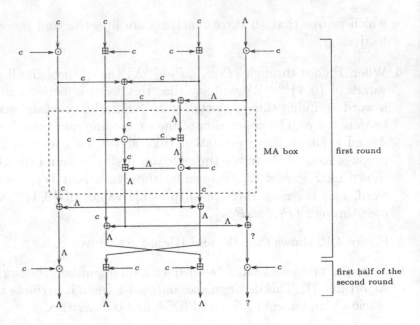

Figure 4.12. Active and constant words propagation through 1.5 round of IDEA

If the oracle $\mathcal{O}$ implements C^*, our distinguisher will give a wrong prediction if W_1, W_2, and W_3 are active words. If we suppose that these are independent random values uniformly distributed over $\{0,1\}^{16}$ we obtain

$$\Pr\left[\mathcal{D}^{C^*} \to 1\right] = \Pr[W_1, W_2, W_3 \text{ are active words}]$$

$$\approx \prod_{i=1}^{3} \Pr[W_i \text{ is an active word}].$$

The probability that $W \in \{W_1, W_2, W_3\}$ is an active word is equal to the probability that $N = 2^{16}$ *nearly*[2] independent and uniformly randomly chosen values of $\{0,1\}^{16}$ are all different (i.e., there is no collision). If we denote $w_1, w_2, \ldots, w_{2^{16}}$ the 2^{16} values taken by W,

---

[2] We will later consider a rigorous computation and see that the approximation made here is reasonably good.

we obtain (as each w_i is drawn independently)

$\Pr[W$ is an active word$]$

$$\begin{aligned}
&= \Pr[w_2 \neq w_1, w_3 \neq w_2, w_3 \neq w_1, \ldots, w_N \neq w_1] \\
&= \Pr[w_2 \neq w_1] \Pr[w_3 \neq w_2, w_3 \neq w_1 \mid w_2 \neq w_1] \cdots \\
&\quad \Pr[w_N \neq w_{N-1}, \ldots, w_N \neq w_1 \mid w_{N-1} \neq w_{N-2}, \ldots, w_{N-1} \neq w_1] \\
&= \left(\frac{N-1}{N}\right) \times \left(\frac{N-2}{N}\right) \times \cdots \times \left(\frac{1}{N}\right) \\
&= \frac{(N-1)!}{N^{N-1}} \\
&= \frac{N!}{N^N} \approx \frac{\sqrt{2\pi N}}{e^N},
\end{aligned}$$

using Stirling's approximation. Therefore,

$$\Pr\left[\mathcal{D}^{C^*} \to 1\right] \approx \left(\frac{\sqrt{2\pi N}}{e^N}\right)^3,$$

so that we finally obtain

$$\mathrm{Adv}^{\mathcal{D}} \approx 1 - \left(\frac{\sqrt{2\pi N}}{e^N}\right)^3,$$

which is approximately $1 - 0.449253 \cdot 10^{-85377}$ for $N = 2^{16}$.

If we do not use the approximation given by the hint.

Suppose $\mathcal{O}$ is implementing C^* and let $\{v_1, v_2, \ldots, v_{2^{16}}\}$ denote the 2^{16} elements of $\{0,1\}^{16}$. The distinguisher will give a wrong prediction if the random permutation implemented by $\mathcal{O}$ verifies the following 2^{16} mappings

$$\begin{cases}
(a, b, c, v_1) & \longrightarrow & (v_{\sigma(1)}, v_{\sigma'(1)}, v_{\sigma''(1)}, *) \\
(a, b, c, v_2) & \longrightarrow & (v_{\sigma(2)}, v_{\sigma'(2)}, v_{\sigma''(2)}, *) \\
\vdots & \vdots & \vdots \\
(a, b, c, v_{2^{16}}) & \longrightarrow & (v_{\sigma(2^{16})}, v_{\sigma'(2^{16})}, v_{\sigma''(2^{16})}, *),
\end{cases} \qquad (4.4)$$

where a, b, c are constant values of $\{0,1\}^{16}$, where $*$ can be any value of $\{0,1\}^{16}$, and where σ, σ' and σ'' are any permutations of $\{1, \ldots, 2^{16}\}$. We wonder how many permutations on $\{0,1\}^{64}$ verify (4.4):

- There are $\left((2^{16})!\right)^3$ different ways to choose σ, σ' and σ''.

Algorithm 21 Description of a distinguisher $\mathcal{D}$ between 1.5 round of IDEA and the uniformly distributed random permutation C^*

Input: A set of 2^{16} plaintexts $\{P_1, \ldots, P_{2^{16}}\}$ with the following shape $(x_1^{(1)}, x_2^{(1)}, x_3^{(1)}, X_4^{(1)})$, where $X_4^{(1)}$ goes through all possible values of $\{0,1\}^{16}$ and where $x_1^{(1)}, x_2^{(1)}, x_3^{(1)}$ are constant values. An oracle $\mathcal{O}$ which is either 1.5 round IDEA or C^*.

Output: 0 (if the guess is that $\mathcal{O}$ implements C^*) or 1 (if the guess is that $\mathcal{O}$ implements 1.5 round of IDEA)

Processing:

1: **for** $i = 1$ to 2^{16} **do**
2:     $(W_1, W_2, W_3, W_4)_i \leftarrow \mathcal{O}(P_i)$
3: **end for**
4: **if** W_1, W_2, and W_3 are active words **then**
5:     output 1
6: **else**
7:     output 0
8: **end if**

- For each one of the 2^{16} mappings of (4.4), there are 2^{16} different ways to choose the $*$'s. This gives a total of $(2^{16})^{2^{16}}$ ways to choose the $*$'s.

- There are $2^{64} - 2^{16}$ input values that still remain to be mapped on $2^{64} - 2^{16}$ output values in a bijective way, which gives $(2^{64} - 2^{16})!$ possibilities.

Finally, there are

$$\left((2^{16})!\right)^3 (2^{16})^{2^{16}} (2^{64} - 2^{16})!$$

different permutations that verify (4.4), so that

$$\Pr\left[\mathcal{D}^{C^*} \to 1\right] = \frac{\left((2^{16})!\right)^3 (2^{16})^{2^{16}} (2^{64} - 2^{16})!}{(2^{64})!}.$$

The exact advantage of the distinguisher is thus

$$\mathrm{Adv}^{\mathcal{D}} = 1 - \frac{\left((2^{16})!\right)^3 (2^{16})^{2^{16}} (2^{64} - 2^{16})!}{(2^{64})!}.$$

Using Stirling's formula, one can obtain

$$\mathrm{Adv}^{\mathcal{D}} \approx 1 - e^{-2N} \left(\sqrt{2\pi N}\right)^3 \sqrt{1 - \frac{1}{N^3}} \left(1 - \frac{1}{N^3}\right)^{N^4} \left(1 - \frac{1}{N^3}\right)^{-N},$$

where $N = 2^{16}$. Furthermore, since N is large, one have

$$(1 - 1/N^3)^{1/2} \approx 1, \ (1 - 1/N^3)^{N^4} \approx e^{-N}, \text{ and } (1 - 1/N^3)^{-N} \approx 1,$$

which leads to the approximation

$$\text{Adv}^D \approx 1 - e^{-3N} \left(\sqrt{2\pi N} \right)^3.$$

As we can see, supposing that W_1, W_2, and W_3 were independent was quite fair, since we obtain the same approximation of the advantage.

8 In order to recover the value of $\left(k_5^{(2)}, k_6^{(2)} \right)$, the cryptanalyst may use Algorithm 22. As the advantage of the distinguisher is huge,

---

Algorithm 22 Key-recovery attack against 2-round IDEA

Input: A set of 2^{16} plaintexts $\{P_1, \ldots, P_{2^{16}}\}$ with the following shape $(x_1^{(1)}, x_2^{(1)}, x_3^{(1)}, X_4^{(1)})$, where $X_4^{(1)}$ goes through all possible values of $\{0, 1\}^{16}$ and where $x_1^{(1)}, x_2^{(1)}, x_3^{(1)}$ are constant values. An oracle $\mathcal{O}$ which implements 2-round IDEA with a randomly chosen (but fixed) key.

Output: the value of $\left(k_5^{(2)}, k_6^{(2)} \right)$

Processing:

1: **for** $i = 1$ to 2^{16} **do**
2:   $C_i \leftarrow \mathcal{O}(P_i)$
3: **end for**
4: **for all** $\left(\hat{k}_5^{(2)}, \hat{k}_6^{(2)} \right) \in \{0,1\}^{16} \times \{0,1\}^{16}$ **do**
5:   **for all** $C \in \{C_1, \ldots, C_{2^{16}}\}$ **do**
6:     Use the guessed value $\left(\hat{k}_5^{(2)}, \hat{k}_6^{(2)} \right)$ of $\left(k_5^{(2)}, k_6^{(2)} \right)$ in order to partially decrypt C and to obtain W_1, W_2, and W_3.
7:   **end for**
8:   **if** W_1, W_2, and W_3 are active words **then**
9:     display $\left(\hat{k}_5^{(2)}, \hat{k}_6^{(2)} \right)$
10:   **end if**
11: **end for**

---

we can consider that whenever Algorithm 22 displays a proposition $\left(\hat{k}_5^{(2)}, \hat{k}_6^{(2)} \right)$, it is a correct guess. The position of $\left(k_5^{(2)}, k_6^{(2)} \right)$ in the list of all 2^{32} possibilities for $\left(\hat{k}_5^{(2)}, \hat{k}_6^{(2)} \right)$ is 2^{31} on average. Each time a key is tested, 2^{16} decryptions are necessary in order to recover W_1,

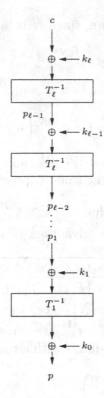

Figure 4.13. Decryption algorithm of the block cipher E

W_2, and W_3. The average complexity of the attack is thus $2^{31} \times 2^{16} = 2^{47}$. Similarly, one can show that the worst case complexity is 2^{48}. Note that decrypting, i.e., obtaining the W_i's, is a very fast operation.

The reference paper for these attacks is [32].

Solution 13   ⋆Fault Attack against a Block Cipher

1 A decryption algorithm for E exists if and only if all functions T_i, $1 \leq i \leq \ell$ are invertible, i.e., are permutations. The decryption algorithm is very similar to the encryption except that the order of the subkeys is inverted and each transformation T_i is replaced by its inverse. The decryption algorithm is shown in Figure 4.13.

2 Looking at the round structure of the block cipher E, we directly notice that $c = T(p_{\ell-1}) \oplus k_\ell$ and $c' = T(p_{\ell-1} \oplus \delta) \oplus k_\ell$. Doing a XOR operation between these two equations leads to the desired

relation

$$c \oplus c' = T(p_{\ell-1}) \oplus T(p_{\ell-1} \oplus \delta).$$

3 It suffices to notice that producing faults on $p_{\ell-1}$ has exactly the same effect as producing the same faults on the subkey $k_{\ell-1}$. The ciphertext c' is unchanged since $p'_{\ell-1} = p_{\ell-1} \oplus \delta = T(p_{\ell-2}) \oplus k_{\ell-1} \oplus \delta$.

4 An element $x \in \{0,1\}^n$ is a candidate for $p_{\ell-1}$ if it satisfies the relation found in Question 2, i.e., if

$$c \oplus c' = T(x) \oplus T(x \oplus \delta).$$

Since $c \oplus c' = (010,000,000,000)$ and $\delta = (001,000,000,000)$, $x = (x_1, x_2, x_3, x_4)$ satisfies the equation if and only if

$$010 = f(x_1) \oplus f(x_1 \oplus 001).$$

Observing Table 4.3, we see that the only candidates satisfying the previous relation are 110 and 111. Therefore, the candidates for $p_{\ell-1}$ are of the form $(11*, ***, ***, ***)$, where the symbol $*$ can be replaced by any bit. In total, this leads to 2^{10} candidates.

Table 4.3. Looking for candidate values for $p_{\ell-1}$

x_1	$x_1 \oplus 001$	$f(x_1) \oplus f(x_1 \oplus 001)$
000	001	001
001	000	001
010	011	101
011	010	101
100	101	110
101	100	110
110	111	010
111	110	010

5 We note that each candidate for $p_{\ell-1}$ defines a unique candidate for $k_\ell = c \oplus T(p_{\ell-1})$. Thus, the number of candidate values for k_ℓ is 2^{10} as well.

6 By definition, $\mathrm{DP}^T(\delta, \delta') = \Pr_{X \in \{0,1\}^{12}}[T(X) \oplus T(X \oplus \delta) = \delta']$, where the probability holds over the uniform distribution of X. This is equal to

$$\frac{|\{x \in \{0,1\}^{12} \mid T(x) \oplus T(x \oplus \delta) = \delta')\}|}{2^{12}} = \frac{2^{10}}{2^{12}} = 2^{-2}.$$

7 As we already noticed in Question 5, the number of subkey candidates is equal to the number of candidates for $p_{\ell-1}$. Therefore, N_ℓ is the cardinality of the set $\{x \in \{0,1\}^n \mid T(x) \oplus T(x \oplus \delta) = \delta'\}$, which allows to conclude that

$$N_\ell = 2^n \cdot \mathrm{DP}^T(\delta, \delta').$$

8 From the experiment, we know that there exists at least one candidate $p_{\ell-1}$ and thus, at least one for k_ℓ also. Furthermore, we know that $x \oplus \delta$ is another candidate for $p_{\ell-1}$ since $\delta \neq 0$. Therefore, we always have at least 2 candidates for k_ℓ. Note that this property directly follows from the fact that a nonzero DP^T is always greater or equal than 2^{-n+1} for any transformation $T : \{0,1\}^n \to \{0,1\}^n$.

9 Since $c \oplus c' = (000, 000, 100, 000)$, the fault occurred between the 7th and 9th position. Otherwise, the third block of 3 bits of $c \oplus c'$ would be equal to 000 by definition of T. Now, we look for the elements $x \in \{0,1\}^3$ such that $f(x) \oplus f(x \oplus \Delta) = 100$ for a bitstring $\Delta \in \{001, 010, 100\}$. This corresponds to the bitstrings $001, 101, 011, 111$, all with the same $\Delta = 100$. Hence, the candidates for $p_{\ell-1}$ are of the form $(***, ***, y, ***)$ where y is an arbitrary element of $\{001, 101, 011, 111\}$. This leads to 2^{11} candidates for k_ℓ.

A reference paper on fault attacks in block ciphers is [6].

Chapter 5

SECURITY PROTOCOLS WITH CONVENTIONAL CRYPTOGRAPHY

Exercises

Exercise 1   Flipping a Coin by Email

Two persons are responsible for correcting an exam on cryptography, none wants to do it, but one, and only one, has to do it. Thus, they want to decide who will correct the exam by flipping a coin. One person chooses "head" or "tail". The other person flips a coin, and the decision is made upon the face up. One problem is that one of them is traveling so they can only communicate remotely over some channel (e.g., Internet or telephone). In order to solve this problem, somebody proposes the following protocol.

- Participant A chooses $x =$ "head" or $x =$ "tail" and picks a random key K. He encrypts x with DES by using K and obtains y.

- Participant A sends y to participant B.

- Participant B flips a coin and tells which face is up to participant A.

- Participant A reveals K.

- Participant B decrypts y with DES by using K and obtains the bet of participant A.

This person claims that it is impossible for participant A "to change his mind" due to the commitment y.

1 By using a birthday-like attack, show that participant A can actually change his mind and cheat with the above protocol.

2 What is the complexity of the above attack?

3 Which cryptographic primitive requirement ensures the validity of the assertion "participant A cannot change his mind"?

4 Correct this protocol to fix the above problem.

▷ Solution on page 130

Exercise 2   Woo-Lam Protocol

In the Woo-Lam protocol (see Figure 5.1), an entity A authenticates himself to another entity B with the help of an authentication server S. We denote a secret key shared by entities X and Y by K_{XY}, and let N_X denote a random value generated by X freshly for each instance of the protocol. The encryption of a message m by a key K is denoted $\{m\}_K$.

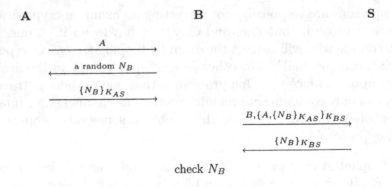

Figure 5.1. The Woo-Lam protocol

1 Prove that the protocol is flawed by showing that a legitimate and malicious entity C can impersonate A to B without any contribution from A.

2 Correct the protocol.

▷ Solution on page 130

Exercise 3 MicroMint I

Let $H : \mathcal{E} \to \mathcal{E}$ be a uniformly distributed random function on a finite set $\mathcal{E}$ of cardinality N, where N is a large number. We let $N_k = N^{\frac{k-1}{k}}$.

1 We call the pair $\{x, y\}$ of $\mathcal{E}$ (where $x \neq y$ and $x, y \in \mathcal{E}$) a collision if $H(x) = H(y)$. What is the expected number of ordered collision pairs (i.e., $\{x, y\}$ and $\{y, x\}$ are counted as one pair), where the expected value is taken over the distribution of H?

2 If we pick cN_2 random elements in $\mathcal{E}$ for some constant $c \geq 1$ and we look at all the corresponding H images, what is the expected number of collisions?

3 If we pick cN_3 random elements in $\mathcal{E}$ and we look at all the corresponding H images, what is the expected number of ordered triplets $\{x, y, z\}$ with pairwise distinct elements such that $H(x) = H(y) = H(z)$?

4 Redo the same question with k-tuple of pairwise distinct elements when we pick cN_k random elements in $\mathcal{E}$. (We call them k-way collisions.)

▷ Solution on page 131

Exercise 4 MicroMint II

Let $H : \mathcal{E} \to \mathcal{E}$ be a function on a finite set $\mathcal{E}$ of cardinality N, where N is a large number. A k-way collision is a k-tuple of pairwise distinct elements in $\mathcal{E}$ such that their corresponding H images are identical. We consider a k-way collision as a "coin" (e.g., the serial number of the e-coin). We assume that every month, the bank chooses a random function H and looks for k-way collisions in order to create new coins. The bank can spend a lot of time and resources in order to create e-coins, and H will be only revealed after all e-coins are produced.

1 Let $N_k = N^{\frac{k-1}{k}}$. For $k = 4$ and $N = 2^{36}$, compute the number of H evaluations, the expected number of produced coins, and the ratio of H evaluations over produced coins when we pick cN_k random elements in $\mathcal{E}$.

2 For the same parameters k and N as above, estimate the cost to forge one valid e-coin.

▷ Solution on page 132

Exercise 5   Bluetooth Pairing Protocol

In this exercise, we study one potential weakness in the real Bluetooth Pairing Protocol. Assume a Bluetooth device A is setting up a pairing protocol with a new peer device B and B happens to be the first challenger (i.e., A authenticates itself to B first). Suppose this pairing protocol between A and B finally passes successfully.

1 Why cannot we place 100% trust on the authenticity of B?

2 What do you propose to fix the above problem?

▷ Solution on page 133

Exercise 6   UNIX Passwords

In this exercise, we consider the UNIX password variant which uses DES (see the textbook [56]).

We would like to crack the UNIX password using an exhaustive search. We assume that the password consists of alphabetical characters only (i.e., a-z and A-Z).

1 Recall the maximum length of a UNIX password.

2 How many different 8-character passwords do we have? Estimate the complexity of the attack and give an upper bound on the Shannon entropy of the password.

3 Now we consider the password which consists of 8 ASCII characters. Redo the previous question.

4 Unlike alphabetical passwords, passwords that consist of ASCII characters generally cannot be remembered by human beings. Propose an improvement to use alphabetical characters for the UNIX password more securely over the standard UNIX password, so that the maximal entropy of UNIX passwords is achieved.

▷ Solution on page 133

Exercise 7   Key Enlargement

In order to increase the security of DES against the exhaustive search, we enlarge the key: we define a new block cipher EDES with 64-bit plaintext blocks which accepts a key K of any size. The key K is first hashed onto a 128-bit string S_0 by $S_0 = \text{MD5}(K)$ and then truncated to its first 56 bits $S = \text{trunc}_{56}(S_0)$. We then define $\text{EDES}_K = \text{DES}_S$.

How can you break this EDES?

▷ Solution on page 134

Solutions

Solution 1   Flipping a Coin by Email

1 The idea is that A could find two keys K and K' such that

$$\mathsf{DES}_K(\text{"head"}) = \mathsf{DES}_{K'}(\text{"tail"}).$$

For this, A proceeds as follows.

- A builds two lists $(\mathsf{DES}_K(\text{"head"}), K)$ and $(\mathsf{DES}_{K'}(\text{"tail"}), K')$ for all K and K' respectively. Both lists are sorted according to the first field of each entry (i.e., $\mathsf{DES}_K(\text{"head"})$ and $\mathsf{DES}_{K'}(\text{"tail"})$ respectively).

- A looks for the collision between the two lists and obtains K, K' such that $\mathsf{DES}_K(\text{"head"}) = \mathsf{DES}_{K'}(\text{"tail"})$.

- After flipping the coin, A reveals either K or K' to B depending on the result of coin flipping.

2 The complexity of the above attack is the collision search between the 64-bit $\mathsf{DES}_K(\text{"head"})$ and $\mathsf{DES}_{K'}(\text{"tail"})$ in the two lists. By the Birthday Paradox, we need to peform about 2^{32} DES evaluations for getting one collision.

3 The cryptographic requirement is the collision-resistance between the two functions $K \mapsto \mathsf{DES}_K(\text{"head"})$ and $K \mapsto \mathsf{DES}_K(\text{"tail"})$.

4 They may use a symmetric block cipher which uses a 128-bit block size, like AES (in this case, this birthday-like attack needs about 2^{64} AES evaluations). Alternatively, they can use a collision-resistant hash function h. Participant A chooses $x \in \{\text{"head"}, \text{"tail"}\}$, picks a random string r, and computes $y = h(x\|r)$. Once B makes his choice, A can finally reveal x and r.

Solution 2   Woo-Lam Protocol

1 Notice that with multiple sessions, the decrypted random number N_B that B finally receives from the server is not linked with the session it belongs to. A malicious user M may initiate two parallel sessions with B, one in his own name and another one in the name of A. B generates two challenges N_{BM} and N_{BA}. M receives N_{BM} and intercepts N_{BA}. M encrypts N_{BA} with K_{MS} and sends the result in

both sessions to B. B constructs the appropriate messages and sends them to the authentication server S. The server S will successfully recover N_{BA} from $\{M, \{N_{BA}\}_{K_{MS}}\}_{K_{BS}}$ and recover some garbage X out of $\{A, \{N_{BA}\}_{K_{MS}}\}_{K_{BS}}$, since it uses K_{AS} in order to decrypt the value $\{N_{BA}\}_{K_{MS}}$. B will receive $\{N_{BA}\}_{K_{BS}}$ and $\{X\}_{K_{BS}}$, believe that he successfully has run the protocol with A and think that someone tried to impersonate M.

2 We may correct the protocol as shown in Figure 5.2.

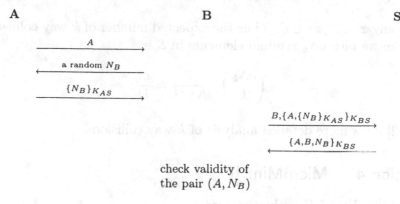

Figure 5.2. The corrected Woo-Lam protocol

Solution 3   MicroMint I

1 Since we have

$$\Pr[H(x) = H(y)|x \neq y] = \frac{1}{N},$$

for any $x, y \in \mathcal{E}$, we know that the expected number of ordered collision pairs in $\mathcal{E}$ is

$$\binom{N}{2} \cdot \frac{1}{N} = \frac{N-1}{2}.$$

2 The expected number of collisions is

$$\binom{cN_2}{2} \cdot \frac{1}{N} \approx \frac{1}{2}(cN_2)^2 \frac{1}{N} = \frac{c^2}{2}.$$

3 Similarly, we know that

$$\Pr[H(x) = H(y) = H(z)|x, y, z \text{ are pairwise distinct}] = \frac{1}{N^2},$$

for any $x, y, z \in \mathcal{E}$ the expected number of collision triplets $\{x, y, z\}$ with pairwise distinct entries is

$$\binom{cN_3}{3} \cdot \frac{1}{N^2} \approx \frac{1}{6}(cN_3)^3 \frac{1}{N^2} = \frac{c^3}{6}.$$

4 Similarly, we have

$$\Pr[H(x_1) = \cdots = H(x_k)|x_1, \ldots, x_k \text{ are pairwise distinct}] = \frac{1}{N^{k-1}}$$

for any $x_1, \ldots, x_k \in \mathcal{E}$. Thus the expected number of k-way collisions when we pick cN_k random elements in $\mathcal{E}$ is

$$\binom{cN_k}{k} \cdot \frac{1}{N^{k-1}} \approx \frac{c^k}{k!}.$$

See [42] for a more detailed analysis of k-way collisions.

Solution 4   MicroMint II

1 The number of H evaluations is

$$cN_k = c \cdot N^{\frac{3}{4}} = c \cdot 2^{27}.$$

According to Question 4 in the last exercise, the expected number of produced coins is

$$\frac{c^k}{k!} = \frac{c^4}{24}.$$

Thus, the ratio of H evaluations over produced coins is

$$\frac{c \cdot 2^{27}}{c^4/24} = \frac{3 \times 2^{30}}{c^3}.$$

2 For the forger to create one coin, he chooses the minimum value of c, i.e., $c = 1$. From previous question, we know that he has to try $cN_k = 2^{27}$ computations to obtain a valid e-coin, whose value is much less compared with the cost of the forger. Notice that the ratio of H evaluations per coin produced decreases in c. It means that the more computation performed the more efficient the coin production becomes.

The interested reader is invited to read [42] for more application details about e-coins in the real life.

Solution 5   Bluetooth Pairing Protocol

1 The reason can be explained as follows. Assuming A follows the protocol honestly, after A authenticates itself, B knows the correct response computed by A's PIN corresponding to B's challenge. Next, B can try exhaustively all possible PIN's on its own to recover A's PIN. Then, B can easily answer any challenge from A and successfully passes the authentication. In the end, A is mistakenly paired with a fake peer B. To conclude, this scenario tells us that the first challenger in the Bluetooth Pairing Protocol could be impersonated by an adversary.

2 One straightforward solution to avoid the above problem is to require PIN number of large bit length, so that the exhaustive search becomes impractical. However, note that in the Bluetooth standard the bit length of the PIN number is defined to be $8L$ bits with $L \in [1, 16]$, which does not exclude the possiblity of an impersonated peer. As an additional caution measure and yet not a countermeasure, the identity of the peer should be recorded down for later use after each execution of the pairing protocol, regardless of success or failure. Indeed, as mentioned in the textbook [56], this measure is already integrated into the Bluetooth authentication protocol, which will, depending on the previous authentication result, lengthen or shorten the waiting period before starting the next protocol with the same device.

The Bluetooth standard is available at [7]. Related studies on the security of pairing protocol are available in [37, 38].

Solution 6   UNIX Passwords

1 UNIX passwords are reduced to their eight leftmost characters. So we have eight *effective* characters.

2 We have $52^8 \approx 2^{45.6}$ different passwords, since we have 52 choices for each character in upper or lower cases. Exhaustive search has a worst case complexity of $2^{45.6}$, and an average complexity of $2^{44.6}$. The entropy is $H(K) \leq 45.6$ with equality if and only if the distribution of the password is uniform, which is not the case in practice.

3 With ASCII characters, we have $7 \times 8 = 56$ bits and thus an entropy up to 56.

4 One possibility consists in hashing the password of arbitrary length
by a cryptographic hash function (see Chapter 3). This generates a
56-bit hashed string, which is used as a DES key (as before).

Solution 7   Key Enlargement

The construction is useless: the goal of the adversary is to recover
the *effective key* in order to decrypt messages rather than to recover the
original key. Note that in this exercise, the *effective key* is S and the
original key is K. Hence he can mount the same attack against DES to
recover S which is enough for decryption.

Chapter 6

ALGORITHMIC ALGEBRA

Exercises

Exercise 1   Captain's Age

The aim of this exercise is to find the very secret age of the Captain. The only information we know is that one year ago, his age was a multiple of 3, in 2 years it will be a multiple of 5, and in 4 years it will be a multiple of 7. Deduce the Captain's age.

Hint: Maybe the Captain is Chinese...

▷ Solution on page 142

Exercise 2   Roots in $\mathbf{Z}_{77}^*$

Compute the 7th root of 23 in $\mathbf{Z}_{77}^*$ by using the Extended Euclid Algorithm and the Square-and-Multiply Algorithm.

▷ Solution on page 142

Exercise 3   ⋆When is $\mathbf{Z}_n^*$ Cyclic?

Let $n > 1$ be an integer, and let $n = p_1^{\alpha_1} \times \cdots \times p_r^{\alpha_r}$ be its decomposition into prime numbers. We assume that for any integers $i \neq j$, we have $p_i \neq p_j$, that p_i is prime, and that $\alpha_i > 0$ for $1 \leq i \leq r$. We consider the multiplicative group $\mathbf{Z}_n^*$. The purpose of this exercise is to find a necessary and sufficient condition on n such that $\mathbf{Z}_n^*$ is a cyclic group, i.e., such that $\mathbf{Z}_n^*$ has a generator.

1 In this question, we assume that $r = 1$ and $p_1 = 2$.

(a) Prove that $\mathbf{Z}_2^*$ is cyclic.

(b) Prove that $\mathbf{Z}_4^*$ is cyclic.

(c) Prove that $\mathbf{Z}_8^*$ is not cyclic.

(d) For $\alpha \geq 3$, deduce that $\mathbf{Z}_{2^\alpha}^*$ is not cyclic.

2 In this question, we assume that $r = 1$ and p_1 is odd. To simplify the notations we let $n = p^\alpha$ where p is an odd prime and α is a positive integer.

(a) What is the order of the group $\mathbf{Z}_n^*$?

(b) Show by induction that $(1 + p)^{p^{\ell-2}} \equiv 1 + p^{\ell-1} \pmod{p^\ell}$ for any integer $\ell \geq 2$.

(c) Show that $g_1 = 1 + p$ is a generator of the subgroup

$$G = \{x \in \mathbf{Z}_n^* \mid x \bmod p = 1\}.$$

(d) Show that there exists an element $g_2 \in \mathbf{Z}_n^*$ such that $g_2 \bmod p$ is a generator of $\mathbf{Z}_p^*$.
Hint: Use the fact that $\mathbf{Z}_p^*$ is cyclic.

(e) Let $g_3 = g_2^{p^{\alpha-1}} \bmod n$. Prove that $g_3 \bmod p$ is also a generator of $\mathbf{Z}_p^*$ and that $g_3^{p-1} \bmod n = 1$.

(f) Show that $\mathbf{Z}_n^*$ is cyclic by proving that $g_1 g_3 \bmod n$ is a generator of $\mathbf{Z}_n^*$.

3 Let $f : \mathbf{Z}_n^* \to \mathbf{Z}_{p_1^{\alpha_1}}^* \times \cdots \times \mathbf{Z}_{p_r^{\alpha_r}}^*$ be the isomorphism defined in the Chinese Remainder Theorem as $f(x) = (x \bmod p_1^{\alpha_1}, \ldots, x \bmod p_r^{\alpha_r})$.

(a) Let $x_i \in \mathbf{Z}_{p_i^{\alpha_i}}^*$ of order k_i for $1 \leq i \leq r$. What is the order of $f^{-1}(x_1, \ldots, x_r)$?

(b) Using the conclusions of Question 1 and Question 2, prove that

$$\begin{cases} \forall i, j \quad i \neq j \;\Rightarrow\; \gcd\left((p_i - 1)p_i^{\alpha_i-1}, (p_j - 1)p_j^{\alpha_j-1} \right) = 1 \\ \forall i \quad p_i = 2 \;\Rightarrow\; \alpha_i < 3. \end{cases}$$

is a necessary and sufficient condition for $\mathbf{Z}_n^*$ to be cyclic.

(c) Deduce that $\mathbf{Z}_n^*$ is cyclic if and only if n is either 2, 4, $2p^\alpha$, or p^α, where p is an odd prime and α is a positive integer.

▷ Solution on page 143

Exercise 4   Finite Fields and AES

The Advanced Encryption Standard (AES) [33] is a block cipher which makes heavy use of finite field operations. The aim of this exercise is to become familiar with the finite field operations performed in the AES. AES uses as only non-linear step a S-box whose core is the multiplicative inverse operation in the finite field $GF(2^8)$

$$
\begin{array}{ccc}
GF(2^8) & \longrightarrow & GF(2^8) \\
x & \longmapsto & x^{-1}.
\end{array}
$$

The 8-bit input of the S-box is then considered as an element of $GF(2^8)$. The designers of AES chose to represent any element of $GF(2^8)$ as a polynomial of degree smaller than 8 with coefficients in $GF(2)$. The addition (respectively the multiplication) in $GF(2^8)$ corresponds to the addition (respectively the multiplication) of polynomials modulo the polynomial $Q \in GF(2)[X]$ of degree 8 defined by $Q(X) = X^8 + X^4 + X^3 + X + 1$.

1 Compute the output of 0x45, i.e., of the polynomial $X^6 + X^2 + 1$ under the inverse operation in $GF(2^8)$.
   Hint: Maybe the Extended Euclid Algorithm will help you...

In AES, the main diffusion step is a linear application defined as follows. The 32-bit blocks are considered as polynomials of degree smaller than 4 over $GF(2^8)$. This linear application consists in multiplying the input polynomial with the fixed polynomial $C \in GF(2^8)[X]$ defined by $C(X) =$ 0x03 $\cdot X^3 +$ 0x01 $\cdot X^2 +$ 0x01 $\cdot X +$ 0x02 modulo the polynomial $X^4 + 1$ defined in $GF(2^8)[X]$ as well. The multiplication in $GF(2^8)[X]$ modulo a fixed polynomial can be written as a matrix multiplication. Indeed we can write $B(X) = C(X) \cdot A(X) \mod X^4 + 1$ as

$$
\begin{pmatrix}
\text{0x02} & \text{0x03} & \text{0x01} & \text{0x01} \\
\text{0x01} & \text{0x02} & \text{0x03} & \text{0x01} \\
\text{0x01} & \text{0x01} & \text{0x02} & \text{0x03} \\
\text{0x03} & \text{0x01} & \text{0x01} & \text{0x02}
\end{pmatrix}
\cdot
\begin{pmatrix}
a_0 \\
a_1 \\
a_2 \\
a_3
\end{pmatrix}
=
\begin{pmatrix}
b_0 \\
b_1 \\
b_2 \\
b_3
\end{pmatrix},
$$

where $A(X) = a_3 \cdot X^3 + a_2 \cdot X^2 + a_1 \cdot X + a_0$ and $B(X) = b_3 \cdot X^3 + b_2 \cdot X^2 + b_1 \cdot X + b_0$.

2 What is the image of the 32-bit block 0x836F13DD (where $a_0 =$ 0x83, $a_1 =$ 0x6F, $a_2 =$ 0x13 and $a_3 =$ 0xDD) under this diffusion step?

3 Propose two different ways to implement the above linear application efficiently on a computer.

▷ Solution on page 145

Exercise 5   ⋆A Special Discrete Logarithm

Let p be a prime and G be the set of all elements $x \in \mathbf{Z}_{p^2}$ satisfying $x \equiv 1 \pmod{p}$.

1 Show that G is a group with the multiplication of $\mathbf{Z}_{p^2}$.

2 Show that $|G| = p$.

3 Show that $L : G \to \mathbf{Z}_p$ defined by $L(x) = \frac{x-1}{p} \bmod p$ is a group isomorphism.

4 Show that $p + 1$ is a generator of G and that the isomorphism L is the logarithm with respect to the basis $p + 1$ in G. In other words, we have

$$(p+1)^{L(x)} \bmod p^2 = x$$

for any $x \in G$.

▷ Solution on page 146

Exercise 6   ⋆Quadratic Residues

Let $n = p_1 \times p_2 \times \cdots \times p_k$ where $p_1, \ldots, p_k$ are distinct odd primes and an integer $k \geq 2$. The element $a \in \mathbf{Z}_n^*$ is said to be a *quadratic residue* (QR) modulo n if there exists an $x \in \mathbf{Z}_n^*$ such that $x^2 \equiv a \pmod{n}$. If no such x exists, then a is called a *quadratic non-residue* (QNR) modulo n. Note that the non-invertible elements of $\mathbf{Z}_n$ are neither quadratic residues nor quadratic non-residues.

1 Find the QR's and QNR's of $\mathbf{Z}_{35}^*$. How many square roots does each of these QR's possess?

2 We call "CRT-transform", the ring isomorphism used in the Chinese Remainder Theorem. Prove that an element $a \in \mathbf{Z}_n^*$ is a QR modulo n if and only if each component of its image under the "CRT-transform" with respect to the moduli $p_1, \ldots, p_k$ is a QR of $\mathbf{Z}_{p_i}^*$.

3 Show that a QR of $\mathbf{Z}_n^*$ has exactly 2^k distinct square roots in $\mathbf{Z}_n^*$.

4 Show that the QR's of $\mathbf{Z}_n^*$ form a subgroup of $\mathbf{Z}_n^*$. What is the order of this subgroup?

5 Show that the product of a QR of $\mathbf{Z}_n^*$ and a QNR of $\mathbf{Z}_n^*$ is always a QNR of $\mathbf{Z}_n^*$.

6 Exhibit some examples in $\mathbf{Z}^*_{35}$ which show that the product of two QNR's of $\mathbf{Z}^*_{35}$ can be either a QR or a QNR of $\mathbf{Z}^*_{35}$.

▷ Solution on page 148

Exercise 7   ⋆Cubic Residues

It is not known whether the RSA decryption problem with $e = 3$ is equivalent to factoring the RSA modulus n or not. In the RSA setup, we have to choose n such that 3 does not divide $\varphi(n)$. Here, we want to study the above equivalence when 3 divides $\varphi(n)$. We consider $n = p \cdot q$ the product of two odd primes.

1 Under which condition on p and q does 3 divide $\varphi(n)$?

2 Let a, b, and m be some integers. Show that linear congruence $ax \equiv b$ (mod m) is solvable in x if and only if $d = \gcd(a, m)$ divides b. Show that in this case, there exists exactly d solutions between 0 and $m - 1$.

3 An element x of $\mathbf{Z}^*_n$ is called a *cubic residue* modulo n if there exists an element $y \in \mathbf{Z}^*_n$ such that $x \equiv y^3$ (mod n). Let CR_n be the set of all cubic residues of $\mathbf{Z}^*_n$.

   ■ Let $x \in \mathrm{CR}_n$. How many cubic roots of x are there when $p \equiv 1$ (mod 3) and $q \equiv 2$ (mod 3)?

   ■ How many cubic roots are there when $p \equiv q \equiv 1$ (mod 3)?

   ■ Assume that 3 divides $\varphi(n)$ and that we get two different cubic roots y and z of a given $x \in \mathrm{CR}_n$. Explain how we can find the factorization of n from $y - z$ and compute the success probability of this method.

4 We still assume that 3 divides $\varphi(n)$. Furthermore, we assume that we have access to an oracle which, given a cubic residue $x \in \mathrm{CR}_n$, outputs one cubic root y of x. Show that we can use it in order to factorize n. Deduce that the RSA decryption problem with $e = 3$ is equivalent to factoring n.

▷ Solution on page 150

Exercise 8   ⋆Generating Generators for $\mathbf{Z}^*_p$

Let p be an odd prime integer.

1 In this question we assume that the factorization of $p - 1$ is known.

(a) Devise an algorithm which checks that an element $g \in \mathbf{Z}_p^*$ is a generator. What is its complexity?

(b) What is the probability that a uniformly distributed random element $g \in \mathbf{Z}_p^*$ is a generator?

(c) Deduce an algorithm that finds a generator of $\mathbf{Z}_p^*$. What is its complexity?

2 In this question we assume that we know some positive integers w, q, B such that $p - 1 = wq$, that the factorization of w is known, and that all prime factors of q are greater than B. Adapt the algorithm of the previous question in order to find a generator $\mathbf{Z}_p^*$ in a probabilistic way. What is its complexity? Give an upper bound for the probability that the output is not a generator?

3 In this question we make *no* assumptions. Exhibit a probabilistic algorithm which generates a generator of $\mathbf{Z}_p^*$. What is its complexity? Give an upper bound for the probability that the output is not a generator?

▷ Solution on page 151

Exercise 9   ⋆Elliptic Curves and Finite Fields I

We consider the finite field $\mathbf{K} = \mathrm{GF}(7) = \mathbf{Z}_7$. As $\mathbf{K}$ is of characteristic 7, an elliptic curve $E_{a,b}$ over $\mathbf{K}$ is defined by

$$E_{a,b} = \{\mathcal{O}\} \cup \{(x,y) \in \mathbf{K}^2 \mid y^2 = x^3 + ax + b\}.$$

1 Compute the multiplication table of the elements of $\mathbf{K}$.

2 Find all the points of $E_{2,1}$. How many points do you find? Is Hasse's Theorem verified?

3 For each point $P \in E_{2,1}$, compute $-P$ and check that it lies on the curve as well.

4 To which group is $E_{2,1}$ isomorphic to? Compute the addition table of $E_{2,1}$.

▷ Solution on page 153

Exercise 10   ⋆Elliptic Curves and Finite Fields II

We consider the finite field $\mathbf{K} = \mathrm{GF}(2^2)$. We know that $\mathrm{GF}(2^2) = \mathbf{Z}_2[X]/(P(X))$, where $P(X)$ is a polynomial of degree 2, irreducible over $\mathbf{Z}_2$. As $\mathbf{K}$ is of characteristic 2, an elliptic curve E_{a_2,a_6} defined over $\mathbf{K}$ is defined by

$$E_{a_2,a_6} = \{\mathcal{O}\} \cup \{(x,y) \in \mathbf{K}^2 \mid y^2 + xy = x^3 + a_2x^2 + a_6\}.$$

1 Show that $P(X) = X^2 + X + 1$ is irreducible over $\mathbf{Z}_2$.

2 Compute the multiplication table of the elements of the field $\mathbf{K} = \mathbf{Z}_2[X]/(X^2 + X + 1)$.

3 Compute $\mathrm{Tr}_{4,2}(X)$. Find all the points of $E_{X,X+1}$. How many points do you find? Is Hasse's Theorem verified?

4 For each point $P \in E_{X,X+1}$, compute $-P$ and check that it lies on the curve as well.

5 Which group is $E_{X,X+1}$ isomorphic to? Compute the addition table of $E_{X,X+1}$.

▷ Solution on page 156

Solutions

Solution 1   Captain's Age

We can write this problem as the following system of equations over $\mathbf{Z}$,

$$\begin{cases} x \equiv 1 \pmod 3 \\ x \equiv 3 \pmod 5 \\ x \equiv 3 \pmod 7, \end{cases}$$

where x denotes the Captain's age. As $3, 5$, and 7 are coprime, we can apply the Chinese Remainder Theorem. Hence, using the transformation given by this theorem, we obtain

$$x = (1 \cdot 5 \cdot 7 \cdot (35^{-1} \bmod 3)$$
$$+ 3 \cdot 3 \cdot 7 \cdot (21^{-1} \bmod 5) + 3 \cdot 3 \cdot 5 \cdot (15^{-1} \bmod 7)) \bmod 105.$$

As $35^{-1} \bmod 3 = 2$, $21^{-1} \bmod 5 = 1$, and $15^{-1} \bmod 7 = 1$, we get $x = 178 \bmod 105 = 73$. Thus, the Captain is 73 years old.

Solution 2   Roots in $\mathbf{Z}_{77}^*$

From classical results on the group $\mathbf{Z}_n^*$, we know that the 7th root of 23 in $\mathbf{Z}_{77}^*$ is given by

$$23^{7^{-1} \bmod \varphi(77)} \bmod 77,$$

where φ denotes the Euler Totient Function. Since this function is multiplicative on the product of two coprime numbers, we have $\varphi(77) = \varphi(11) \cdot \varphi(7) = 10 \cdot 6 = 60$. Applying the Extended Euclidean Algorithm we obtain

$$1 = 2 \cdot 60 - 17 \cdot 7.$$

This immediately gives the inverse of 7 modulo 60 which is equal to $-17 \bmod 60 = 43$. Hence, it remains to compute

$$23^{43} \bmod 77 = ((((23^2)^2 \cdot 23)^2)^2 \cdot 23)^2 \cdot 23 \bmod 77 = 23$$

after having noticed that the binary representation of 43 is 101011.

Solution 3   ⋆When is $\mathbf{Z}_n^*$ Cyclic?

1 (a) $\mathbf{Z}_2^* = \{1\}$ which is trivially generated by 1.

(b) $\mathbf{Z}_4^* = \{1,3\}$ which is generated by the element 3.

(c) $\mathbf{Z}_8^* = \{1,3,5,7\}$. All non-neutral elements have order 2, so none of them has order 4.

(d) If g generates $\mathbf{Z}_{2^\alpha}^*$, then $g \bmod 8$ must generate $\mathbf{Z}_8^*$ which is not possible. So, we have a contradiction on the existence of such a generator g.

2 (a) By classical properties of the Euler Totient Function φ, we know that $|\mathbf{Z}_n^*| = \varphi(p^\alpha) = (p-1)p^{\alpha-1}$.

(b) The assertion obviously holds for $\ell = 2$. We now assume that $(1+p)^{p^{\ell-2}} \equiv 1+p^{\ell-1} \pmod{p^\ell}$ for some $\ell \geq 2$. This is equivalent to say that there exists an integer k satisfying $0 \leq k < p$ and $(1+p)^{p^{\ell-2}} \equiv 1+p^{\ell-1}+kp^\ell \pmod{p^{\ell+1}}$. If we raise this equality to the power p, we obtain

$$(1+p)^{p^{\ell-1}} \equiv \sum_{j=0}^{p} \binom{p}{j} p^{(\ell-1)j}(1+kp^\ell)^{p-j} \pmod{p^{\ell+1}}.$$

Since $\binom{p}{j}p^{(\ell-1)j} \bmod p^{\ell+1} = 0$ for any integer $j \geq 2$ and $\binom{p}{1} = p$, we have

$$(1+p)^{p^{\ell-1}} \equiv 1+p^\ell \sum_{j=0}^{p-1} \binom{p-1}{j} k^j p^{\ell j} \pmod{p^{\ell+1}}.$$

As $p^{\ell j} \equiv 0 \pmod{p^{\ell+1}}$ for $j > 0$, we finally have

$$(1+p)^{p^{\ell-1}} \equiv 1+p^\ell \pmod{p^{\ell+1}}.$$

This shows that the assertion holds for $\ell+1$ provided it holds for ℓ, which concludes the proof.

(c) Since G contains $p^{\alpha-1}$ elements, we have to show that

$$g_1^{p^{\alpha-1}} \bmod p^\alpha = 1$$

and $g_1^{p^{\alpha-2}} \bmod p^\alpha \neq 1$. Applying result of the previous question with $\ell = \alpha$ and $\ell = \alpha+1$, we deduce that

$$g_1^{p^{\alpha-2}} \equiv 1+p^{\alpha-1} \not\equiv 1 \pmod{p^\alpha}$$

and $g_1^{p^{\alpha-1}} \equiv 1 + p^\alpha \pmod{p^{\alpha+1}}$. Reducing the last equality modulo p^α shows that $g_1^{p^{\alpha-1}} \equiv 1 \pmod{p^\alpha}$.

(d) Since $\mathbf{Z}_p^*$ is cyclic there exists an element $g_2 \in \mathbf{Z}_p^*$ which generates $\mathbf{Z}_p^*$. g_2 can also be considered as an element of $\mathbf{Z}_n^*$.

(e) Since $p^{\alpha-1} \equiv 1 \pmod{p-1}$ we have $g_3 \equiv g_2 \pmod{p}$. Furthermore, we have

$$g_3^{p-1} \equiv g_2^{(p-1)p^{\alpha-1}} \equiv g_2^{\varphi(n)} \equiv 1 \pmod{n}.$$

(f) Let $g = g_1 g_3 \bmod n$. We have $g^{p^{\alpha-1}} \bmod n = g_3^{p^{\alpha-1}} \bmod n$ which is equal to g_3 modulo p by the previous questions. Therefore, we get $g^{p^{\alpha-1}} \bmod n \neq 1$, which means that there must be the factor $p-1$ in the order of g. Next we have $g^{(p-1)p^{\alpha-2}} \bmod n = (g_1^{p^{\alpha-2}})^{p-1} \bmod n$. We know that $g_1^{p^{\alpha-2}} \bmod n$ is an element of G different from 1. We also know that an element of G different from 1 has an order which divides $p^{\alpha-1}$. Therefore, $g^{(p-1)p^{\alpha-2}} \bmod n \neq 1$ which shows that the order of g is a multiple of $p^{\alpha-1}$. Thus, we deduce that g has the full order and generates $\mathbf{Z}_n^*$.

3 (a) Since f is an isomorphism, the order of $f^{-1}(x_1, \ldots, x_r)$ is equal to the order of $(x_1, \ldots, x_r)$. By definition of the order, we have to find the smallest integer λ such that $x_i^\lambda \bmod p_i^{\alpha_i} = 1$ for all $1 \leq i \leq r$. This is equivalent to say that λ must be a multiple of the order of x_i for all $1 \leq i \leq r$. Since λ is the smallest integer which satisfies this property, we have $\lambda = \mathrm{lcm}(k_1, \ldots, k_r)$.

(b) $\mathbf{Z}_n^*$ is cyclic if and only if there exists a generator. Let g be such a generator and let $f(g) = (g_1, \ldots, g_r)$. Each g_i must clearly be a generator of $\mathbf{Z}_{p_i^{\alpha_i}}^*$, otherwise g would not be a generator of $\mathbf{Z}_n^*$. Hence, if $p_j = 2$ for $1 \leq j \leq r$, this implies that $\alpha_j < 3$ by Question 1. Moreover, by the formula of the previous question, the least common multiple of all $(p_i - 1)p_i^{\alpha_i - 1}$ for $1 \leq i \leq r$ is equal to their product since $|\mathbf{Z}_n^*| = \prod_{i=1}^r (p_i - 1)p_i^{\alpha_i - 1}$. This implies that the integers $(p_i - 1)p_i^{\alpha_i - 1}$ are pairwise coprime.

Conversely, if the primes p_i's satisfy the condition given in the question we know that $\mathbf{Z}_{p_i^{\alpha_i}}$ is cyclic for $1 \leq i \leq r$. If we consider a generator g_i of $\mathbf{Z}_{p_i^{\alpha_i}}$ for $1 \leq i \leq r$ and compute $g = f^{-1}(g_1, \ldots, g_r)$. Now, using the formula of the previous question shows that the order of g is maximal, i.e., g is a generator of $\mathbf{Z}_n^*$.

(c) If we have two odd primes p_i and p_j then $p_i - 1$ and $p_j - 1$ are not coprime (they are both even). So, we have at most one odd prime factor of n. If we have a power of 2 greater than 8 the second condition does not hold. Conversely, if we have either 2, 4, or a single odd prime and a power of 2 which is 1 or 2, then the conditions hold.

For further readings about the structure of $\mathbf{Z}_n^*$, we refer to Chapter 4 of the book of Ireland and Rosen [22].

Solution 4   Finite Fields and AES

1 Applying the Extended Euclid Algorithm on the inputs $X^8 + X^4 + X^3 + X + 1$ and $X^6 + X^2 + 1$ leads to the equality

$$1 = (X^5 + X^4 + 1)(X^6 + X^2 + 1) + (X^3 + X^2)(X^8 + X^4 + X^3 + X + 1).$$

Therefore, we deduce that

$$(X^6 + X^2 + 1) \cdot (X^5 + X^4 + 1) \equiv 1 \pmod{X^8 + X^4 + X^3 + X + 1}$$

and that the output of this inverse operation is 0x31.

2 First, we need to compute the multiplications $0x02 \cdot a_i$ and $0x03 \cdot a_i$ in $GF(2^8)$ for $i = 0, 1, 2, 3$. Below, we give the results of these operations.

$$
\begin{aligned}
X \cdot (X^7 + X + 1) &\equiv X^4 + X^3 + X^2 + 1 \pmod{Q} \\
(X + 1) \cdot (X^7 + X + 1) &\equiv X^7 + X^4 + X^3 + X^2 + X \pmod{Q} \\
X \cdot (X^6 + X^5 + X^3 + X^2 + X + 1) &\equiv X^7 + X^6 + X^4 + X^3 + X^2 + X \pmod{Q} \\
(X + 1) \cdot (X^6 + X^5 + X^3 + X^2 + X + 1) &\equiv X^7 + X^5 + X^4 + 1 \pmod{Q} \\
X \cdot (X^4 + X + 1) &\equiv X^5 + X^2 + X \pmod{Q} \\
(X + 1) \cdot (X^4 + X + 1) &\equiv X^5 + X^4 + X^2 + 1 \pmod{Q} \\
X \cdot (X^7 + X^6 + X^4 + X^3 + X^2 + 1) &\equiv X^7 + X^5 + 1 \pmod{Q} \\
(X + 1) \cdot (X^7 + X^6 + X^4 + X^3 + X^2 + 1) &\equiv X^6 + X^5 + X^4 + X^3 + X^2 \pmod{Q}
\end{aligned}
$$

Computing the corresponding linear combinations, we get $b_0 = X^6 + X^5 + X$, $b_1 = X^7 + X^5 + X^4 + X^2 + 1$, $b_2 = X^7 + X^5 + X^4 + X^2 + X$, $b_3 = X^6 + X + 1$. Thus, we finally obtain 0x62B5B643 as output.

3 On a computer, a $GF(2^8)$ addition can be implemented by a (bitwise) XOR operation. The multiplication of an element $a \in GF(2^8)$ by X corresponds to a left-shit of the coefficients of a, followed by a conditional XOR. Namely, if the polynomial corresponding to a contains the monomial X^7, we have to perform a XOR with the polynomial

$Q(X) = X^8 + X^4 + X^3 + X + 1$. Similarly, the multiplication by $X+1$ corresponds to a multiplication by X followed by a XOR operation. These operations will typically be used on 8-bit architectures (like smartcards). On a 32-bit architecture, the matrix multiplication may be implemented as 3 XOR's and 4 table-lookups:

$$\begin{pmatrix} 0x02 & 0x03 & 0x01 & 0x01 \\ 0x01 & 0x02 & 0x03 & 0x01 \\ 0x01 & 0x01 & 0x02 & 0x03 \\ 0x03 & 0x01 & 0x01 & 0x02 \end{pmatrix} \cdot \begin{pmatrix} a_0 \\ a_1 \\ a_2 \\ a_3 \end{pmatrix} =$$

$$a_0 \cdot \underbrace{\begin{pmatrix} 0x02 \\ 0x01 \\ 0x01 \\ 0x03 \end{pmatrix}}_{T_0[a_0]} + a_1 \cdot \underbrace{\begin{pmatrix} 0x03 \\ 0x02 \\ 0x01 \\ 0x01 \end{pmatrix}}_{T_1[a_1]} + a_2 \cdot \underbrace{\begin{pmatrix} 0x01 \\ 0x03 \\ 0x02 \\ 0x01 \end{pmatrix}}_{T_2[a_2]} + a_3 \cdot \underbrace{\begin{pmatrix} 0x01 \\ 0x01 \\ 0x03 \\ 0x02 \end{pmatrix}}_{T_3[a_3]} \cdot$$

Each table needs $256 \cdot 32 = 8192$ bits, i.e., 1024 bytes of memory. Note that it is possible to only use one table if one is willing to accept three more 32-bit rotations.

For further readings about the AES, we refer to the book of Daemen and Rijmen [13].

Solution 5 ⋆A Special Discrete Logarithm

1 We show that $G = \{x \in \mathbf{Z}_{p^2} \mid x \equiv 1 \pmod{p}\}$ with the multiplication modulo p^2 is a group. Below, we prove the different conditions G should fulfill to be a group.

- **(Closure)** Let $a, b \in G$. By definition of G, we have $a \equiv b \equiv 1 \pmod{p}$. Hence, $ab \equiv 1 \pmod{p}$, which means that $ab \in G$.

- **(Associativity)** The associativity follows from the associativity of the multiplication in $\mathbf{Z}_{p^2}$.

- **(Neutral element)** The neutral element $e \in G$ has to satisfy $a \cdot e = e \cdot a = a$ for any $a \in G$. The element $1 \in G$ satisfies this property since it is the neutral element in $\mathbf{Z}_{p^2}$.

- **(Inverse element)** We have to show, that for any $a \in G$, there exists an element $b \in G$ such that $a \cdot b \equiv 1 \pmod{p}$. We can write $a = 1 + kp$ for an integer k such that $0 \le k < p$. Similarly, we set $b = 1 + \ell p$ for an integer ℓ such that $0 \le \ell < p$. From the equation

$$(1 + kp) \cdot (1 + \ell p) \equiv 1 + (k + \ell)p \pmod{p^2},$$

we deduce that b is the inverse of a if and only if $k + \ell \equiv 0$ (mod p). Thus, each element $a = 1 + kp \in G$ has $b = 1 + (p - k)p$ as inverse.

Since the multiplication in $\mathbf{Z}_{p^2}$ is commutative, note that G is commutative as well.

2 Any element a of $\mathbf{Z}_{p^2}$ can be written in the unique form $a = a_1 + a_2 p$, where a_1 and a_2 are unique integers satisfying $0 \leq a_1, a_2 \leq p - 1$. We can conclude the proof by noticing that any element a of $\mathbf{Z}_{p^2}$ lies in G if and only if the corresponding integer $a_1 = 1$.

3 We show that $L : G \rightarrow \mathbf{Z}_p$ defined by $L(x) = \frac{x-1}{p}$ mod p is a group isomorphism.

- **(Homomorphism)** We first show that L is a group homomorphism. Let $a = 1 + kp$ with $0 \leq k < p$ and $b = 1 + \ell p$ with $0 \leq \ell < p$ be elements of G. We have

$$
\begin{aligned}
L(a \cdot b) &= L\left((1 + kp)(1 + \ell p) \bmod p^2\right) \\
&= L(1 + (k + \ell)p) \\
&= \frac{1 + (k + \ell)p - 1}{p} \bmod p \\
&= k + \ell \bmod p
\end{aligned}
$$

and

$$
\begin{aligned}
L(a) + L(b) &= \frac{1 + kp - 1}{p} + \frac{1 + \ell p - 1}{p} \bmod p \\
&= k + \ell \bmod p.
\end{aligned}
$$

- **(Injectivity)** Since L is an homomorphism, it suffices to show that its kernel contains only the neutral element. Let $a = 1 + kp$ with $0 \leq k < p$ such that $L(a) = 0$. This is equivalent to

$$\frac{1 + kp - 1}{p} = k = 0,$$

which shows that the kernel is trivial, i.e., is equal to $\{0\}$.

- **(Surjectivity)** The surjectivity simply follows from the injectivity, since the two sets G and $\mathbf{Z}_p$ have the same finite cardinality. More details about this fact are given in Exercise 1 of Chapter 1.

4 We have to show that any element $a \in G$ can be written as a power of $p + 1$. Using the binomial theorem, we have

$$(p+1)^n \bmod p^2 = \sum_{i=0}^{n} \binom{n}{i} p^i \bmod p^2$$
$$= 1 + np.$$

Thus, it is clear that $p + 1$ generates G. For $y \in G$,

$$y = \log_{p+1}(x) \iff x = (p+1)^y \bmod p^2.$$

Since $(p+1)^y \bmod p^2 = 1 + py$, we finally obtain

$$y = \frac{x-1}{p} \bmod p = L(x).$$

This logarithm function plays an important role for the Okamoto-Uchiyama cryptosystem [34]. This cryptosystem is studied in Exercise 1 of Chapter 9.

Solution 6   ⋆Quadratic Residues

1 We find the QR's of $\mathbf{Z}_{35}^*$ using Table 6.1 which contains the square of all elements in $\mathbf{Z}_{35}^*$.

Table 6.1. Squares in $\mathbf{Z}_{35}^*$

$1^2 = 1$	$2^2 = 4$	$3^2 = 9$	$4^2 = 16$
$6^2 = 1$	$8^2 = 29$	$9^2 = 11$	$11^2 = 16$
$12^2 = 4$	$13^2 = 29$	$16^2 = 11$	$17^2 = 9$
$18^2 = 9$	$19^2 = 11$	$22^2 = 29$	$23^2 = 4$
$24^2 = 16$	$26^2 = 11$	$27^2 = 29$	$29^2 = 1$
$31^2 = 16$	$32^2 = 9$	$33^2 = 4$	$34^2 = 1$

Hence, by looking at the values of Table 6.1, we obtain the set QR_{35} of all QR's modulo 35

$$\mathrm{QR}_{35} = \{1, 4, 9, 11, 16, 29\}.$$

Then, the set QNR_{35} of the non-quadratic residues is

$$\text{QNR}_{35} = \{2, 3, 6, 8, 12, 13, 17, 18, 19, 22, 23, 24, 26, 27, 31, 32, 33, 34\}.$$

We observe that every QR has four square roots.

2 By definition, the "CRT-transform" of an element $a \in \mathbf{Z}_n^*$ with respect to $p_1, \ldots, p_k$ is $(a \bmod p_1, \ldots, a \bmod p_k)$. We have to show that

$$a \in \text{QR}_n \iff a \bmod p_i \in \text{QR}_{p_i} \text{ for } 1 \le i \le k.$$

By definition, there exists an $x \in \mathbf{Z}_n^*$ such that $a = x^2 \bmod n$. Then, $a \bmod p_i = x^2 \bmod p_i$ is trivially a QR in $\mathbf{Z}_{p_i}$ for any $1 \le i \le k$. Conversely, one can write by assumption the "CRT-transform" of the element a as $(x_1^2, x_2^2, \ldots, x_k^2) \in \mathbf{Z}_{p_1}^* \times \cdots \times \mathbf{Z}_{p_k}^*$. Since the "CRT-transform" is a ring isomorphism, we deduce that a is the square of an element x having $(x_1, \ldots, x_k)$ as image under the "CRT-transform". Hence, $a = x^2 \bmod n$ is in QR_n.

3 From the previous question, we know that a quadratic residue $a \in \mathbf{Z}_n^*$ has an image of the form $(x_1^2, x_2^2, \ldots, x_k^2)$ under the "CRT-transform". Since $\mathbf{Z}_{p_i}$ is a field, x_i^2 has exactly 2 square roots in $\mathbf{Z}_{p_i}$ for $1 \le i \le k$, namely $\pm x_i$. Therefore, we have 2^k square roots in total since we have two square roots for each "CRT-component".

4 By definition of a subgroup, it suffices to show that $ab^{-1} \in \text{QR}_n$ whenever $a, b \in \text{QR}_n$. There exist two elements $x, y \in \mathbf{Z}_n^*$ satisfying $a = x^2$ and $b = y^2$. From this, we have $ab^{-1} = x^2 \cdot (y^2)^{-1} = (xy^{-1})^2$, which concludes the proof.

As every element of QR_n has 2^k square roots, the order of QR_n is equal to $\varphi(n)/2^k$.

5 Let $a, b \in \mathbf{Z}_n^*$, with $a \in \text{QR}_n$ and $b \in \text{QNR}_n$. From Question 2, we know that there exists an integer $1 \le j \le k$ such that $b_j = b \bmod p_j$ is in QNR_{p_j}. Hence,

$$b^{\frac{p_j-1}{2}} \not\equiv 1 \pmod{p_j}.$$

As

$$a^{\frac{p_j-1}{2}} \equiv 1 \pmod{p_j},$$

we have

$$(ab)^{\frac{p_j-1}{2}} \not\equiv 1 \pmod{p_j},$$

which means that ab is not a QR modulo n.

6 Consider the elements $2, 3 \in \text{QNR}_{35}$. The element $6 = 2 \cdot 3 \bmod 35$ does not lie in QNR_{35}. In the contrary, if we take $2, 18 \in \text{QNR}_{35}$, we observe that $2 \cdot 18 \equiv 1 \pmod{35}$.

Solution 7   ⋆Cubic Residues

1 Since $\varphi(n) = (p-1)(q-1)$, 3 divides n if and only if $p \equiv 1 \pmod 3$ or $q \equiv 1 \pmod 3$ (or both).

2 If the congruence $ax \equiv b \pmod m$ is solvable, then m must divide $ax - b$. Since d divides m and a, it is clear that d divides b. Conversely, assume that d divides b. It follows that $b = kd$ for some integer k. We know that there exists a Bézout's Identity $d = \alpha a + \mu m$ for some integers α and μ. It follows that

$$b = kd = k\alpha a + k\mu m = (k\alpha)a + (k\mu)m$$

and hence $k\alpha$ is a solution of the congruence $ax \equiv b \pmod m$. It is not hard to see that each element of the form

$$x_i = x_0 + \frac{im}{d} \text{ where } i = 0, \ldots, d-1$$

is a solution if x_0 is any solution. Moreover, the solutions are distinct modulo m. It remains to show that any arbitrary solution c of $ax \equiv b \pmod m$ is equal to some x_i. Indeed, since $ac \equiv ax_0 \equiv b \pmod m$, it follows that m divides $a(c - x_0)$. But $d = \gcd(a, m)$ and hence $\frac{m}{d}$ divides $(c - x_0)$.

3 Given a generator g of $\mathbf{Z}_p^*$ where p is an odd prime, a cubic root can be written as $g^j \equiv g^{3i} \pmod p$ for two integers i and j. Equivalently, we can write $j \equiv 3i \pmod{p-1}$.

From the previous question, $j \equiv 3i \pmod{p-1}$ possesses three solutions if $\gcd(p-1, 3) = 3$ and a single solution if $\gcd(p-1, 3) = 1$. By using the Chinese Remainder Theorem, we conclude that $x = y^3 \pmod{pq}$ possesses three cubic roots when $p \equiv 1 \pmod 3$ and $q \equiv 2 \pmod 3$ and nine cubic roots when $p \equiv q \equiv 1 \pmod 3$.

We now have $y \neq z$ such that $y^3 \equiv z^3 \equiv x \pmod{pq}$ two different cubic roots of x at disposal. We have $y^3 - z^3 \equiv (y-z)(y^2+yz+z^2) \equiv 0 \pmod{pq}$. The probability that $\gcd(y - z, n)$ is a non-trivial factor of $n = pq$ is equal to

$$\Pr\left[y \equiv z \pmod p, \, y \not\equiv z \pmod q\right]$$
$$+ \Pr\left[y \not\equiv z \pmod p, \, y \equiv z \pmod q\right].$$

Note that if $y \not\equiv z \pmod{p}$ and $y \not\equiv z \pmod{q}$, then $x \not\equiv y \pmod{pq}$ but the method will fail to reveal a *non-trivial* factor. The above probability is equal to $\frac{2}{3}$ if $p \equiv 2 \pmod 3$ and $q \equiv 1 \pmod 3$ and if $p \equiv 1 \pmod 3$ and $q \equiv 2 \pmod 3$. It is equal to $\frac{4}{9}$ when $p \equiv q \equiv 1 \pmod 3$. The overall success probability is thus equal to

$$\frac{2}{3} \cdot \frac{2}{3} + \frac{1}{3} \cdot \frac{4}{9} = \frac{16}{27},$$

for a random modulus $n = p \cdot q$ with $3 \mid \varphi(n)$ and p, q odd.

4 Given an oracle which can compute cubic roots in $\mathbf{Z}_n^*$, it is possible to factorize n is the following way. We generate randomly a $y \in \mathbf{Z}_n^*$ and we compute $x = y^3 \bmod n$. We give then x to the oracle, and with a probability equal to $\frac{16}{27}$, it will output a $z \neq y$ allowing to factorize n. Conversely, we can use the factorization of n to compute cubic roots by using the Chinese Remainder Theorem. Thus, computing cubic roots and factorizing n are equivalent.

Solution 8   ⋆Generating Generators for $\mathbf{Z}_p^*$

1 In what follows, we denote

$$p - 1 = p_1^{\alpha_1} \times \cdots \times p_r^{\alpha_r}$$

where the p_i's are distinct primes such that $p_1 < p_2 < \cdots < p_r$, and where the α_i's are positive integers.

(a) By the Lagrange Theorem, we know that the order of g is a factor of $p - 1$. To be ensured that the order is maximal, we need to check that this one is not a factor of $\frac{p-1}{p_i}$ for all $1 \leq i \leq r$. Hence, for $i = 1, \ldots, r$ we check that

$$g^{\frac{p-1}{p_i}} \bmod p \neq 1.$$

Since this algorithm consists in computing r modular exponentiations, its average complexity is $\mathcal{O}(r\ell^3)$ with $\ell = \log_2(p)$.

(b) For a generator g and an integer i, we know that g^i is another generator if and only if there exists some j such that $g^{ij} \equiv g \pmod p$ (i.e., such that $ij \equiv 1 \pmod{p-1}$), which happens if and only if i is invertible modulo $p - 1$. Hence we have $\varphi(p-1)$ generators of $\mathbf{Z}_p^*$ in total. The probability that a random $g \in \mathbf{Z}_p^*$ is a generator is thus

$$\frac{\varphi(p-1)}{p-1} = \left(1 - \frac{1}{p_1}\right) \times \cdots \times \left(1 - \frac{1}{p_r}\right).$$

This can be quite small. Actually, since p_1 must be equal to 2, we know that this probability is less than $\frac{1}{2}$. We also notice that it is greater than $\frac{1}{2^r}$.

(c) We simply pick a random $g \in \mathbf{Z}_p^*$, check if it is a generator using the test of the first question, and iterate until the test succeeds. The average complexity of this algorithm is

$$\mathcal{O}\left(\frac{r\ell^3}{\left(1 - \frac{1}{p_1}\right) \times \ldots \times \left(1 - \frac{1}{p_r}\right)} \right).$$

In practice, it is enough for regular p. However, this is not so efficient when $p - 1$ is the product of small different primes.

2 Let s be the integer such that $p_s \leq B < p_{s+1}$. The problem here is that we cannot perform the test on the first question on the prime factors of q. We can still apply the algorithm of the previous question with all p_i's which are factors of w, i.e., for those with $i = 1, \ldots, s$. This may produce a fake generator whose order is wq' for a given factor $q' < q$ of q. The complexity is

$$\mathcal{O}\left(\frac{s\ell^3}{\left(1 - \frac{1}{p_1}\right) \times \cdots \times \left(1 - \frac{1}{p_s}\right)} \right).$$

Let $\Pr[\text{fake}]$ be the probability that we pick such a fake generator. Let β_i be the probability that the order of the picked candidate for g has an order which is a factor of $\frac{p-1}{p_i}$. We have $\Pr[\text{fake}] \leq \beta_{s+1} + \cdots + \beta_r$. Let g be a generator of $\mathbf{Z}_p^*$. A random element of $\mathbf{Z}_p^*$ can be written $g^i \bmod p$ for an integer $1 \leq i \leq p - 1$. Its order is a factor of $\frac{p-1}{p_i}$ only if i is a multiple of p_i which holds with probability less than $\frac{1}{p_i}$. From this and the assumption that $p_i \geq B$ for $s + 1 \leq i \leq r$, we obtain $\Pr[\text{fake}] \leq \frac{r-s}{B}$. Since $p \geq p_1 \times \cdots \times p_s \times B^{r-s}$, we obtain $r - s \leq \frac{\ell}{\log_2(B)}$ and thus,

$$\Pr[\text{fake}] \leq \frac{\ell}{B \log_2(B)}.$$

3 For a given B we can look for all factors of $p - 1$ which are less than B and then apply the algorithm of the previous question. The complexity of this first phase is $\mathcal{O}(B\ell^3)$ by using trial division. Thus,

the overall complexity is

$$
\mathcal{O}\left(\frac{s\ell^3}{\left(1 - \frac{1}{p_1}\right) \times \cdots \times \left(1 - \frac{1}{p_s}\right)} + B\ell^3\right).
$$

The upper bound that the output is not a generator is again $\frac{\ell}{B\log_2(B)}$.

Solution 9 ⋆Elliptic Curves and Finite Fields I

1 The multiplication table of the elements of **K** is given in Table 6.2.

Table 6.2. Multiplication table of $\mathbf{Z}_7$

*	0	1	2	3	4	5	6
0	0	0	0	0	0	0	0
1	0	1	2	3	4	5	6
2	0	2	4	6	1	3	5
3	0	3	6	2	5	1	4
4	0	4	1	5	2	6	3
5	0	5	3	1	6	4	2
6	0	6	5	4	3	2	1

Another useful table for this exercise is given in Table 6.3.

Table 6.3. Square and cubic elements of $\mathbf{Z}_7$

x	x^2	x^3
0	0	0
1	1	1
2	4	1
3	2	6
4	2	1
5	4	6
6	1	6

2 Let $P = (x, y)$ be a point of $E_{2,1}$.

- If $x = 0$, y must satisfy $y^2 = 1$, so that $(0, 1)$ and $(0, 6)$ are points of $E_{2,1}$.
- If $x = 1$, y must satisfy $y^2 = 4$, so that $(1, 2)$ and $(1, 5)$ are points of $E_{2,1}$.

- If $x = 2$, y must satisfy $y^2 = 6$, which is impossible.
- If $x = 3$, y must satisfy $y^2 = 6$, which is impossible.
- If $x = 4$, y must satisfy $y^2 = 3$, which is impossible.
- If $x = 5$, y must satisfy $y^2 = 3$, which is impossible.
- If $x = 6$, y must satisfy $y^2 = 5$, which is impossible.

Finally $E_{2,1} = \{\mathcal{O}, (0,1), (0,6), (1,2), (1,5)\}$ and thus $|E_{2,1}| = 5$. According to Hasse's Theorem, we should have $||\mathbf{K}| + 1 - |E_{2,1}|| \leq 2\sqrt{|\mathbf{K}|}$. As $||\mathbf{K}| + 1 - |E_{2,1}|| = 7 + 1 - 5 = 3$ and $2\sqrt{|\mathbf{K}|} = 2\sqrt{7} > 3$, everything is fine.

3 Table 6.4 confirms that $-P$ lies on the curve as well.

Table 6.4.   Inverse elements of $E_{2,1}$

P	$\mathcal{O}$	$(0,1)$	$(0,6)$	$(1,2)$	$(1,5)$
$-P$	$\mathcal{O}$	$(0,6)$	$(0,1)$	$(1,5)$	$(1,2)$

4 As $E_{2,1}$ is a group of prime order, each of its elements (except $\mathcal{O}$) is a generator. This is because the order of an element should divide $|E_{2,1}|$, which is prime, so that the order of an element is either 1 (this is only the case for $\mathcal{O}$) or $|E_{2,1}|$. We choose for example $G = (1,2)$ as a generator. Consider the mapping

$$\varphi: \quad \mathbf{Z}_5 \quad \longrightarrow \quad E_{2,1}$$
$$\gamma \quad \longmapsto \quad \gamma G.$$

It is easy to show that φ is a group isomorphism. From

$$\begin{aligned} \varphi(\alpha + \beta) &= (\alpha + \beta)G \\ &= \alpha G + \beta G \quad \text{(by associativity of } + \text{ in } E_{2,1}) \\ &= \varphi(\alpha) + \varphi(\beta), \end{aligned}$$

φ is a group homomorphism. As

$$\begin{aligned} \varphi(\gamma) = 0 &\Rightarrow \gamma G = \mathcal{O} \\ &\Rightarrow \gamma = 0 \quad \text{(as } G \text{ is a generator of } E_{2,1}), \end{aligned}$$

φ is injective. As $|\mathbf{Z}_5| = |E_{2,1}|$, φ is an isomorphism. Therefore, $E_{2,1}$ is isomorphic to $\mathbf{Z}_5$. Note that an isomorphism is *very* useful to compute the addition table of the points of the elliptic curve. Indeed, after some computations, one can obtain Table 6.5.

Table 6.5. Elements generated by a generator G in $E_{2,1}$

G	$2G$	$3G$	$4G$	$5G$
$(1,2)$	$(0,1)$	$(0,6)$	$(1,5)$	$\mathcal{O}$

From the definition of the isomorphism φ, we have the following correspondence between the elements of $E_{2,1}$ and of $\mathbf{Z}_5$:

$$\mathcal{O} \leftrightarrow 0$$
$$(1,2) \leftrightarrow 1$$
$$(0,1) \leftrightarrow 2$$
$$(0,6) \leftrightarrow 3$$
$$(1,5) \leftrightarrow 4$$

The addition table of the elements of $\mathbf{Z}_5$ is given in Table 6.6.

Table 6.6. Addition table of $\mathbf{Z}_5$

+	0	1	2	3	4
0	0	1	2	3	4
1	1	2	3	4	0
2	2	3	4	0	1
3	3	4	0	1	2
4	4	0	1	2	3

From this, we easily obtain the addition table of the elements of $E_{2,1}$ which is given in Table 6.7.

Table 6.7. Addition table of $E_{2,1}$

+	$\mathcal{O}$	$(1,2)$	$(0,1)$	$(0,6)$	$(1,5)$
$\mathcal{O}$	$\mathcal{O}$	$(1,2)$	$(0,1)$	$(0,6)$	$(1,5)$
$(1,2)$	$(1,2)$	$(0,1)$	$(0,6)$	$(1,5)$	$\mathcal{O}$
$(0,1)$	$(0,1)$	$(0,6)$	$(1,5)$	$\mathcal{O}$	$(1,2)$
$(0,6)$	$(0,6)$	$(1,5)$	$\mathcal{O}$	$(1,2)$	$(0,1)$
$(1,5)$	$(1,5)$	$\mathcal{O}$	$(1,2)$	$(0,1)$	$(0,6)$

Table 6.8.   Multiplication table of $GF(2^2)$

*	0	1	X	$X+1$
0	0	0	0	0
1	0	1	X	$X+1$
X	0	X	$X+1$	1
$X+1$	0	$X+1$	1	X

Solution 10   ⋆Elliptic Curves and Finite Fields II

1 As P is a polynomial of degree 2, the only non-trivial factorization would be a product of two polynomials of degree 1. Therefore, P is irreducible over $\mathbf{Z}_2$ if and only if P has no roots in $\mathbf{Z}_2$. As $P(0) = P(1) = 1$, we see that it is indeed the case. Therefore, P is irreducible.

One should note that the fact that a polynomial has no root does not necessarily imply that it is irreducible. For example, the polynomial $X^4 + X^2 + 1$ has no root in $\mathbf{Z}_2$ although it is not irreducible, as $X^4 + X^2 + 1 = (X^2 + X + 1)^2$.

2 The multiplication table of the elements of $\mathbf{K}$ is given Table 6.8. Another useful table for this exercise is given in Table 6.9.

3 By definition, for any $x \in GF(2^2)$,

$$\mathrm{Tr}_{4,2}(x) = x + x^2.$$

Therefore, $\mathrm{Tr}_{4,2}(X) = X + X^2 = 1$. Let $P = (x, y) \in \mathbf{K}^2$ be a point of $E_{X,X+1}$.

- If $x = 0$, y must satisfy $y^2 = X + 1$, so that $(0, X)$ is a point of $E_{X,X+1}$.
- If $x = 1$, y must satisfy $y^2 + y = 0$, so that $(1, 0)$ and $(1, 1)$ are points of $E_{X,X+1}$.

Table 6.9.   Square and cubic elements of $GF(2^2)$

x	x^2	x^3
0	0	0
1	1	1
X	$X+1$	1
$X+1$	X	1

Table 6.10. Inverse elements of $E_{X,X+1}$

P	$\mathcal{O}$	$(0, X)$	$(1, 0)$	$(1, 1)$	$(X, 1)$	$(X, X+1)$
$-P$	$\mathcal{O}$	$(0, X)$	$(1, 1)$	$(1, 0)$	$(X, X+1)$	$(X, 1)$

Table 6.11. Elements generated by a generator G of $E_{X,X+1}$

G	$2G$	$3G$	$4G$	$5G$	$6G$
$(1, 0)$	$(X, 1)$	$(0, X)$	$(X, X+1)$	$(1, 1)$	$\mathcal{O}$

- If $x = X$, y must satisfy $y^2 + X \cdot y = X + 1$, so that $(X, 1)$ and $(X, X+1)$ are points of $E_{X,X+1}$.
- If $x = X + 1$, y must satisfy $y^2 + (X + 1) \cdot y = 1$, which is impossible.

Finally, $E_{X,X+1} = \{\mathcal{O}, (0, X), (1, 0), (1, 1), (X, 1), (X, X+1)\}$ and we get $|E_{X,X+1}| = 6$. According to Hasse's Theorem, we should have

$$||\mathbf{K}| + 1 - |E_{X,X+1}|| \leq 2\sqrt{|\mathbf{K}|}.$$

As $||\mathbf{K}| + 1 - |E_{X,X+1}|| = |-1| = 1$ and $2\sqrt{|\mathbf{K}|} = 4 > 1$, everything is fine.

4 Table 6.10 confirms that $-P$ lies on the curve as well.

5 We can wonder if one of the points is a generator of the group. Obviously, $(0, X)$ is not a generator as $-(0, X) = (0, X)$, so that $2 \cdot (0, X) = \mathcal{O}$. Let $G = (1, 0)$. After some computations, we can find Table 6.11. Therefore, G is a generator of $E_{X,X+1}$, which is a cyclic group. Another cyclic group with 6 elements one might think of is $(\mathbf{Z}_6, +)$. Consider the mapping

$$\varphi: \begin{array}{ccc} \mathbf{Z}_6 & \longrightarrow & E_{X,X+1} \\ \gamma & \longmapsto & \gamma G. \end{array}$$

It is easy to show that φ is a group isomorphism. From

$$\begin{aligned} \varphi(\alpha + \beta) &= (\alpha + \beta)G \\ &= \alpha G + \beta G \qquad \text{(by associativity of $+$ in $E_{X,X+1}$)} \\ &= \varphi(\alpha) + \varphi(\beta), \end{aligned}$$

φ is a group homomorphism. As

$$\begin{aligned} \varphi(\gamma) = 0 &\Rightarrow \gamma G = \mathcal{O} \\ &\Rightarrow \gamma = 0 \qquad \text{(as G is a generator of $E_{X,X+1}$),} \end{aligned}$$

Table 6.12. Addition table of $\mathbf{Z}_6$

+	0	1	2	3	4	5
0	0	1	2	3	4	5
1	1	2	3	4	5	0
2	2	3	4	5	0	1
3	3	4	5	0	1	2
4	4	5	0	1	2	3
5	5	0	1	2	3	4

φ is injective. As $|\mathbf{Z}_6| = |E_{X,X+1}|$, φ is an isomorphism. Therefore, $E_{X,X+1}$ is isomorphic to $\mathbf{Z}_6$. Note that an isomorphism is *very* useful to compute the addition table of the points of the elliptic curve. From the definition of the isomorphism φ, we have the following correspondence between the elements of $E_{X,X+1}$ and of $\mathbf{Z}_6$:

$$\mathcal{O} \leftrightarrow 0$$
$$(1,0) \leftrightarrow 1$$
$$(X,1) \leftrightarrow 2$$
$$(0,X) \leftrightarrow 3$$
$$(X,X+1) \leftrightarrow 4$$
$$(1,1) \leftrightarrow 5$$

The addition table of the elements of $\mathbf{Z}_6$ is given in Table 6.12. From this, we easily obtain the addition table of the elements of $E_{X,X+1}$ which is given in Table 6.13.

Table 6.13. Addition table of $E_{X,X+1}$

+	$\mathcal{O}$	$(1,0)$	$(X,1)$	$(0,X)$	$(X,X+1)$	$(1,1)$
$\mathcal{O}$	$\mathcal{O}$	$(1,0)$	$(X,1)$	$(0,X)$	$(X,X+1)$	$(1,1)$
$(1,0)$	$(1,0)$	$(X,1)$	$(0,X)$	$(X,X+1)$	$(1,1)$	$\mathcal{O}$
$(X,1)$	$(X,1)$	$(0,X)$	$(X,X+1)$	$(1,1)$	$\mathcal{O}$	$(1,0)$
$(0,X)$	$(0,X)$	$(X,X+1)$	$(1,1)$	$\mathcal{O}$	$(1,0)$	$(X,1)$
$(X,X+1)$	$(X,X+1)$	$(1,1)$	$\mathcal{O}$	$(1,0)$	$(X,1)$	$(0,X)$
$(1,1)$	$(1,1)$	$\mathcal{O}$	$(1,0)$	$(X,1)$	$(0,X)$	$(X,X+1)$

Chapter 7

ALGORITHMIC NUMBER THEORY

Exercises

Exercise 1   ⋆Rho Method and Distinguished Points

Let f be a function from a finite set E into itself and x_0 be a given element of E. The sequence defined by $x_i = f(x_{i-1})$ for $i \in \mathbf{N}$ has the shape of the Greek character ρ, i.e., is composed of a first part $x_0, \ldots, x_{q-1}$ (the "*tail*") and a second part $x_q, \ldots, x_{q+\ell-1}$ (the "*loop*") such that $x_{q+\ell} = x_q$ for two integers ℓ and q. We assume that q and ℓ are the smallest integers such that $x_{q+\ell} = x_q$. The goal of this exercise is to design an algorithm for determining q, ℓ, x_{q-1}, and $x_{q+\ell-1}$ when $q > 0$. We assume that for a random pair (x_0, f), the average values of q and ℓ are equal to $\sqrt{\frac{\pi |E|}{8}}$ (for more details, see Section 2.1.6 of [29] and the article of Flagolet and Odlyzko [17]) and that it is possible to store some pairs (x, S) in memory, where $x \in E$ and S is any piece of information. Furthermore, we can perform two instructions, each costing one unit of time, $\mathrm{Mem}(x, S)$ which stores the pair (x, S) and $\mathrm{Val}(x)$ which gives back for any x the last S value such that (x, S) has been stored or the symbol $\perp$ otherwise.

1 Propose a simple algorithm which finds for any (f, x_0) the values q, ℓ, x_{q-1}, and $x_{q+\ell-1}$.

- What is the average number of operations?
- What is the average number of f evaluations?

- What is the average memory size?

2 Propose an algorithm that only requires a constant size memory.

- What is the average number of operations?
- What is the average number of f evaluations?

Hint: Consider a concurrent sequence y_i defined by $y_0 = x_0$ and $y_i = f(f(y_{i-1}))$ for $i \in \mathbf{N}$. The algorithm will determine the smallest $i > 0$ such that $x_i = y_i$. It remains to establish its relation with ℓ.

3 In what follows, we try to reduce the number of operations with a moderate increase of the memory requirement. For this purpose, we store so-called "*distinguished points*" of E. These points are determined by a function T from E to {true, false} ($T(x)$ depends on the value x but not on the position of x in the sequence). The distinguished points are the x's such that $T(x) =$ true. The function T is chosen at the beginning in a random way with a distribution such that for any x, the probability that $T(x) =$ true is equal to $\frac{1}{m}$ for a fixed integer m. In the following questions, we assume that $m \ll q, \ell$.

- Use this structure for solving the problem.
- What is the average number of operations?
- What is the average number of f evaluations?
- What is the average number of pairs to store?

▷ Solution on page 165

Exercise 2   ⋆Factorization

Factorize the following numbers:

- $2^{32} - 1$
- $2^{64} - 1$
- $3^{32} - 1$

Hint: Remember some algebraic identities!

▷ Solution on page 169

Exercise 3   ⋆Prime Numbers

Show that $2^8 + 1$ and $2^{16} + 1$ are prime numbers.
Hint: Look at the structure of the group $\mathbf{Z}_p^*$, when p is a prime!

▷ Solution on page 170

Exercise 4   ⋆Factoring $n = p \cdot q$

Assume that $n = p \cdot q$, where p and q are distinct primes.

1 Compute $S = n + 1 - \varphi(n)$.

2 What are the roots of the polynomial equation $x^2 - Sx + n$? Give some explicit expressions for these roots and explain how p and q can be found with the help of a simple integer square-roots algorithm.

3 Find the factorization n for the following two cases:

- $n = 667$, $\varphi(n) = 616$
- $n = 15049$, $\varphi(n) = 14800$

▷ Solution on page 170

Exercise 5   Strong Prime Numbers

We call *strong prime number* an odd prime number p such that $\frac{p-1}{2}$ is prime as well. Prove that we can generate ℓ-bit strong prime numbers with a complexity of $\mathcal{O}(\ell^5)$.
Hint: Make the heuristic assumption that m and $2m + 1$ behave like independent random odd numbers when m is a random odd number.

▷ Solution on page 170

Exercise 6   Complexity of Eratosthenes Sieve

We assume to have a table S of n elements which are all equal to **true** at disposal. We consider algorithms 23 to 27.

1 What can we deduce from table S once it has been processed by one of these algorithms?

Algorithm 23

```
1:  S[1] ← false
2:  i ← 2
3:  while i ≤ n do
4:     if S[i] = true then
5:        j ← 2i
6:        while j ≤ n do
7:           S[j] = false
8:           j ← j + i
9:        end while
10:    end if
11:    i ← i + 1
12: end while
```

Algorithm 24

```
1:  S[1] ← false
2:  i ← 2
3:  while i ≤ n do
4:     j ← 2i
5:     while j ≤ n do
6:        S[j] = false
7:        j ← j + i
8:     end while
9:     i ← i + 1
10: end while
```

Algorithm 25

```
1:  S[1] ← false
2:  i ← 2
3:  while i ≤ n do
4:     if S[i] = true then
5:        j ← i + 1
6:        while j ≤ n do
7:        .  if i divides j then
8:              S[j] = false
9:           end if
10:          j ← j + 1
11:       end while
12:    end if
13:    i ← i + 1
14: end while
```

Algorithm 26

```
1:  S[1] ← false
2:  i ← 2
3:  while i ≤ n do
4:     j ← 2
5:     while j < i do
6:        if j divides i then
7:           S[i] ← false
8:        end if
9:        j ← j + 1
10:    end while
11:    i ← i + 1
12: end while
```

Algorithm 27

```
1:  S[1] ← false
2:  i ← 2
3:  while i ≤ n do
4:     j ← 2
5:     while j ≤ √i do
6:        if j divides i then
7:           S[i] ← false
8:        end if
9:        j ← j + 1
10:    end while
11:    i ← i + 1
12: end while
```

2 We denote by $2 = p_1 < p_2 < \cdots < p_k$ the sequence of all prime numbers smaller than n. A consequence of Mertens' Second Theorem [27] is that

$$\sum_{i=1}^{k} \frac{1}{p_i} \underset{n \to \infty}{\sim} \log \log(n).$$

Using this property, find the complexity of each of these algorithms.

3 Write an algorithm in the spirit of the formers which factorizes an integer n.

▷ Solution on page 171

Exercise 7   ⋆Hash Function Based on Arithmetics

Let $p = 2p' + 1$ and $q = 2q' + 1$ be two s-bit long primes such that p' and q' are prime numbers. Let $n = pq$ and g be an element of $\mathbf{Z}_n^*$ of order $p'q'$.

1 How should p, q, p', q' be generated? What is the complexity of this generation in terms of s?

2 How should g be generated? What is the complexity of this generation?

We now assume that p, q, p', q' are unknown and that only n and g are public. For a message m, which is represented by an integer of arbitrary size, we define the hash function $H(m) = g^m \bmod n$. This defines a hash function.

3 Show that finding collisions on H is equivalent to factorizing n.
   Hint: Show first that it is possible to find an integer k such that $\lambda(n)$ divides k.

4 Show that inverting H is at least as hard as solving the discrete logarithm problems with respect to the base g in $\mathbf{Z}_p^*$ and $\mathbf{Z}_q^*$.

▷ Solution on page 173

Solutions

Solution 1   ⋆Rho Method and Distinguished Points

1 Algorithm 28 solves our problem. In this algorithm, for any x_i we store the pair $S = (i, x_{i-1})$, which is sufficient to recover the information as soon as we meet a value for the second time. Algorithm 28

Algorithm 28 A simple algorithm that finds q, ℓ, x_{q-1}, and $x_{q+\ell-1}$

Input: the function $f : E \to E$, a point $x_0 \in E$
Output: q, ℓ, x_{q-1}, and $x_{q+\ell-1}$
Processing:
  1: $i \leftarrow y \leftarrow 0$
  2: $x \leftarrow x_0$
  3: **while** $\mathrm{Val}(x) = \perp$ **do**
  4:    $\mathrm{Mem}(x, (i, y))$
  5:    $i \leftarrow i + 1$
  6:    $y \leftarrow x$
  7:    $x \leftarrow f(x)$
  8: **end while**
  9: $q \leftarrow (\mathrm{Val}(x))_1$
  10: $\ell \leftarrow i - q$
  11: $x_{q-1} \leftarrow (\mathrm{Val}(x))_2$
  12: $x_{q+\ell-1} \leftarrow y$

---

needs about $\sqrt{\frac{\pi|E|}{2}}$ f-evaluations and $\mathcal{O}\left(\sqrt{|E|}\right)$ operations in total. It needs furthermore a storage capacity of $\mathcal{O}(\sqrt{|E|})$.

2 Algorithm 29 shows a method relying on the idea mentioned in the hint. The situation is represented in Figure 7.1. When $x_i = y_i$ for the first time, the iteration $x_i = f(x_{i-1})$ has made i calls to the function f, while the iteration $y_i = f(f(y_{i-1}))$ has made $2i$ calls to f. We denote this i by ℓ_m. We have $x_{\ell_m} = y_{\ell_m}$ and thus, $2\ell_m = \ell_m + k\ell$ for some integer k. Consequently, $\ell_m = k\ell$ so that the total number of iterations ℓ_m is a multiple of ℓ. Let us consider x_q and y_q. We have $y_q = x_{2q} = x_{q+j}$ for some integer $0 \le j < \ell$. This means that the distance from y_q to x_q is equal to $\ell - j$ (see Figure 7.2). At each iteration of the loop in Algorithm 29 Part 1, this distance is decreased by one, as the y_i's are twice as fast as the x_i's. Therefore,

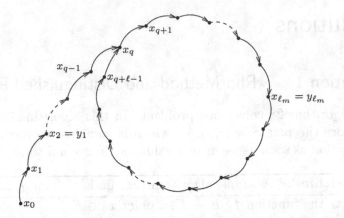

Figure 7.1. Applying Pollard's rho method in order to find collisions

after $q + \ell - j$ iterations, the distance is zero, i.e., $\ell_m = q + \ell - j$, so that $q < \ell_m \leq q + \ell$. The value of ℓ_m is computed by the end of Algorithm 29 Part 1.

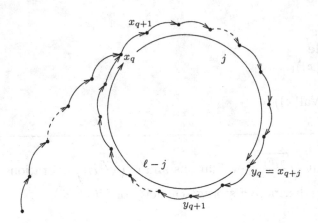

Figure 7.2. Distance from y_q to x_q

In Part 2 of this algorithm, we start simultaneously from x_{ℓ_m} and x_0. As $\ell_m = k\ell$ is a multiple of ℓ, we always get index values having a difference equal to a multiple of ℓ. The first time we get two equal elements, it must therefore be at the point x_q. This allows to find x_{q-1} and q.

Finally, Part 3 of Algorithm 29 allows to deduce ℓ and $x_{q+\ell-1}$. In this part, it is sufficient to iterate f, starting from x_q, until we get x_q again.

Algorithm 29 Finding collisions using the Pollard rho method

Input: the function $f : E \to E$, a point $x_0 \in E$
Output: q, ℓ, x_{q-1}, and $x_{q+\ell-1}$
Processing - Part 1: Finding the smallest ℓ_m such that $x_{\ell_m} = y_{\ell_m}$
  1: $i \leftarrow 1$
  2: $x \leftarrow f(x_0)$
  3: $y \leftarrow f(x)$
  4: **while** $x \neq y$ **do**
  5: $\quad i \leftarrow i + 1$
  6: $\quad x \leftarrow f(x)$
  7: $\quad y \leftarrow f(f(y))$
  8: **end while**
  9: $\ell_m \leftarrow i$
 10: $x_{\ell_m} \leftarrow x$
Processing - Part 2: Finding x_{q-1} and q
 11: $y \leftarrow x_{\ell_m}$
 12: $x \leftarrow x_0$
 13: $z \leftarrow \perp$
 14: $i \leftarrow 0$
 15: **while** $x \neq y$ **do**
 16: $\quad z \leftarrow x$
 17: $\quad x \leftarrow f(x)$
 18: $\quad y \leftarrow f(y)$
 19: $\quad i \leftarrow i + 1$
 20: **end while**
 21: $q \leftarrow i$
 22: $x_{q-1} \leftarrow z$
 23: $x_q \leftarrow x$
Processing - Part 3: Finding $x_{q+\ell-1}$ and ℓ
 24: $i \leftarrow 0$
 25: $z \leftarrow x_q$
 26: $x \leftarrow f(z)$
 27: **while** $x \neq x_q$ **do**
 28: $\quad z \leftarrow x$
 29: $\quad x \leftarrow f(x)$
 30: $\quad i \leftarrow i + 1$
 31: **end while**
 32: $\ell \leftarrow i$
 33: $x_{q+\ell-1} \leftarrow z$

This algorithm needs $\mathcal{O}(\sqrt{|E|})$ operations, including $9\sqrt{\frac{\pi|E|}{8}}$ f evaluations.

3 The main idea is to memorize information concerning the distinguished points only. Each time we encounter a distinguished point, we store its value together with its index. We detect a loop at the first distinguished point belonging to the loop, i.e., for the smallest integer $i \geq q$ such that x_i is a distinguished point (see Figure 7.3).

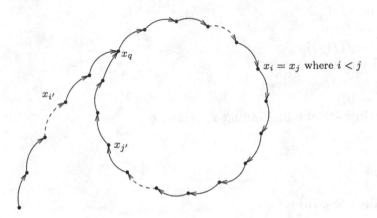

Figure 7.3. A method using distinguished points

After one lap, we have $x_j = x_i$ and we directly deduce $\ell = j - i$. In order to find q we look for $x_{i'}$ and $x_{j'}$, the distinguished points preceeding x_i and x_j in the list, respectively. Note that $x_{i'}$ is the last distinguished point of the tail ($i' < q$) while $x_{j'}$ lies in the loop. The distance from $x_{i'}$ to x_i is $i - i'$ and the one from $x_{j'}$ to x_j is $j - j'$. Assume $j - j' > i - i'$. We begin by iterating $(j - j') - (i - i')$ times the function f on $x_{j'}$. The point we obtain is at distance $i - i'$ from x_j, just as $x_{i'}$ is from x_i. As both points are at equal distance from $x_i = x_j$, they also are at equal distance from x_q. If we now iterate f simultaneously on both points, a collision will occur in x_q. The case where $j - j' < i - i'$ is similar, except that we start by iterating $(i - i') - (j - j')$ times the function f on $x_{i'}$. In case of equality, this step is not necessary.

In order to evaluate the complexity, we need to compute the mean distance between the anchorage point x_q and the distinguished point x_i. This is approximately equal to

$$\sum_{i=0}^{+\infty} i \left(1 - \frac{1}{m}\right)^{i-1} \frac{1}{m} = m.$$

The mean distance between $x_{i'}$ and the anchorage point x_q is m as well. So, this algorithm needs $\mathcal{O}(\sqrt{|E|} + m)$ operations, including $\sqrt{\frac{\pi|E|}{2}} + 3m$ evaluations of the function f. It needs furthermore a storage capacity of $\mathcal{O}\left(\frac{1}{m}\sqrt{\frac{\pi|E|}{2}}\right)$ pairs.

Solution 2 ⋆Factorization

Using the algebraic identity $(a+b) \cdot (a-b) = a^2 - b^2$, we get

$$2^{32} - 1 = (2^{16} + 1) \cdot (2^{16} - 1).$$

The first factor is a prime, the second one may be written as

$$2^{16} - 1 = (2^8 + 1) \cdot (2^8 - 1).$$

$2^8 + 1$ being prime, we use the same procedure to write

$$2^8 - 1 = (2^4 + 1)(2^4 - 1) = 3 \cdot 5 \cdot 17.$$

Finally,

$$2^{32} - 1 = 3 \cdot 5 \cdot 17 \cdot 257 \cdot 65537.$$

Similarly, $2^{64} - 1 = (2^{32} + 1)(2^{32} - 1)$. We know the factorization of the second part of this product. After some computational work,

$$2^{32} + 1 = 641 \cdot 6700417,$$

where 6700417 is prime. Hence,

$$2^{64} - 1 = 3 \cdot 5 \cdot 17 \cdot 257 \cdot 641 \cdot 65537 \cdot 6700417.$$

Finally, $3^{32} - 1 = (3^{16} + 1) \cdot (3^{16} - 1)$, where $3^{16} - 1 = (3^8 - 1) \cdot (3^8 + 1)$ and $3^8 - 1 = (3^4 + 1)(3^4 - 1)$. As $3^4 + 1 = 2 \cdot 41$ and $3^4 - 1 = 2^4 \cdot 5$, we can write

$$3^{32} - 1 = 2^5 \cdot 5 \cdot 41 \cdot (3^8 + 1) \cdot (3^{16} + 1),$$

its complete factorization being

$$3^{32} - 1 = 2^7 \cdot 5 \cdot 17 \cdot 41 \cdot 193 \cdot 21523361.$$

Again, note that showing the primality of 21523361 requires intensive computational work.

Solution 3   ⋆Prime Numbers

Let n be a positive integer. We know that the order of the multiplicative group $\mathbf{Z}_n^*$ is $\varphi(n)$. If $\varphi(n) = n - 1$, it means that among the n elements of $\mathbf{Z}_n = \{0, 1, 2, \ldots, n-1\}$, only 0 is not invertible modulo n. This means that n is prime. In that case, we also know that $\mathbf{Z}_n^*$ is cyclic. Consequently, it is sufficient to find an element a in $\mathbf{Z}_n^*$ such that $\text{ord}(a) = n - 1$ to show that n is prime. This is the strategy we will apply here.

We let $n = 2^8 + 1 = 257$ and $a = 3$. We can show (using a square-and-multiply algorithm for example) that $a^{256} \equiv 1 \pmod{n}$. Thus, according to the Lagrange Theorem, $\text{ord}(a)|256$. Similarly, we can show that $a^{128} \not\equiv 1 \pmod{n}$. We conclude that $\text{ord}(a) = 256$, and thus, that $2^8 + 1 = 257$ is a prime number.

Similarly, when $n = 2^{16} + 1$, it can be shown that the order of $a = 3$ in $\mathbf{Z}_n^*$ is equal to 2^{16}, so that $2^{16} + 1$ is a prime number.

Solution 4   ⋆Factoring $n = p \cdot q$

1 $S = n + 1 - \varphi(n) = n + 1 - (n - p - q + 1) = p + q$.

2 The roots of this polynomial equation are p and q, because

$$(x - p)(x - q) = x^2 - (p + q)x + pq = x^2 - Sx + n.$$

It suffices to solve this polynomial equation to obtain p and q.

3 Applying the famous formula for solving equation of second order provides

$$p, q = \frac{S \pm \sqrt{S^2 - 4n}}{2}.$$

Thus, we obtain $p = 29$ and $q = 23$ for the first problem and $p = 149$ and $q = 101$ for the second one.

Solution 5   Strong Prime Numbers

Let us consider Algorithm 30. Obviously, the number displayed by the algorithm is a strong prime. To compute the complexity of Algorithm 30, we need to recall that the probability that an ℓ-bit random number is a prime is $\Omega\left(\frac{1}{\ell}\right)$ (as there are $\Omega\left(\frac{\log n}{n}\right)$ prime numbers smaller than n). As a primality test, we can use the Miller-Rabin algorithm, whose complexity is in $\mathcal{O}(\ell^3)$ (see [56] for more details about this test, in particular about its success probability as it is a probabilistic algorithm).

As we make the assumption that q and $p = 2q + 1$ behave like random odd number (as far as primality is concerned), the probability that they are both prime is approximately $\frac{1}{\ell^2}$. The main loop of the algorithm will then be performed approximately ℓ^2 times before a strong prime is found. Each time, either one or two Miller-Rabin tests are performed, so that the total complexity of the algorithm is $\mathcal{O}(\ell^5)$.

Note that in Algorithm 30, we can also choose p at random and, in the case it is prime, compute $q = \frac{p-1}{2}$ and run the primality test on q. The complexity would be the same, as p and q have almost the same size. Considering now the case where $p = aq + 1$ and q is often much smaller than p (as it is the case in the DSS scheme for example), it is more efficient to test whether q is a prime or not first.

Algorithm 30 Strong primes generation

Input: the bit-size ℓ of the desired strong prime. An `isPrime()` subroutine that takes a positive integer as an input and answers `true` when the integer is prime, or `false` if it is not

Output: an ℓ-bit strong prime

Processing:

1: **loop**
2:     choose $q \in \{0,1\}^{\ell-1}$ at random (such that q is odd)
3:     **if** isPrime(q) **then**
4:         $p \leftarrow 2q + 1$
5:         **if** isPrime(p) **then**
6:             output p and exit
7:         **end if**
8:     **end if**
9: **end loop**

Solution 6   Complexity of Eratosthenes Sieve

1 All these algorithms return a table where only the entries of S corresponding to prime indices are marked **true**.

Algorithms 23, 24, and 25 work in a very similar way. In Algorithm 25, one tests each number i smaller than n and if it is prime, one tests each number j with $i < j \leq n$, marking j as non-prime if it is divisible by i. Algorithm 24 does the same but marks directly as non-primes the multiples of i and does not treat the other numbers. Algorithm 23 does the same as Algorithm 24, but only for the prime numbers, in order to avoid to mark the same element several times.

Algorithm 26 and Algorithm 27 use another strategy. The first one tests all the numbers i smaller than n and checks whether j divides i. If it is the case, then i is a non-prime. Algorithm 27 applies the same principle, but is restricted to the numbers $i \leq \sqrt{n}$. Note that if n has a divisor greater than $\sqrt{n}$ then it must also have one smaller too.

2 Using the consequence of Mertens' Second Theorem we get the following complexities.

- Algorithm 23:

$$n + \sum_{i=1}^{k(n)} \frac{n}{p_i} = \mathcal{O}(n \log \log n)$$

- Algorithm 24:

$$\sum_{i=2}^{n} \frac{n}{i} = \mathcal{O}(n \log n)$$

- Algorithm 25:

$$n + \sum_{i=1}^{k(n)} (n - p_i) = \mathcal{O}\left(\frac{n^2}{\log n}\right)$$

In order to compute previous complexity, we used the fact that $n - p_i$ is upper bounded by n. This is the right complexity order, since we can show that it is not possible to do better by lower bounding the first terms of the sum by $n/2$, knowing that there are in the order of $\frac{n}{2} \log n$ such terms.

- Algorithm 26:

$$\sum_{i=1}^{n} i = \mathcal{O}(n^2)$$

- Algorithm 27:

$$\sum_{i=1}^{n} \sqrt{i} \sim \int_{0}^{n} \sqrt{x}\, dx = \mathcal{O}(n^{\frac{3}{2}})$$

3 A possible solution is Algorithm 31 whose complexity is between $\mathcal{O}(\log_2 n)$ and $\mathcal{O}(\sqrt{n})$. Namely, in the best case we have to factorize a power of 2 and in the worst case a modulus which is the product of two primes having the same size.

Algorithm 31 Factorization of n

Input: an integer n
Output: the factorization of n
Processing:

  1: $i \leftarrow 2$
  2: **while** $i \leq \sqrt{n}$ **do**
  3:     **while** i divides n **do**
  4:        output i
  5:        $n \leftarrow \frac{n}{i}$
  6:     **end while**
  7:     $i \leftarrow i+1$
  8: **end while**
  9: **if** $n \neq 1$ **then**
10:     output n
11: **end if**

Solution 7   ⋆Hash Function Based on Arithmetics

1 We first generate p' and q' until p and q are prime. This method is also the one used in Exercise 5. The complexity is $\mathcal{O}(s^5)$.

2 First, we note that g is such that $g \bmod p$ has order p' in $\mathbf{Z}_p^*$ and $g \bmod q$ has order q' in $\mathbf{Z}_q^*$. Since the subgroup of the square elements in $\mathbf{Z}_p^*$ (resp. $\mathbf{Z}_q^*$) is cyclic of order p' (resp. q'), it suffices to pick a random square $g \in \mathbf{Z}_n^*$ until $g \bmod p \neq 1$ and $g \bmod q \neq 1$. Note that in a cyclic group of prime order, all elements except the neutral element are generators.

3 If $g^m \equiv g^{m'} \pmod{n}$ then $m - m'$ is a multiple of $p'q'$. As by definition, $\lambda(n) = \mathrm{lcm}(2p', 2q') = 2\mathrm{lcm}(p', q') = 2p'q'$, $2(m - m')$ is a multiple of the exponent $\lambda(n)$ of the group $\mathbf{Z}_n^*$. As for RSA, we can factorize n from a multiple of the exponent $\lambda(n)$ using a similar algorithm as the primality test of Miller-Rabin. For more details about this algorithm, we refer to the textbook [56].

4 Assume we are given some elements $x \in \mathbf{Z}_p^*$ and $y \in \mathbf{Z}_q^*$ which are in the subgroups generated by $g \bmod p$ and $g \bmod q$ respectively. By using the Chinese Remainder Theorem, we can find an element $a \in \mathbf{Z}_n^*$ such that $a \bmod p = x$ and $a \bmod q = y$. If we are able to invert H, we can obtain an integer m such that $g^m \bmod n = a$. Reducing the last equality modulo p and q, shows that $m \bmod p'$ (resp. $m \bmod q'$) is the discrete logarithm of x (resp. y) with respect to g in $\mathbf{Z}_p^*$ (resp. $\mathbf{Z}_q^*$).

Chapter 8

ELEMENTS OF COMPLEXITY THEORY

Exercises

Exercise 1   ⋆Regular Language

Describe the strings denoted by the regular language over the binary alphabet $\sum = \{0, 1\}$:

- 0(0|1)*1

- (0|1)*1(0|1)(0|1)

- 0*10*10*10*

▷ Solution on page 177

Exercise 2   ⋆Finite State Automaton

Find the regular language over the binary alphabet $\sum = \{0, 1\}$ accepted by the finite state automaton in Figure 8.1.

▷ Solution on page 177

Exercise 3   ⋆Turing Machine

Of the class of recursively enumerable languages, there is an important subclass called *recursive languages*. A language L is defined to be *recursive* if there exists a Turing machine M that satisfies the following:

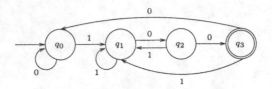

Figure 8.1. The finite state automaton

- if the input $w \in L$, then M eventually enters the halting state q_{accept} and accepts it;

- if $w \notin L$, then M eventually enters the halting state q_{reject} and rejects it;

- the set F of all final states of M is defined to be $F = \{q_{accept}\}$.

1 Prove that a recursive language is recursively enumerable.

2 Prove that if L is a recursive language, so is its complement $\bar{L}$.

▷ Solution on page 177

Exercise 4   ⋆Graph Colorability I

Given an undirected graph with n nodes $v_1, \ldots, v_n$ and E edges e_{ij}'s, where e_{ij} means that n_i and n_j are connected by one edge, we call it k-colorable (for a fixed k) if each node in the graph can be assigned one color out of k colors such that none edge in the graph connects two nodes of the same color. Propose an algorithm to solve the graph 2-colorability problem in polynomial time.

▷ Solution on page 178

Exercise 5   ⋆Graph Colorability II

Show by reduction that if the decision version of the 3-SAT problem has a polynomial time algorithm, then so does the decision problem of the 3-colorability of a graph. Note that 3-SAT stands for the satisfiability problem for boolean expressions in 3-CNF, which means that the problem input consists of formulae in conjunctive normal form with the limitation to a maximum of three literals per clause.

▷ Solution on page 178

Solutions

Solution 1 ⋆Regular Language

- $0(0|1)^*1$ denotes any string of at least 2 bits with the prefix 0 and the suffix 1.

- $(0|1)^*1(0|1)(0|1)$ denotes any string of at least 3 bits, whose third least significant bit is 1.

- $0^*10^*10^*10^*$ denotes any string with exactly 3 ones.

Solution 2 ⋆Finite State Automaton

We first note that a "1" always sends to q_1, from any other state. From there, a "00" will always lead to the final state q_3. Thus, all strings of the form $(0|1)^*100$ are accepted. This corresponds to any binary string with the suffix 100.

We now prove that no other string can be accepted. The terminating state q_3 can only be reached from q_2, with a "0". Similarly, q_2 can only be reached from q_1, with a "0". q_1 can be reached from any state, but always with a "1". Thus, an accepted string must end by "100". Consequently, $(0|1)^*100$ is the only regular language accepted by the finite state automaton of Figure 8.1

Solution 3 ⋆Turing Machine

1 By definition, we know that the recursively enumerable language requires the existence of a Turing machine, such that it eventually enters a final state q_{accept} (and halts) for all inputs in the language, but it may never halt on the input that is not in the language. Therefore, a recursive language is always recursively enumerable.

2 From the last question, we know that there exists a Turing machine (denoted M) that accepts L, which has two halting states q_{accept} and q_{reject} with the set of all final states $F = \{q_{\text{accept}}\}$. We modify M as follows (where M' denotes the modified Turing machine): for all the state transitions involving q_{accept} or q_{reject}, we replace q_{accept} (resp. q_{reject}) by q_{reject} (resp. q_{accept}); define the set F' of all final states for M' as $F' = \{q_{\text{accept}}\}$. To complete the proof, it suffices to check the following:

- for any $w \notin \bar{L}$ (i.e., $w \in L$), M' eventually enters the halting state q_{reject} and rejects it;

- for any $w \in \bar{L}$ (i.e., $w \notin L$), M' eventually enters the final state q_{accept} to accept it and halts.

Solution 4   ⋆Graph Colorability I

Let c_i denote the color of the node n_i. As we are working on the 2-colorability problem of the graph, we let $c_i \in \{0, 1\}$. For each edge e_{ij} in the graph, we write down one linear equation

$$c_i \oplus c_j = 1,$$

describing that this edge must connect two nodes of distinct colors. This way, we obtain E linear equations in n binary variables. It is well known that the problem of solving linear equations takes polynomial time. Therefore, the problem of solving 2-colorability of a graph is indeed in **P**.

Solution 5   ⋆Graph Colorability II

We adopt the same notations as in the previous exercise. Let $c_i = (c_i^1, c_i^2, c_i^3)$ denote the color of the node n_i, which is a 3-bit binary vector. We put the constraints

$$\begin{aligned}
(c_i^1 c_i^2) \text{ OR } (c_i^1 c_i^3) \text{ OR } (c_i^1 c_i^3) &= 0 \\
c_i^1 \text{ OR } c_i^2 \text{ OR } c_i^3 &= 1
\end{aligned}$$

to describe that one and only one of the coordinate of c_i must equal one for each n_i. For each edge e_{ij}, we add the constraint

$$c_i^1 c_j^1 \text{ OR } c_i^2 c_j^2 \text{ OR } c_i^3 c_j^3 = 0$$

to describe that adjacent nodes must have different colors. Therefore, we can transform the above constraints into determining existence of a truth value of each literal such that the following expression is TRUE:

$$(c_1^1 \text{ OR } c_1^2 \text{ OR } c_1^3) \text{ AND}$$
$$(\neg c_1^1 \text{ OR } \neg c_1^2) \text{ AND}(\neg c_1^1 \text{ OR } \neg c_1^3) \text{ AND}(\neg c_1^2 \text{ OR } \neg c_1^3) \text{ AND}$$

$$\vdots$$

$$(c_n^1 \text{ OR } c_n^2 \text{ OR } c_n^3) \text{ AND}$$
$$(\neg c_n^1 \text{ OR } \neg c_n^2) \text{ AND}(\neg c_n^1 \text{ OR } \neg c_n^3) \text{ AND}(\neg c_n^2 \text{ OR } \neg c_n^3) \text{ AND}$$

$$\vdots$$

$$(\neg c_i^1 \text{ OR } \neg c_j^1) \text{ AND}(\neg c_i^2 \text{ OR } \neg c_j^2) \text{ AND}(\neg c_i^3 \text{ OR } \neg c_j^3) \text{ AND}$$

$$\vdots$$

It is therefore easy to see that if the decision version of the 3-SAT problem has a polynomial time algorithm, then so does the decision problem of the 3-colorability of a graph.

Chapter 9

PUBLIC KEY CRYPTOGRAPHY

Exercises

Exercise 1   *Okamoto-Uchiyama Cryptosystem

Let p be a prime number and let G be the set of all $x \in \mathbf{Z}_{p^2}$ such that $x \equiv 1 \pmod{p}$. In Exercise 5 of Chapter 6, we have proven that G is a group with the multiplication of $\mathbf{Z}_{p^2}$, that $|G| = p$, that $L : G \to \mathbf{Z}_p$ defined by $L(x) = \frac{x-1}{p}$ is a group isomorphism, that $p+1$ is a generator of G, and that L is the logarithm with respect to the basis $p+1$ in G.

We now define the public-key cryptosystem of Okamoto-Uchiyama [34] which was proposed in 1998.

Key Generation: We first choose two large primes p and q greater than 2^k for some fixed k and we compute $n = p^2 q$. Then, we randomly choose $g \in \mathbf{Z}_n^*$ such that $g^{p-1} \pmod{p^2}$ has the multiplicative order of p. Finally, we compute $h = g^n \bmod n$. The public key is (n, g, h) and the secret key is (p, q).

Encryption: Let $m \in \mathbf{N}$ such that $0 < m < 2^{k-1}$ be a plaintext. Pick $r \in \mathbf{Z}_n^*$ uniformly at random. The ciphertext c is defined by

$$c = g^m h^r \bmod n.$$

Decryption: One can recover the message m with

$$m = \frac{L(c^{p-1} \bmod p^2)}{L(g^{p-1} \bmod p^2)} \bmod p.$$

Show that the decryption is well defined, i.e., that $L(c^{p-1} \bmod p^2)$ and $L(g^{p-1} \bmod p^2)$ are two elements in $\mathbf{Z}_p$. Show that the decryption indeed recovers the original plaintext.

▷ Solution on page 188

Exercise 2   RSA Cryptosystem

The aim of this exercise is to introduce the first public-key cryptosystem [43]. It was published in 1978 by Rivest, Shamir, and Adleman.

The RSA public-key cryptosystem is defined as follows. Let p and q be two prime numbers, let $n = p \cdot q$ and $\phi = (p - 1) \cdot (q - 1)$. Select a random integer e with $1 < e < \phi$ such that $\gcd(e, \phi) = 1$. Compute d such that $1 < d < \phi$ and $e \cdot d \equiv 1 \pmod{\phi}$. The public-key is (n, e) and the corresponding private key is (n, d). The encryption of a message m is defined by

$$c = m^e \bmod n$$

and the decryption by

$$m = c^d \bmod n.$$

Prove that the decryption works.

Hint: Although it is not the case, Rivest, Shamir, and Adleman could be Chinese researchers...

▷ Solution on page 188

Exercise 3   RSA for Paranoids

The purpose of this exercise is to study a variant of the RSA cryptosystem with a very large modulus which was proposed by Shamir [48].

1 Let us consider the regular RSA cryptosystem with $n = pq$ with p and q primes of s bits. What is the complexity of generating this key in terms of s?

Instead of taking p and q of same size, we take a prime p of s bits and a random number q (not necessarily prime, whose factorization is not necessarily known) of size ts (e.g., with $t \approx 10$) and we take $n = pq$ as in RSA. Assuming that messages m are integers of length less than s, i.e., $m \in \{0, 1, \ldots, 2^{s-1} - 1\}$, we encrypt m by computing $E(m) = m^e \bmod n$ like in RSA. The public key is the pair (n, e) as well.

2 What is the restriction on e in order to make E injective?

3 Under this restriction, explain how to decrypt.

4 What are the complexities of the encryption, the decryption, and the key generation?

5 When e is smaller than t, show that anyone can decrypt an intercepted ciphertext.

6 Show that finding the factor p of n is equivalent to the decryption problem.

7 Deduce that we can perform a chosen ciphertext attack in order to recover the secret key.

8 How to thwart this attack?

▷ Solution on page 189

Exercise 4   RSA - Common Moduli

We assume that two entities Alice and Bob use RSA public keys with the same modulus n but with different public exponents e_1 and e_2.

1 Prove that Alice can decrypt messages sent to Bob.

2 Prove that Eve can decrypt a message sent to Alice *and* Bob provided that $\gcd(e_1, e_2) = 1$.

▷ Solution on page 191

Exercise 5   Networked RSA

We want to set up the RSA cryptosystem in a network of n users.

1 How many prime numbers do we have to generate?

2 We want to reduce this number by generating a smaller pool of prime numbers and making combinations of two of these primes: for each user, we pick a new pair of two of these primes in order to set up his key. Show how one user can factorize the modulus of some other user.

3 Show how anyone can factorize all moduli for which at least one prime factor has been used in at least one other modulus.

▷ Solution on page 191

Exercise 6   Repeated RSA Encryption

A surprising cryptanalyst trick is to try repeated encryption of the ciphertext. It might happen, even for a secure-looking cryptosystem that the plaintext is retrieved from a small number of these encryptions. This is of course a fatal flaw of the scheme.

1 Let $n = 35$ be an RSA modulus, m be a plaintext, and c the corresponding ciphertext. Check that $E(c) = m^{e^2} \bmod 35 = m$ for any legitimate public exponent e (i.e., for any e such that $0 < e < \varphi(35)$ and $\gcd(e, \varphi(35)) = 1$) which shows that this modulus leads to a completely insecure RSA cryptosystem.

2 By generalizing the results of Question 1, explain how to mount a so-called *cycling attack* in order to try to decrypt a ciphertext c given the corresponding public key (n, e).

3 Try to explain under which condition such an attack will be efficient. Propose a solution to defeat this attack when generating RSA parameters.

▷ Solution on page 191

Exercise 7   Modified Diffie-Hellman

After having studied the Diffie-Hellman protocol, a young cryptographer decides to implement it. In order to simplify the implementation, he decides to use the *additive* group $(\mathbf{Z}_p, +)$ instead of the multiplicative one $(\mathbf{Z}_p^*, \cdot)$. As an experienced cryptographer, what do you think about this new protocol?

▷ Solution on page 193

Exercise 8   ⋆Rabin Cryptosystem

Below, we consider the Rabin cryptosystem [40] which was proposed in 1979.

Setup: Generate two primes p, q such that $p \equiv q \equiv 3 \pmod 4$, set $n = p \cdot q$ and pick a uniformly distributed random element $B \in \mathbf{Z}_n$.

Public Key: $K_p = (B, n)$

Secret Key: $K_s = (B, p, q)$

Encryption: A message $x \in \mathbf{Z}_n$ is encrypted by computing $E(x) = x(x + B) \bmod n$.

Decryption: Let $y \in \mathbf{Z}_n$ be a ciphertext. The decrypted plaintext $D(y)$ is one of the four square roots of $\frac{B^2}{4} + y$ minus $\frac{B}{2}$.

1 Explain how it is possible to compute the square roots in $\mathbf{Z}_n$.

2 Notice that the decryption is non-deterministic. Show that we can make the decryption deterministic by adding some redundancy in the plaintext.

3 Show that if one can factorize n then one can break the Rabin cryptosystem.

4 Show that the Rabin cryptosystem can be completely broken by a chosen-ciphertext attack.
   Hint: Show how to factorize n if one can play with a decryption oracle which takes a ciphertext as an input, and outputs one of the four possible plaintexts at random.

▷ Solution on page 193

Exercise 9   ⋆Paillier Cryptosystem

In 1999, Pascal Paillier [36] proposed a trapdoor permutation that we will study in this exercise. Let p and q be two distinct odd primes such that $\gcd(n, (p-1)(q-1)) = 1$, where $n = p \cdot q$. Let $g \in \mathbf{Z}_{n^2}^*$ such that the order of g is a multiple of n. Paillier's trapdoor permutation is defined by

$$F_g: \quad \mathbf{Z}_n^* \times \mathbf{Z}_n \quad \longrightarrow \quad \mathbf{Z}_{n^2}^*$$
$$(r, m) \quad \longmapsto \quad r^n \cdot g^m \bmod n^2.$$

1 Show that the sets $\mathbf{Z}_n^* \times \mathbf{Z}_n$ and $\mathbf{Z}_{n^2}^*$ have the same cardinality.

2 Let $\lambda(n)$ be the smallest positive integer such that $x^{\lambda(n)} \bmod n = 1$ for any $x \in \mathbf{Z}_n^*$. Show that

$$w^{n \cdot \lambda(n)} \bmod n^2 = 1,$$

for any $w \in \mathbf{Z}_{n^2}^*$.

3 **Bijectivity.** In this part, we prove that the function F_g is bijective.

 (a) Argue why it suffices to show the injectivity of F_g to prove that it is bijective.

(b) Show that

$$F_g(r_1, m_1) = F_g(r_2, m_2) \Rightarrow g^{\lambda(n)(m_2 - m_1)} \equiv 1 \pmod{n^2}.$$

(c) Show that F_g is injective.
   Hint: Show that $\gcd(n, \lambda(n)) = 1$.

4 We consider now a variant of this scheme called the RSA-Paillier cryptosystem (see [11, 12]) which is defined as follows.

> **Key Generation:** Let s be an integer. Pick two different odd primes p and q of size $\frac{s}{2}$ bits, an element $e \in \mathbf{Z}_n$ such that $\gcd(e, \lambda(n)) = 1$. Set $n = pq$ and $d = e^{-1} \bmod \lambda(n)$.

> **Public Key:** (e, n)

> **Secret Key:** (d, n)

> **Encryption:** To encrypt a message $m \in \mathbf{Z}_n$, we pick a random $r \in \mathbf{Z}_n^*$ and compute the ciphertext $c = r^e(1 + mn) \bmod n^2$.

(a) Evaluate the complexity of the key generation and encryption algorithms in terms of s.

(b) Explain how the decryption algorithm works.

(c) Evaluate the complexity of the decryption algorithm in terms of s.

▷ Solution on page 194

Exercise 10   ⋆Naccache-Stern Cryptosystem

The aim of this exercise is to study the Naccache-Stern cryptosystem proposed in 1998 [31]. We first give the description of this cryptosystem.

> **Key Generation:** Let $n = pq$ be a modulus of two large odd primes p and q such that $p = 2au + 1$ and $q = 2bv + 1$, where a and b are also two large distinct primes and where u and v are chosen as follows. Consider 10 small (e.g., about 10 bits) odd pairwise distinct primes $r_1, r_2, \ldots, r_{10}$ and set $u = \prod_{i=1}^{5} r_i$ and $v = \prod_{i=6}^{10} r_i$. Set also $\sigma = uv$. Let $g \in \mathbf{Z}_n^*$ be an element which generates a subgroup whose order is a multiple of σab.

> **Public Key:** $K_p = (n, g)$

> **Secret Key:** $K_s = (p, q)$

Note that a, b, and the r_i's can easily be found from p and q. So, these elements are implicitly in the secret key.

Encryption: Let m be an integer lying in $\{1, 2, \ldots, \sigma\}$. We encrypt m by computing $g^m \bmod n$. In practice, since the sender of m does not know σ, he encrypts messages that are smaller than a lower bound of σ.

1 What is the impact on the security of this cryptosystem if we set $a = b = 1$ in the key generation?

2 Devise an algorithm which generates n.

3 What is the asymptotic complexity of this algorithm expressed in terms of the size of p, q and of a, b? Assume that p and q have the same size denoted by ℓ_1 (in bits) and a and b have the same size denoted by ℓ_2 (in bits).

4 Show that the size of the largest cyclic subgroup of $\mathbf{Z}_n^*$ is equal to $2ab\sigma$.
   Hint: Take a generator g_1 of $\mathbf{Z}_p^*$ and a generator g_2 of $\mathbf{Z}_q^*$.

5 Let H be a commutative group of order t such that $t = cd$, where c is a prime number and d is a positive integer coprime with c. Let $h \in H$. Prove that if $h^d \neq 1$, then the order of h is a multiple of c.
   Hint: Try a proof by contradiction!

6 Deduce an algorithm for testing whether a given element $g \in \mathbf{Z}_n^*$ has order at least σab or not.

7 Show that the encryption function defined on $\{1, 2, \ldots, \sigma\} \subset \mathbf{N}$ is injective.

8 Using the secret key K_s, show how we can retrieve the message m from the ciphertext $c = g^m \bmod n$.
   Hint: Adapt the algorithm of Pohlig-Hellman.

▷ Solution on page 196

Solutions.

Solution 1   ⋆Okamoto-Uchiyama Cryptosystem

By Fermat's Little Theorem, we know that $g^{p-1} \equiv 1 \pmod{p}$ and that $c^{p-1} \equiv 1 \pmod{p}$. Therefore, $c^{p-1} \bmod p^2 \in G$ and $g^{p-1} \bmod p^2 \in G$, so that the decryption function is well defined.

Now, we show that the decryption works. First, we have

$$
\begin{aligned}
c^{p-1} \pmod{p^2} &\equiv (g^m h^r)^{p-1} \pmod{p^2} \\
&\equiv \left(g^m g^{p^2 qr}\right)^{p-1} \pmod{p^2} \\
&\equiv \left(g^{p(p-1)}\right)^{pqr} g^{m(p-1)} \pmod{p^2} \\
&\equiv 1 \cdot \left(g^{p-1}\right)^m \pmod{p^2}.
\end{aligned}
$$

Thus, we have

$$
\frac{L\left(c^{p-1} \bmod p^2\right)}{L\left(g^{p-1} \bmod p^2\right)} \bmod p = \frac{L\left(g^{m(p-1)} \bmod p^2\right)}{L\left(g^{p-1} \bmod p^2\right)} \bmod p.
$$

Since, L is a group homomorphism, we deduce that

$$
L(g^{m(p-1)} \bmod p^2) = m \cdot L(g^{p-1} \bmod p^2) \bmod p.
$$

Thus,

$$
\frac{L\left(c^{p-1} \bmod p^2\right)}{L\left(g^{p-1} \bmod p^2\right)} \bmod p = m
$$

which proves that the decryption function indeed recovers the original plaintext.

More details on the Okamoto-Uchiyama cryptosystem are given in the original article [34].

Solution 2   RSA Cryptosystem

Since $ed \equiv 1 \pmod{\phi}$, there exists an integer k such that $ed = 1 + k\phi$. Now, if $\gcd(m, p) = 1$, by Fermat's Little Theorem we have

$$
m^{p-1} \equiv 1 \pmod{p}.
$$

Raising both sides of this congruence to the power $k(q-1)$ and then multiplying both sides by m yields

$$
m^{1+k(p-1)(q-1)} \equiv m \pmod{p}.
$$

Noting that this congruence is also valid if $\gcd(m, p) = p$ (in which case, both sides are congruent to 0 modulo p), we conclude that in any case,

$$m^{ed} \equiv m \pmod{p}.$$

Using the same arguments, we obtain

$$m^{ed} \equiv m \pmod{q}.$$

Finally, since p and q are distinct primes, and thus coprime, it follows by the Chinese Remainder Theorem that

$$m^{ed} \equiv m \pmod{n}.$$

This concludes the proof. If we assume that $m \in \mathbf{Z}_n^*$, we directly prove that decryption works using the following fact from group theory. If G is a group and g is an element of G, then $g^{|G|} = 1$, where $|G|$ denotes the order of G. In RSA, the group we consider is $\mathbf{Z}_n^*$ and its order is ϕ. Hence,

$$m^{ed} \equiv m^{1+k\phi} \equiv m \cdot \left(m^\phi\right)^k \equiv m \pmod{n}.$$

For more details about RSA, we refer to the original article [43].

Solution 3   RSA for Paranoids

1 The bottleneck is making an s-bit prime number, which can be done in $\mathcal{O}(s^4)$.

2 For plain RSA, the condition would be $\gcd(e, (p-1)(q-1)) = 1$. Here q is not a prime, and its factorization is not even known, so that computing $\varphi(pq)$ is not an easy task. We can guess that the condition we are looking for is $\gcd(e, p-1) = 1$. We now show that this is sufficient to make E injective. For any $m_1, m_2 \in \{0, 1, \dots, 2^{s-1} - 1\}$, we have

$$E(m_1) = E(m_2) \;\Rightarrow\; m_1^e \equiv m_2^e \pmod{pq}$$
$$\Rightarrow\; m_1^e \equiv m_2^e \pmod{p}.$$

As $\gcd(e, p-1) = 1$, we can find (using the Extended Euclid Algorithm) two integers u, v such that $ue - v(p-1) = 1$. Therefore

$$E(m_1) = E(m_2) \;\Rightarrow\; m_1^{ue} \equiv m_2^{ue} \pmod{p}$$
$$\Rightarrow\; m_1^{1+v(p-1)} \equiv m_2^{1+v(p-1)} \pmod{p}$$
$$\Rightarrow\; m_1 \equiv m_2 \pmod{p},$$

using Fermat's Little Theorem. Finally, as $m_1 < p$ and $m_2 < p$, the last condition is sufficient to show that $m_1 = m_2$.

3 As $\gcd(e, p-1) = 1$, we can compute $d = e^{-1} \bmod (p-1)$, so that there exists some $k \in \mathbf{Z}$ such that $ed = 1 + k(p-1)$. To decrypt, we compute

$$E(m)^d \bmod p = m^{ed} \bmod p = m^{1+k(p-1)} \bmod p = m \ ,$$

using Fermat's Little Theorem.

4 Encryption is a modular exponentiation, so that the complexity is $\mathcal{O}(s^3 t^2)$ (exponent is of length s, multiplication of st-bit long integers is quadratic). Similarly, decryption's complexity is $\mathcal{O}(s^3)$ (integers are s-bit long). We can accept $\mathcal{O}(s^3)$ for both complexities if t is considered as a constant. The complexity of the key generation is the same as for plain RSA, that is, $\mathcal{O}(s^4)$ (prime generation).

5 If e is smaller than t, $m^e \bmod n$ is simply m^e, since $m^e < n$. So, anyone can extract eth roots over $\mathbf{Z}$ and decrypt the ciphertext c.

6 Clearly, the knowledge of p enables to compute the secret key and thus to decrypt. Conversely, suppose we can decrypt, i.e., we have access to a decryption machine that takes as an input any ciphertext and returns as an output the result of the decryption process on the ciphertext. We choose to submit the encryption of a *large* plaintext m such that $p < m < 2p$ (even if p is not known yet, such a m can be chosen as we know the size of p). We can write m as $m = p + u$, where $u < p$. The decryption machine allows to recover u easily. Indeed, if we submit the ciphertext $m^e \bmod n$ the decryption machine returns

$$m^{ed} \bmod p = (p+u)^{ed} \bmod p = u^{ed} \bmod p = u \ ,$$

as u was chosen smaller than p. Knowing m and u allows to recover p as $p = m - u$. Note that the same kind of ideas can be applied to the Rabin cryptosystem.

7 This works as in Question 6, since we have a decryption oracle at disposal.

8 To thwart this attack, one can add some redundancy in the message before encryption, and check the redundancy after decryption before disclosing the result.

More details about this variant of RSA are given in the original article [48]. We also refer to an article of Gilbert et al. [19] which shows a similar chosen ciphertext attack and which argues why the redundancy should be added carefully.

Solution 4   RSA - Common Moduli

1 Given a modulus n, a public exponent e_A and the corresponding private key d_A, it is possible to recover the factorization of n (see the textbook [56]). Then, Alice uses the factorization of n in order to recover $\varphi(n)$ and to compute Bob's private key d_B with the help of his public exponent e_B.

2 If $\gcd(e_A, e_B) = 1$, then Eve can compute two integers x and y such that $e_A \cdot x + e_B \cdot y = 1$ by using the Extended Euclid Algorithm. Then, Eve uses the two ciphertexts c_A and c_B in the following way

$$c_A^x \cdot c_B^y \equiv m^{e_A x} \cdot m^{e_B y} \equiv m^{e_A x + e_B y} \equiv m \pmod{n}.$$

For further readings about this topic, we suggest an article of Simmons [49] and another one of DeLaurentis [15].

Solution 5   Networked RSA

1 Each user needs 2 primes, thus one needs a total of $2n$ prime numbers.

2 A malicious user Eve can proceed as follows. She can factorize her own modulus by using her private exponent d (see the textbook [56]) and try to divide other moduli with her prime numbers. All the moduli sharing a prime with hers will then be broken.

3 Eve does not need to own a public key generated from the prime numbers pool. By taking the greatest common divisor of all possible pairs of moduli, she will be able to factorize all moduli for which at least one prime factor has been used in at least one other modulus.

Solution 6   Repeated RSA Encryption

1 Since $E(c) \equiv c^e \equiv m^{e^2} \pmod{n}$, it is sufficient to show that $e^2 \equiv 1 \pmod{\varphi(n)}$ for all legitimate e, i.e., for all $e \in \mathbf{Z}^*_{\varphi(35)}$. We have $\varphi(35) = \varphi(5) \cdot \varphi(7) = 4 \cdot 6 = 24$. Table 9.1 confirms the validity of the above statement.

2 Since an RSA encryption is a permutation on the message space $\{0, 1, \ldots, n-1\}$, a positive integer k such that $c^{e^k} \equiv c \pmod{n}$ must exist. In this case, $c^{e^{k-1}} \equiv m \pmod{n}$. This observation leads to Algorithm 32, called a *cycling attack*.

Table 9.1.   Squares of $\mathbf{Z}_{24}^*$

legitimate e	e^2 (mod 24)
1	$1^2 \equiv 1 \equiv 1$ (mod 24)
5	$5^2 \equiv 25 \equiv 1$ (mod 24)
7	$7^2 \equiv 49 \equiv 1$ (mod 24)
11	$11^2 \equiv 121 \equiv 1$ (mod 24)
13	$13^2 \equiv 169 \equiv 1$ (mod 24)
17	$17^2 \equiv 289 \equiv 1$ (mod 24)
19	$19^2 \equiv 361 \equiv 1$ (mod 24)
23	$23^2 \equiv 529 \equiv 1$ (mod 24)

3 Let $n = pq$. A t-times iterated encryption in an RSA cryptosystem reveals the plaintext m if and only if

$$m^{e^u} \equiv m \pmod{n} \tag{9.1}$$

for some $u \leq t$. This is equivalent to

$$e^u \equiv 1 \pmod{\mathrm{ord}_n(m)}$$

for some $u \leq t$, where $\mathrm{ord}_n(m)$ denotes the order of the element m in the group $\mathbf{Z}_n^*$. Hence, the minimal number of encryptions needed to recover the plaintext is $\mathrm{ord}_{\mathrm{ord}_n(m)}(e)$.

If we consider Equation (9.1) modulo p, we can deduce that $e^u \equiv 1$ (mod $\mathrm{ord}_p(m)$). For a prime number p' dividing $p-1$, the probability

---

Algorithm 32 Cycling attack against RSA

Input: an RSA public key (n, e), a ciphertext $c = m^e \bmod n$, and an upper bound N on the number of encryptions
Output: either the plaintext m or `Failure`
Processing:
1: $k \leftarrow 1$
2: $s \leftarrow c$
3: **for** $k = 1, \ldots, N$ **do**
4:      $m \leftarrow s$
5:      $s \leftarrow s^e \bmod n$
6:      **if** $s = c$ **then**
7:          output m and stop
8:      **end if**
9: **end for**
10: output `Failure` and stop

---

for a random $m \in \mathbf{Z}_n^*$ to have an order in $\mathbf{Z}_p^*$ which is a multiple of p' is $1 - 1/p'$, since $\mathbf{Z}_p^*$ is cyclic of order $p - 1$. When this holds, we must have $e^u \equiv 1 \pmod{p'}$. Using similar arguments, we can show that for a random $e \in \mathbf{Z}_{\varphi(n)}^*$, the probability for u to be a multiple of a prime number $p'' \mid p' - 1$ is $1 - 1/p''$ as well. Therefore, a solution to thwart this attack would be to choose p (and similarily for q) such that $p - 1$ has a large prime factor p' where $p' - 1$ again has a large prime factor p''.

Nevertheless, it has been shown that the probability for a cycling attack to succeed is negligible if the primes p and q are just chosen at random with a sufficient size. For this, we refer to an article of Rivest and Silverman [45].

This cycling attack was proposed by Simmons [50] in 1977 and the above countermeasure can be found in an article of Rivest [41] published in 1978.

Solution 7 Modified Diffie-Hellman

If we transpose the Diffie-Hellman in the additive group $(\mathbf{Z}_p, +)$, the intractibility of the discrete logarithm problem is no longer satisfied. The exponentation is transposed to a multiplication, while the discrete logarithm operation becomes equivalent to a division (i.e., to a multiplication with an inverse element). As computing the inverse (with respect to the multiplication) of an element in $\mathbf{Z}_p$ is an easy task with the Extended Euclid Algorithm, the security of such a modified Diffie-Hellman protocol is completely jeopardized!

Solution 8 ⋆Rabin Cryptosystem

1 As $p \equiv q \equiv 3 \pmod{4}$, one can easily compute the square roots of an element $c \in \mathbf{Z}_n^*$ modulo p and modulo q as follows

$$s_1 = c^{\frac{p+1}{4}} \bmod p$$
$$s_2 = c^{\frac{q+1}{4}} \bmod q.$$

Then, using the "CRT-transform", we compute the square roots modulo $n = p \cdot q$. Namely, using the Extended Euclid Algorithm, we find two integers a and b such that $ap + bq = 1$, and then compute

$$x = aps_1 + bqs_2 \bmod n$$
$$y = aps_1 - bqs_2 \bmod n.$$

The four square roots of c are $x, -x, y, -y$. Note that it is possible that $\gcd(c, n) \neq 1$, i.e., $c \notin \mathbf{Z}_n^*$. In this case, $s_1 = 0$ and/or $s_2 = 0$ and there is either 1 or 2 distinct square root(s).

2 If we fix, for instance, the 64 most significant bits of the message, the probability that decrypting the ciphertext in a correct way and getting *two* square roots having the same first 64 bits is in the order of 2^{-64}. Similarly, if the ciphertext is not valid, we get a square root having the same pattern with a probability 2^{-64}.

3 If we can factorize n, then we can recover the secret key.

4 While provably secure against a passive adversary, the Rabin public-key cryptosystem is vulnerable to a chosen-ciphertext attack. This attack works as follows. One chooses a random value $r \in \mathbf{Z}_n^*$ and computes $c = r(r+B) \bmod n$. Then, c is submitted to the decryption machine, which decrypts c and returns some plaintext m. Since the decryption machine does not know r, and r is randomly chosen, the plaintext m is not necessarily equal to r. The two elements $s = r + \frac{B}{2} \bmod n$ and $s' = m + \frac{B}{2} \bmod n$ correspond to two random square roots of $\frac{B^2}{4} + c$ in $\mathbf{Z}_n^*$. With probability $\frac{1}{2}$, s and s' are such that $s \not\equiv \pm s' \pmod{n}$, in which case $\gcd(s - s', n) = \gcd(r - m, n)$ is one of the prime factors of n.[1] If $s \equiv \pm s' \pmod{n}$, then the attack has to be iterated.

Solution 9 ⋆Paillier Cryptosystem

1 First, we recall that $|\mathbf{Z}_m^*| = \varphi(m)$ for any $m \in \mathbf{N}$. Hence, the cardinality of $\mathbf{Z}_n^*$ is equal to $\varphi(n) = (p-1)(q-1)$ and the cardinality of $\mathbf{Z}_{n^2}^*$ is equal to $\varphi(p^2 q^2) = p(p-1)q(q-1) = n\varphi(n)$. It remains to observe that $|\mathbf{Z}_n^* \times \mathbf{Z}_n| = |\mathbf{Z}_n^*| \cdot |\mathbf{Z}_n| = \varphi(n)n$.

2 We provide two different solutions for this question. By definition of the Carmichael function λ, it suffices to show that $\lambda(n^2)$ divides $n \cdot \lambda(n)$. By a classical formula of the Carmichael function, we have $\lambda(n^2) = \mathrm{lcm}(p(p-1), q(q-1))$. Since $\gcd(n, (p-1)(q-1)) = 1$, we obtain $\lambda(n^2) = n \cdot \mathrm{lcm}(p-1, q-1) = n\lambda(n)$.

Alternatively, we can compute $w^{n \cdot \lambda(n)} \bmod n^2$. As $w \in \mathbf{Z}_{n^2}^*$ we know that $\gcd(w, n^2) = 1$, which is equivalent to say that $\gcd(w, n) = 1$.

---

[1]Remember the following fact. Let x, y and n be integers such that $x^2 \equiv y^2 \pmod{n}$, but $x \not\equiv \pm y \pmod{n}$. Then, n divides $x^2 - y^2 = (x - y)(x + y)$ but divides neither $(x - y)$ nor $(x + y)$. Hence, $\gcd(x - y, n)$ is a non-trivial factor of n.

Therefore, $w \in \mathbf{Z}_n^*$ and thus $w^{\lambda(n)} \bmod n = 1$, so that there exists some $k \in \mathbf{Z}$ such that $w^{\lambda(n)} = 1 + k \cdot n$. Then, using Newton's binomial formula, we have

$$w^{n \cdot \lambda(n)} = (1 + k \cdot n)^n = 1 + \underbrace{\sum_{i=1}^{n} \binom{n}{i} (k \cdot n)^i}_{\text{divisible by } n^2}.$$

Finally, we clearly have $w^{n \cdot \lambda(n)} \bmod n^2 = 1$.

3 (a) Since the domain and the codomain of F_g have the same cardinality, showing the injectivity of F_g is sufficient for showing its bijectivity.

(b) We have

$$F_g(r_1, m_1) = F_g(r_2, m_2) \;\Rightarrow\; r_1^n \cdot g^{m_1} \equiv r_2^n \cdot g^{m_2} \pmod{n^2}$$
$$\Rightarrow\; r_1^n \cdot g^{m_1 - m_2} \equiv r_2^n \pmod{n^2}$$

as g is invertible modulo n^2. Noting that $r_1, r_2 \in \mathbf{Z}_n^*$ implies that $r_1, r_2 \in \mathbf{Z}_{n^2}^*$ (as being coprime with n is equivalent to being coprime with n^2), we can apply the result of Question 2. We deduce that $F_g(r_1, m_1) = F_g(m_2, r_2)$ implies

$$r_1^{n \cdot \lambda(n)} \cdot g^{(m_1 - m_2) \cdot \lambda(n)} \equiv r_2^{n \cdot \lambda(n)} \pmod{n^2}$$

and

$$g^{(m_1 - m_2) \cdot \lambda(n)} \equiv 1 \pmod{n^2}.$$

(c) We prove the injectivity of F_g by showing that $F_g(r_1, m_1) = F_g(r_2, m_2) \Rightarrow r_1 = r_2$ and $m_1 = m_2$. In the previous question, we obtained $g^{(m_1 - m_2) \cdot \lambda(n)} \equiv 1 \pmod{n^2}$. This means that the order of g divides $(m_1 - m_2)\lambda(n)$. But the order of g is a multiple of n, so that

$$n \mid (m_1 - m_2) \cdot \lambda(n). \tag{9.2}$$

Clearly, as $\lambda(n)$ divides the group order (note that λ is the order of an element and use Lagrange's Theorem), it divides $\varphi(n)$. Moreover we assumed that $\gcd(n, \varphi(n)) = 1$. Therefore $\gcd(n, \lambda(n)) = 1$, so that (9.2) implies that $n \mid m_1 - m_2$, i.e.,

$$m_1 \equiv m_2 \pmod n.$$

Showing that $r_1 = r_2$ is easy as

$$r_1^n \equiv r_2^n \pmod{n^2} \;\Rightarrow\; (r_1 \cdot r_2^{-1})^n \equiv 1 \pmod n$$
$$\Rightarrow\; r_1 \cdot r_2^{-1} \equiv 1 \pmod n$$

as the order of an element cannot divide n (as it must divide $\varphi(n)$ and as $\gcd(n, \varphi(n)) = 1$). Therefore, we have

$$r_1 \equiv r_2 \pmod{n}.$$

4 (a) Since the biggest amount of computation is required for the prime number generation, the complexity of the key generation algorithm is $\mathcal{O}(s^4)$. The complexity of the encryption algorithm is essentially due to a modular exponentiation, so it is $\mathcal{O}(s^3)$.

(b) We first try to retrieve r. We notice that $c \equiv r^e \pmod{n}$. As $ed \equiv 1 \pmod{\lambda(n)}$, there exists some $k \in \mathbf{Z}$ such that $ed = 1 + k \cdot \lambda(n)$. Thus

$$c^d \equiv r^{ed} \equiv r \cdot (r^{\lambda(n)})^k \equiv r \pmod{n}$$

by definition of $\lambda(n)$. As $r < n$, we have shown that $c^d \bmod n = r$, so that we can retrieve r (using the secret key). Moreover, we have

$$c \cdot r^{-e} - 1 \equiv m \cdot n \pmod{n^2}.$$

But as $m < n$, $m \cdot n < n^2$, we have shown that

$$(c \cdot r^{-e} - 1) \bmod n^2 = m \cdot n,$$

and thus

$$\frac{(c \cdot r^{-e} - 1) \bmod n^2}{n} = m.$$

(c) The essential computations are some modular exponentiations. Thus the complexity of the decryption algorithm is $\mathcal{O}(s^3)$.

More details about the Paillier cryptosystem are given in [36]. For further readings about the RSA-Paillier cryptosystem, we refer to [11, 12].

Solution 10   ⋆Naccache-Stern Cryptosystem

1 If $a = b = 1$, we notice that $p = 2u + 1$ and $q = 2v + 1$. Since the r_i's are very small, the size of the primes p and q is also small, e.g., 50 bits. Thus, due to the modulus size, we can retrieve the secret key easily by factoring n. This can be done efficiently in the following way. Since u and v are products of small odd primes, $p - 1$ and $q - 1$ are smooth integers. Thus, we can factorize n efficiently using the Pollard $p - 1$ method in most cases. Note that since the

r_i's are distinct, the largest prime of u is not equal to that of v. This avoids some pathological cases of the Pollard $p - 1$ method. Thus, the security impact is dramatic since we can retrieve the secret key from the public key quite efficiently in most cases.

2 Since p and q are of the same form, it suffices to consider only the generation of p. The algorithm first consists in picking small primes $r_1, \ldots, r_5$ and computing u. Then, we pick a randomly of a given size until it passes the primality test of Miller-Rabin. For each a that passes the Miller-Rabin test, we compute $p = 2au + 1$ and test its primality with Miller-Rabin. If p passes the test, we are done. Otherwise we start again with another element a.

3 The asymptotic complexity of computing u (resp. v) is constant (asymptotically negligible) since the length of primes $r_1, \ldots, r_{10}$ is small and fixed. The largest computation is due to the generation of the large primes a and p (resp. b and q). Generating a prime number a of size ℓ_2 has an asymptotic complexity of $\mathcal{O}(\ell_2^4)$. This value a will lead to an integer $p = 2au + 1$ which is prime with a probability of about $\Omega(\frac{1}{\ell_1})$. Hence, the final asymptotic complexity for generating p (resp. q) is $\mathcal{O}(\ell_2^4 \ell_1)$. If we take into account the Miller-Rabin test on p, a more precise evaluation of the complexity is $\mathcal{O}(\ell_2^4 \ell_1 + \ell_1^4)$.

4 We choose an element $g \in \mathbf{Z}_n^*$ such that $g \bmod p = g_1$ and $g \bmod q = g_2$, where g_1 (resp. g_2) is a generator of $\mathbf{Z}_p^*$ (resp. $\mathbf{Z}_q^*$). The order of g is then the smallest integer j such that $g_1^j \equiv 1 \pmod{p}$ and $g_2^j \equiv 1 \pmod{q}$. This j is then the smallest integer which is a multiple of $p-1$ and $q-1$, namely $j = \mathrm{lcm}(p-1, q-1)$. Here, $\gcd(\frac{p-1}{2}, \frac{q-1}{2}) = 1$ and j is then equal to $2abuv = 2ab\sigma$.

5 Suppose first that the order of h is not a multiple of c. Since the order of h must divide $t = cd$, we deduce that the order of h divides d (since this one does not contain any c in its prime decomposition). This leads to $h^d = 1$, which is a contradiction.

6 We have to check that $g^{\varphi(n)/a} \neq 1$, $g^{\varphi(n)/b} \neq 1$ and $g^{\varphi(n)/r_i} \neq 1$ for all $i = 1, \ldots, 10$. If all these relations hold, we deduce that the order of g is at least equal to σab since $a, b, r_1, \ldots, r_{10}$ are pairwise distinct primes (more precisely, the order of g is at least as large as the least common multiple integer of $a, b, r_1, \ldots, r_{10}$).

7 Assume we have $g^m \equiv g^{m'} \pmod{n}$ for $m, m' \in \mathbf{N}$. Since g has an order which is a multiple of σ, we have $m \equiv m' \pmod{\sigma}$. Thus, $m = m'$ and our encryption function is injective on the set $\{1, \ldots, \sigma\}$.

8 Since the message m is smaller than σ, the problem of retrieving m is equivalent to retrieve the discrete logarithm of the ciphertext c modulo σ with respect to g. To this end, we determine the value m_i of this discrete logarithm modulo r_i for $i = 1, \ldots, 10$ and then, by applying the "CRT-transform", we get m (such that $m \equiv m_i$ (mod r_i)). The value m_i can be found from c as in the Pohlig-Hellman algorithm, namely,

$$m_i = \log_{g^{\varphi(n)/r_i} \bmod n} \left(c^{\varphi(n)/r_i} \right)$$

for all $i = 1, \ldots, 10$. To summarize, one just need to apply the Pohlig-Hellman algorithm, except that the discrete logarithm computations are restricted to the r_i's instead of all prime numbers dividing the order of the subgroup generated by g.

For further readings about the Nacchache-Stern cryptosystem, we refer to the original article [31].

Chapter 10

DIGITAL SIGNATURES

Exercises

Exercise 1   Lazy DSS

We consider the DSS signature algorithm with parameters p, q, g, a hash function H, and a secret key x.

Let us consider a lazy signer who has precomputed one pair (k, r) satisfying $r = (g^k \bmod p) \bmod q$ and who always uses the same one for generating a signature. Show how to attack him and recover his secret key.

▷ Solution on page 205

Exercise 2   ⋆DSS Security Hypothesis

We consider the DSS signature algorithm with parameters p, q, g, a hash function H, and a public key y.

1 If the discrete logarithm problem is easy in the subgroup of $\mathbf{Z}_p^*$ spanned by g, show that anyone can forge signatures. What is the complexity of this attack when Shanks baby-step giant-step algorithm is used?

2 If H is not one-way, show that we can forge a (m, r, s) triplet so that (r, s) is a valid signature for the message m with the public key y. Apply this attack to SHA-1 by using brute force. What is its complexity?

3 If H is not collision resistant, show that we can forge a given signature with a chosen-message attack. Apply this attack to SHA-1 by using brute force. What is its complexity?

4 If the parameter k of DSS is predictable, show that we can deduce the secret key from a valid signature. What is the complexity of this attack when using brute force?

▷ Solution on page 205

Exercise 3   DSS with Unprotected Parameters

In a network of users we use DSS signatures with the given parameters p, q, g. We assume that each registered user U has a secret key x_U and a public key $y_U = g^{x_U} \bmod p$. For each pair (U, y_U), an authority delivers a certificate C_U which binds y_U to U. So, when Alice wants to send a signed message to Bob she just has to provide the triplet (Alice, $y_{\text{Alice}}, C_{\text{Alice}}$) and the signed message to Bob. Then, Bob checks that the certificate C_{Alice} is valid. After this, he verifies the signature with the public key y_{Alice}. If these tests passed, Bob is finally ensured that the message comes from Alice.

1 We assume that when Bob gets a new valid certified key (U, y_U, C_U) he puts (U, y_U) in a directory so that Alice does not need to send her triplet each time she sends a message. What happens if the integrity of the directory is not protected? Namely, show that an adversary Eve who can modify Bob's directory can impersonate Alice and forge a signed message which will be accepted by Bob as coming from Alice.

How can we address this problem without having to protect the integrity of the directory?

2 We assume that the certificate C_U is simply the DSS signature of (U, y_U) with the authority key. In order to verify the certificates, Bob needs to keep $y_{\text{Authority}}$ in memory. What happens if the integrity of $y_{\text{Authority}}$ in his memory is not protected? Show that Eve can forge a fake certificate.

The parameters p, q, g are also kept in memory. Similarly, we wonder what happens if the integrity of these parameters is not protected.

3 Show that if g can be replaced by 0 in Bob's memory, then Eve can forge a fake certificate.

4 We now assume that Bob checks that $g \neq 0$. Show that if g can be replaced by another element of the subgroup spanned by g, then Eve can forge a fake certificate.

▷ Solution on page 206

Exercise 4 Ong-Schnorr-Shamir Signature

Let n be a large composite modulus (of unknown factorization), k and s be two elements of $\mathbf{Z}_n^*$ such that $s^2 \equiv -k \pmod{n}$. We also consider a cryptographic hash function $H : \{0,1\}^* \to \mathbf{Z}_n$. Devise a digital signature scheme which uses a public key $K_p = k$, a secret key $K_s = s$ and such that the verification of a signature $\sigma = (x, y) \in \mathbf{Z}_n$ of a message m consists in checking that

$$x^2 + ky^2 \equiv H(m) \pmod{n}.$$

Note: This scheme was proposed by Ong, Schnorr, and Shamir in 1984 [35]. It was proven insecure by Pollard and Schnorr in 1987 [39].

▷ Solution on page 207

Exercise 5 Batch Verification of DSS Signatures

In this exercise, we consider a variant of the DSS signature from which we remove some modulo q operations. Namely, r is computed as $r = g^k \bmod p$ and the verification consists in checking that

$$r = g^{\frac{H(m)}{s} \bmod q} y^{\frac{r}{s} \bmod q} \bmod p.$$

All the other operations of this DSS variant are identical to those of the original DSS. For the sake of simplicity, this variant will simply be called DSS throughout the exercise.

We recall that g generates a subgroup of $\mathbf{Z}_p^*$ of order q. We denote by ℓ_p and ℓ_q the respective sizes of p and q in bits.

Assume that we have n DSS signatures to verify. We need to check n triplets (m_i, r_i, s_i), where m_i is the ith message and (r_i, s_i) is the corresponding signature, for $1 \le i \le n$. We assume that all signatures come from the same signer and correspond to the same public key y and the same parameters p, q, and g.

1 What is the complexity of sequentially verifying all the signatures in terms of ℓ_p, ℓ_q, and n? (You can neglect the computation time of the hash function.)

In order to speed up the verification of the signatures, we will perform a "batch verification", namely we will check all the signatures at the same time. We consider a set $\mathcal{A}$ of N pairwise coprime numbers in $\mathbf{Z}_q^*$ which are smaller than an upper bound $B < \sqrt{q}$. Then, we pick n different elements $a_1, \ldots, a_n$ in $\mathcal{A}$. We define

$$R = r_1^{a_1} r_2^{a_2} \cdots r_n^{a_n} \bmod p,$$

$$G = \frac{a_1 H(m_1)}{s_1} + \frac{a_2 H(m_2)}{s_2} + \cdots + \frac{a_n H(m_n)}{s_n} \bmod q,$$

$$Y = \frac{a_1 r_1}{s_1} + \frac{a_2 r_2}{s_2} + \cdots + \frac{a_n r_n}{s_n} \bmod q.$$

A batch verification of these n signatures consists in verifying that

$$R = g^G y^Y \bmod p.$$

2 Show that the batch verification succeeds when all the signatures (m_i, r_i, s_i) for $1 \leq i \leq n$ are valid.

3 What is the complexity of the verification in terms of n, ℓ_p, ℓ_q, and B?

4 Let γ_1 and γ_2 be two elements of the subgroup generated by g such that $\gamma_1 \neq 1$ and $\gamma_2 \neq 1$. Show that there exists at most one pair $(a_1, a_2) \in \mathcal{A} \times \mathcal{A}$ with $a_1 \neq a_2$ satisfying

$$\gamma_1^{a_1} \gamma_2^{a_2} \equiv 1 \pmod{p}.$$

Hint: Given two such pairs (a_1, a_2) and (a_1', a_2') deduce that $a_1' = a_1$ and $a_2 = a_2'$ from $a_1 a_2' = a_1' a_2$.

5 Let α_1, β_1, α_2, β_2 be arbitrary elements of the subgroup generated by g, such that $\alpha_1 \neq \beta_1$ and $\alpha_2 \neq \beta_2$. Using result of the previous question, show that there exists at most one pair $(a_1, a_2) \in \mathcal{A} \times \mathcal{A}$ with $a_1 \neq a_2$ satisfying

$$\alpha_1^{a_1} \alpha_2^{a_2} \equiv \beta_1^{a_1} \beta_2^{a_2} \pmod{p}.$$

In what follows, for any invalid signature triplet (m, r, s) we assume that r lies in the subgroup generated by g.

6 For $n = 2$, show that for any pair of triplets of DSS signatures (m_1, r_1, s_1) and (m_2, r_2, s_2) such that at least one is invalid, the probability that the batch verification fails is greater than or equal to

$$1 - \frac{1}{N^2 - N}.$$

Hint: Separate the cases where one or two signatures are invalid. For the latter case, use the previous question.

7 Using the parameters $p = 11$, $q = 5$, $g = 4$, $y = 3 = 4^4 \bmod 11$, $n = 2$, $a_1 = 1$, and $a_2 = 2$, exhibit an example, where at least one signature is invalid but the batch verification passes. We do not require to find the m_i's here, but only the digests $h_1 = H(m_1)$ and $h_2 = H(m_2)$.

▷ Solution on page 207

Exercise 6   Ring Signatures

The goal of this exercise is to make the reader familiar with the concept of ring signature which was first formalized by Shamir et al. [44].

A ring signature is a cryptographic primitive allowing each user to anonymously sign as a member of an ad-hoc set of users (called a "ring of users"). Any verifier can thus be convinced that the message was signed by a member of the ring. Moreover, it should not be possible for the verifier to determine which member of the ring actually signed the message. Another required property of a ring signature is that the signer does not need any cooperation of any other members of the ring in the signing step. There is furthermore no setup scheme for the ring itself so that the signer can simply define the ring by giving a list of the members. We only assume that each user is already associated to a public key of some digital signature scheme such as RSA and that all public keys are authenticated.

We first consider the case of a ring composed only by two members Alice and Bob. We propose a ring signature in which Alice is able to sign a message for the ring (Bob and herself) and where Colin can verify that this signature was indeed signed either by Alice or Bob.

Alice (resp. Bob) has an RSA public key denoted $P_A = (e_A, n_A)$ (resp. $P_B = (e_B, n_B)$). The RSA signature of a message x with respect to a public key $P = (e, n)$ is denoted $E_P(x) = x^e \bmod n$. Let h be a hash function that hashes messages of any length to s-bit digests. All RSA moduli are assumed to be $(s + 1)$-bit long. We describe below the ring signature scheme.

Signature Generation: Alice hashes a message $m \in \{0, 1\}^*$ and obtains $h(m) \in \{0, 1\}^s$. She then picks a random element x_B in $\mathbf{Z}^*_{n_B}$ and computes $y_B = E_{P_B}(x_B)$. Alice computes $x_A = E_{P_A}^{-1}(y_B \oplus h(m))$ with her secret key. The signature of m is (A, B, x_A, x_B), where A is Alice's identity and B is Bob's one.

Verification: Colin checks that $E_{P_A}(x_A) \oplus E_{P_B}(x_B) = h(m)$ holds.

1 Explain how an adversary could forge a message with a valid signature (A, B, x_A, x_B) if h is not preimage resistant.

2 Does h have to be collision resistant in order to ensure the security of this scheme?

3 Assume that an adversary is given a challenged message m and that $s = 1024$. We also assume that this adversary has two tables of the same size at his disposal. The tables T_A and T_B respectively contain several pairs of the form $(w_A, E_{P_A}(w_A))$ and $(w_B, E_{P_B}(w_B))$ for some random $w_A \in \mathbf{Z}^*_{n_A}$ and $w_B \in \mathbf{Z}^*_{n_B}$. Explain how the adversary can use these tables in order to forge a valid signature for m. Estimate roughly the size of these tables in order for this attack to work with a probability greater than 0.1.

4 Generalize this scheme to rings of arbitrary size N.
   Notation: Each member of the ring U_i has an RSA public key $P_i = (n_i, e_i)$ and
   $$E_{P_i}(x) = x^{e_i} \bmod n_i,$$
   for $1 \leq i \leq N$.

▷ Solution on page 210

Solutions

Solution 1   Lazy DSS

Let us consider the signatures of two different messages m and m'. We can write both signatures as (r, s) and (r, s') respectively. We have

$$s = \frac{H(m) + xr}{k} \bmod q$$

$$s' = \frac{H(m') + xr}{k} \bmod q.$$

We can find k by computing

$$k = \frac{H(m) - H(m')}{s - s'} \bmod q.$$

Then, we compute $r = (g^k \bmod p) \bmod q$ and finally, we can recover x by computing

$$x = \frac{ks - H(m)}{r} \bmod q.$$

Solution 2   ⋆DSS Security Hypothesis

1 We compute the discrete logarithm of the public key with respect to the base g and obtain the secret key which trivially allows to sign any message. The Shanks baby-step giant-step algorithm has a complexity in $\Omega(\sqrt{q})$.

2 We can easily forge a triplet (h, r, s) as follows. Pick random elements α and β in $\mathbf{Z}_q^*$. Then, compute

$$r = (g^\alpha y^\beta \bmod p) \bmod q, \quad s = \frac{r}{\beta} \bmod q, \quad \text{and} \quad h = s\alpha \bmod q.$$

From this, we see that a message m such that $H(m) = h$ passes the DSS verification with the signature (r, s), since

$$r = \left(g^{\frac{h}{s} \bmod q} y^{\frac{r}{s} \bmod q} \bmod p \right) \bmod q$$

holds. If we invert H on h, we obtain a valid (m, r, s) triplet. We can invert SHA-1 by brute force in 2^{160} computations.

3 For two different messages m_1 and m_2, we create a collision $H(m_1) = H(m_2)$, then we ask for the signature (r, s) of m_1. The (m_2, r, s) triplet is a valid forged one. By the Birthday Paradox we can do it within 2^{80} computations when the hash function is SHA-1.

4 If we can guess k we can compute $x = \frac{sk - H(m)}{r} \bmod q$. By brute force, guessing k requires within $\Omega(q)$ trials.

Solution 3   DSS with Unprotected Parameters

1 Eve can replace Alice's public key y_{Alice} by her own public key y_{Eve} in Bob's memory. Then, Eve can send a message signed with her own secret key. Bob will finally verify the signature using Eve's public key believing he is using that of Alice.

To protect himself against this attack, Bob can store the certificate C_{Alice} and always check the validity of the tuple (Alice, $y_{\text{Alice}}, C_{\text{Alice}}$) before verifying any signature from Alice.

2 Eve can replace the key of the authority by her own public key and create fake certificates. Hence, she can assign a new public key to Alice (whose secret key is known by Eve) with a fake certificate in Bob's memory. We conclude by saying that at least $y_{\text{Authority}}$ must be protected.

3 If g is replaced by 0, then any signature on a message m with $r = 0$ will be valid since the test

$$r = \left(g^{\frac{H(m)}{s} \bmod q} y^{\frac{r}{s} \bmod q} \bmod p \right) \bmod q$$

will succeed for any $y \in \mathbf{Z}_p$. Therefore, it is trivial for Eve to forge fake signatures and thus, fake certificates.

4 One solution consists in replacing g by 1. In this case, we can forge valid signatures by picking $\alpha \in \mathbf{Z}_q^*$ at random and take $r = (y_{\text{Authority}}^{\alpha} \bmod p) \bmod q$ and $s = \frac{r}{\alpha} \bmod q$.

Another solution consists in using the method for forging a valid (h, r, s) triplet and then deducing a new useful value for g. For this, we pick $\alpha, \beta \in \mathbf{Z}_q^*$ at random and take

$$r = (g^{\alpha} y_{\text{Authority}}^{\beta} \bmod p) \bmod q$$

and $s = \frac{r}{\beta} \bmod q$. Then, we compute $i = \frac{s\alpha}{H(m)} \bmod q$ and replace g by $g^i \bmod p$.

An additional possible solution is obtained as follows. We replace g by $y_{\text{Authority}}^i \bmod p$ for a value $i \in \mathbf{Z}_q^*$ picked at random and use the signature algorithm with $x_{\text{Authority}} = \frac{1}{i} \bmod q$.

Solution 4   Ong-Schnorr-Shamir Signature

The signature generation of this scheme should consist in computing two elements $x, y \in \mathbf{Z}_n^*$ using the secret key s such that

$$x^2 + ky^2 \equiv x^2 - s^2 y^2 \equiv H(m) \pmod{n}.$$

Applying a classical algebraic identity, we obtain

$$(x + sy)(x - sy) \equiv H(m) \pmod{n}.$$

This equation can easily be solved by introducing two new variables a and b such that $ab = H(m)$, $a = x - sy$ and, $b = x + sy$ (all equations are considered in $\mathbf{Z}_n$). The two last equations allow to provide expressions of x and y which depend on a and b, namely, $x = (a + b)2^{-1}$ and $y = (b - a)(2s)^{-1}$. It remains to solve the relation between a and b in order to express the signature with one degree of freedom. This finally leads to

$$x = (H(m)a^{-1} + a)2^{-1} \quad \text{and} \quad y = (H(m)a^{-1} - a)(2s)^{-1}.$$

Hence, the signature generation consists in picking an invertible element $a \in \mathbf{Z}_n^*$ at random and computing x and y according to the above equation.

More details about this signature scheme are given in [35].

Solution 5   Batch Verification of DSS Signatures

1 The verification complexity of a DSS signature is mainly due to two modular exponentiations which have a complexity of $\mathcal{O}(\ell_p^2 \ell_q)$. Hence, the total complexity is $\mathcal{O}(n\ell_p^2 \ell_q)$.

2 Since all signatures are valid, we know that

$$r_i \equiv g^{\frac{H(m_i)}{s_i} \bmod q} y^{\frac{r_i}{s_i} \bmod q} \pmod{p}$$

holds for any $1 \leq i \leq n$. Hence, by raising the above equation to the power a_i and then multiplying these equations together, we have

$$R \equiv \prod_{i=1}^n r_i^{a_i} \equiv \prod_{i=1}^n g^{\frac{a_i H(m_i)}{s_i} \bmod q} y^{\frac{a_i r_i}{s_i} \bmod q} \equiv g^G y^Y \pmod{p}.$$

3 The computation of the coefficients Y and G can be considered as negligible in comparison to a modular exponentiation. The computation of R requires $\mathcal{O}(n\ell_p^2 \log(B))$ since all exponents are smaller than B and performing the verification requires two modular exponentiations, i.e., of complexity $\mathcal{O}(\ell_p^2 \ell_q)$. Thus, in total the complexity is $\mathcal{O}(\ell_p^2(n \log(B) + \ell_q))$.

4 We assume the existence of a pair $(a_1, a_2) \in \mathcal{A} \times \mathcal{A}$ with $a_1 \neq a_2$ such that

$$\gamma_1^{a_1} \gamma_2^{a_2} \equiv 1 \pmod{p}. \tag{10.1}$$

We will show that this pair is unique. Let $(a_1', a_2') \in \mathcal{A} \times \mathcal{A}$ such that $a_1' \neq a_2'$ and

$$\gamma_1^{a_1'} \gamma_2^{a_2'} \equiv 1 \pmod{p}, \tag{10.2}$$

be another pair. From equations (10.1) and (10.2), we obtain

$$\gamma_1 \equiv \left(\frac{1}{\gamma_2}\right)^{\frac{a_2}{a_1} \bmod q} \pmod{p}$$

$$\gamma_1 \equiv \left(\frac{1}{\gamma_2}\right)^{\frac{a_2'}{a_1'} \bmod q} \pmod{p},$$

which leads to

$$\gamma_2^{a_1' a_2} \equiv \gamma_2^{a_1 a_2'} \pmod{p}.$$

Hence, we have

$$a_1' a_2 \equiv a_1 a_2' \pmod{q}$$

and since $B < \sqrt{q}$, we get $a_1' a_2 = a_1 a_2'$. By the assumptions on the elements a_1, a_1', a_2, a_2', we must have $a_1' = a_1$ and $a_2' = a_2$.

5 If we set $\gamma_1 = \alpha_1/\beta_1 \bmod p$ and $\gamma_2 = \alpha_2/\beta_2 \bmod p$, we notice that the statement we have to prove is equivalent to the one of the previous question, as $\gamma_1 \neq 1$ and $\gamma_2 \neq 1$. Furthermore, these two elements are elements of the subgroup generated by g. The assumptions of the previous question are fulfilled.

6 We first consider the case where exactly one signature is invalid. Without loss of generality, we assume that only (m_1, r_1, s_1) is invalid, which means that

$$r_1 \neq g^{\frac{H(m_1)}{s_1} \bmod q} y^{\frac{r_1}{s_1} \bmod q} \bmod p$$

$$r_2 = g^{\frac{H(m_2)}{s_2} \bmod q} y^{\frac{r_2}{s_2} \bmod q} \bmod p.$$

Raising the first equation to the power a_1 and the second one to the power a_2 and multiplying them together shows that

$$r_1^{a_1} r_2^{a_2} \not\equiv g^{\frac{a_1 H(m_1)}{s_1} + \frac{a_2 H(m_2)}{s_2} \bmod q} y^{\frac{a_1 r_1}{s_1} + \frac{a_2 r_2}{s_2} \bmod q} \pmod{p}$$

for any $(a_1, a_2) \in \mathcal{A} \times \mathcal{A}$. Thus, the batch verification fails with probability 1. Secondly, we assume that the two signatures are invalid, i.e.,

$$r_i \neq g^{\frac{H(m_i)}{s_i} \bmod q} y^{\frac{r_i}{s_i} \bmod q} \bmod p \quad \text{for } i = 1, 2.$$

Applying the result of the previous question to $\alpha_i = r_i$ and

$$\beta_i = g^{\frac{H(m_i)}{s_i} \bmod q} y^{\frac{r_i}{s_i} \bmod q} \bmod p \quad \text{for } i = 1, 2,$$

we know that there exists at most one pair $(a_1, a_2) \in \mathcal{A} \times \mathcal{A}$ with $a_1 \neq a_2$ which passes the batch verification. Finally, since

$$|\{(a_1, a_2) \in \mathcal{A} \times \mathcal{A} \mid a_1 \neq a_2\}| = N^2 - N$$

we can conclude that the probability that the batch verification succeeds is smaller than or equal to

$$\frac{1}{N^2 - N}.$$

7 We consider the parameters given in the hint and we first look for the elements α_1, α_2, β_1, and β_2 lying in the subgroup generated by the element $g = 4$ in $\mathbf{Z}_{11}^*$, satisfying $\alpha_1 \neq \beta_1$, $\alpha_2 \neq \beta_2$, and

$$\alpha_1 \alpha_2^2 \equiv \beta_1 \beta_2^2 \pmod{11}.$$

By looking at the subgroup $\langle g \rangle = \{1, 3, 4, 5, 9\}$, one can choose $\alpha_1 = 4$, $\beta_1 = 3$, $\alpha_2 = 5$ and $\beta_2 = 9$, since $4 \cdot 5^2 \equiv 3 \cdot 9^2 \equiv 1 \pmod{11}$. We set $r_1 = \alpha_1 = 4$, $r_2 = \alpha_2 = 5$. It remains to solve

$$3 = 4^{\frac{h_1}{s_1} \bmod 5} 3^{\frac{4}{s_1} \bmod 5} \bmod 11$$
$$9 = 4^{\frac{h_2}{s_2} \bmod 5} 3^{\frac{5}{s_2} \bmod 5} \bmod 11.$$

Taking the discrete logarithm of the above equation with respect to $g = 4$ leads to the equations

$$4 = \frac{h_1}{s_1} + \frac{16}{s_1} \bmod 5$$
$$3 = \frac{h_2}{s_2} + \frac{20}{s_2} \bmod 5.$$

Choosing $s_1 = 2$, $h_1 = 2$, $s_2 = 1$, $h_2 = 3$ satisfies the above equations. Finally, the triplets $(h_1, r_1, s_1) = (2, 4, 2)$ and $(h_2, r_2, s_2) = (3, 5, 1)$ have the desired properties.

For more details about this topic, we refer to the original article [30].

Solution 6   Ring Signatures

1 For any $x_A \in \mathbf{Z}_{n_A}^*$ and $x_B \in \mathbf{Z}_{n_B}^*$, the adversary can find a preimage of $E_{P_A}(x_A) \oplus E_{P_B}(x_B)$ under the hash function h. In this case, he has found a valid signature for this preimage m, since he obviously passes signature's verification $h(m) = E_{P_A}(x_A) \oplus E_{P_B}(x_B)$.

2 If h is not collision resistant, an adversary can find two messages $m \neq m'$ with the same digest. Noting that in this case, a valid signature for m is also a valid signature for m' leads to the conclusion that h definitely must be collision resistant in order to prevent an adversary to easily forge a signature.

3 The adversary can build a third table T_h by performing a XOR operation between each element that is on the right of the table T_A with $h(m)$. He then looks for a collision between the right values of the pairs of tables T_h and T_B. If we consider the two values $E_{P_A}(w_A)$, $E_{P_B}(w_B)$ involved in such a collision, we have $E_{P_A}(w_A) \oplus h(m) = E_{P_B}(w_B)$, which shows that the tuple (A, B, w_A, w_B) is a valid ring signature.

As mentioned in the textbook [56], the probability that a collision occurs between the two previous tables T_h and T_B is given by the approximation $1 - e^{\theta_h \theta_B}$, where $\theta_h \sqrt{2^{1024}}$ and $\theta_B \sqrt{2^{1024}}$ respectively correspond to the number of entries in table T_h and in table T_B. We see that the probability becomes non-negligible when the size of the tables is about 2^{512}.

4 Without loss of generality, we assume that the signer is the user U_N. The signer picks $N - 1$ values $x_i \in \mathbf{Z}_{n_i}^*$ randomly for $1 \leq i \leq N - 1$ and computes $y_i = E_{P_i}(x_i)$. He then computes

$$x_N = E_{P_N}^{-1}(y_1 \oplus y_2 \oplus \cdots \oplus y_{N-1} \oplus h(m)).$$

As a verification, the verifier has to check the equality

$$E_{P_1}(x_1) \oplus E_{P_2}(x_2) \oplus \cdots \oplus E_{P_N}(x_N) = h(m).$$

For further readings about ring signatures, we suggest the original article of Shamir et al. [44].

Chapter 11

CRYPTOGRAPHIC PROTOCOLS

Exercises

Exercise 1   Breaking the RDSA Identification Scheme

An identification scheme is an interactive protocol in which a prover wants to convince a verifier that he knows some private information. It can be used, for instance, in access control. The original RDSA identification scheme was proposed by Ingrid Biehl, Johannes Buchmann, Safuat Hamdy, and Andreas Meyer in [2]. The security issues about this scheme were raised by Pierre-Alain Fouque and Guillaume Poupard in [18].

Let s and t be some given security parameters (e.g., $s = 1024$ bits and $t = 160$ bits). We assume that the prover and the verifier have set up some public parameters, that the prover (only) has a private key, and that the verifier has the public key of the prover. Those values are set up as follows.

Public Parameters: a large integer n of size s, an element $\gamma \in \mathbf{Z}_n^*$, a prime q of size t

Private Key: an integer $a \in [2, q - 1]$

Public Key: $\alpha = \gamma^a \bmod n$

Following the identification scheme on Figure 11.1, the prover convinces the verifier that he knows the private key without disclosing it.

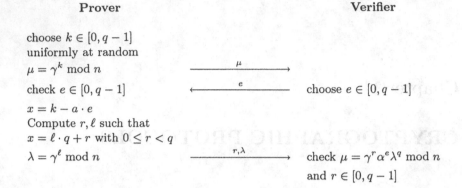

Figure 11.1. The RDSA identification scheme

1 What is the complexity of the generation of the public parameters? What is the complexity of the generation of the private/public key pair? Cite all the algorithms that are needed in both cases.

2 What is the total bit length of the messages exchanged between the prover and the verifier in the worst case?

3 Show that the verification process should work, i.e., show that $\mu = \gamma^r \alpha^e \lambda^q \bmod n$ when the prover and the verifier follow the protocol specifications.

Obviously, no information about the prover's private information should leak, not even to the verifier. We will now see that this scheme is flawed as a *malicious* verifier can recover some of the bits of the private key.

4 A malicious verifier chooses $e = 0$. Compute ℓ, r, λ in this case. Does the malicious verifier recover any information about the secret key in this case?

5 A malicious verifier chooses $e = 1$. Depending on k and a, compute ℓ, r, λ in this case.

6 Deduce from the previous question that the verifier learns one bit of the secret key (with high probability) after a few runs of the protocol.

We denote by $\lfloor x \rceil$ the greatest integer less than or equal to x. We will see that the verifier can recover *several* bits of the private key.

7 Show that $\ell = \lfloor \frac{-a \cdot e}{q} \rfloor + \varepsilon$, where $\varepsilon = 0$ or 1.

8 Deduce from the last question that the size of ℓ is approximately equal to the size of e. Show that the verifier can exploit this to easily recover ℓ from λ when e is short.

9 Show that $\left| a - \frac{-\ell \cdot q}{e} \right| < \frac{2q}{e}$.

10 Denoting δ the size of e, show that the last inequality allows the verifier to recover $\delta - 1$ bits of the private key by selecting a short e.

▷ Solution on page 220

Exercise 2 ⋆A Blind Signature Protocol for a Variant of DSA

An interesting variant of signature schemes is a blind signature protocol. The basic purpose of such a protocol is to enable a sender A to obtain a valid signature σ for a message m from a signer B such that B does not see the value of m nor σ. Later on, if B sees (m, σ), he can verify that σ is genuine. However he is unable to link (m, σ) to a specific instance of the protocol producing (m, σ). A useful scenario of the blind signature protocol is electronic cash application between a customer A and the bank B, where a message m might represent a monetary value A can spend.

A blind signature protocol requires the following components.

- A digital signature mechanism for the signer B. Let $\mathcal{S}_B(m)$ denote the signature generation scheme for B on m, and let $\mathcal{V}(m, \sigma)$ taking value in {valid, invalid} denotes the signature verification output for σ on m.

- A blinding function $\mathcal{F}_A$ and an unblinding function $\mathcal{G}_A$ (both $\mathcal{F}_A$ and $\mathcal{G}_A$ are known only to A), such that the following property holds:

$$\mathcal{S}_B\left(\mathcal{F}_A(m)\right) \to \sigma \Rightarrow \mathcal{V}\left(m, \mathcal{G}_A(\sigma)\right) = \texttt{valid}.$$

Note that the same signature verification scheme is used for the blind signature protocol based on the underlying signature mechanism. Thus B can easily verify the signature afterwards without knowledge of $\mathcal{F}_A$ and $\mathcal{G}_A$.

We first describe a variant of DSA as follows.

Public Parameters: a prime p, a prime factor q of $p - 1$ and an element $g \in \mathbf{Z}_p^*$ of order q

Setup: The signer chooses an element $x \in \mathbf{Z}_q$ uniformly at random and computes $y = g^x \bmod p$.

Secret Key: x

Public Key: y

Signature Generation: Given the message m and the hash function $H : \{0,1\}^* \to \mathbf{Z}_q^*$, the signer chooses an element $k \in \mathbf{Z}_q$ uniformly at random and computes

$$
\begin{aligned}
r &= (g^k \bmod p) \bmod q \\
s &= kH(m) + xr \bmod q
\end{aligned}
$$

The signature for m is the pair (r, s).

Algorithm 33 The blind signature protocol for a variant DSA

Public Parameters and Key Setup:
1: a prime p, a prime factor q of $p - 1$ and an element $g \in \mathbf{Z}_p^*$ of order q
2: B chooses a random $x \in \mathbf{Z}_q$ and computes $y = g^x \bmod p$.

Secret Key: x

Public Key: y

Blind Signature Setup:
3: B chooses a random $k' \in \mathbf{Z}_q$ and computes $R' = g^{k'} \bmod p$.
4: if $R' \bmod q = 0$, B goes back to step 3.
5: B sends R' to A.

Blinding $\mathcal{F}_A$:
6: A chooses random $\alpha, \beta \in \mathbf{Z}_q$ and computes $R = R'^{\alpha} g^{\beta} \bmod p$.
7: if $R \bmod q = 0$, A goes back to step 6.
8: A computes $m' = \alpha H(m) R' R^{-1} \bmod q$ and sends it to B.

Signing:
9: B computes $s' = k'm' + R'x \bmod q$ and sends it to A.

Unblinding $\mathcal{G}_A$:
10: A computes $r = R \bmod q$ and $\boxed{s = \cdots}$ to obtain a genuine signature (r, s) for m by B finally.

---

1 Let ℓ_p and ℓ_q denote the respective bit length of p and q. What is the asymptotic complexity of computing r and s respectively, given $H(m)$?

2 Show how to verify the signature (r, s) on m for the variant of DSA.

3 Read the blind signature protocol (Algorithm 33) based on above variant of DSA. Briefly explain why it is necessary to avoid

$$
R \bmod q = 0
$$

in step 7.

4 Find a computable expression of s for A in Step 10 such that (r, s) is a genuine signature by B, i.e., (r, s) successfully passes the signature verification phase as answered in Question 2.

5 Assuming that $(g^\beta \bmod p) \bmod q$ is uniformly distributed over $\mathbf{Z}_q$, show that m' is uniformly distributed over $\mathbf{Z}_q^*$ for any fixed $R', H(m)$, and nonzero α. Deduce that B receives no information about $H(m)$ with knowledge of R' and m' from the execution of the blind signature protocol.

▷ Solution on page 222

Exercise 3   ⋆Fiat-Shamir Signature I

We study the security of the following Fiat-Shamir signature scheme based on the basic Fiat-Shamir protocol (see the textbook [56]).

Setup: The signer generates two random distinct primes p and q, and computes $n = pq$. He keeps p, q secret. He then selects a random integer $s \in \mathbf{Z}_n^*$ and computes $v = s^{-2} \bmod n$.

Secret Key: s

Public Key: v, n

Signature Generation: Given a message m and the hash function $H : \{0, 1\}^* \to \{0, 1\}$, the signer picks a random $r \in [1, n-1]$ and computes $x = r^2 \bmod n$, $e = H(m \| x)$, $y = rs^e \bmod n$. The signature is the pair (e, y).

Verification: Upon the reception of signature (e, y) with the message m, the verifier computes $w = y^2 v^e \bmod n$, then $e' = H(m \| w)$. He compares e' with e and accepts the signature if $e = e'$, otherwise rejects it.

1 Explain why p and q must be distinct.

2 Prove that the signature verification scheme works.

3 Show that an adversary can forge a valid signature for a given message m in a probabilistic way.

4 Is the above problem fixed by choosing $H : \{0, 1\}^* \to \{0, 1\}^k$ with a fixed larger k?

▷ Solution on page 223

Exercise 4   ⋆Fiat-Shamir Signature II

Consider $H : \{0,1\}^* \rightarrow \{0,1\}^k$ with some fixed positive integer k. Propose a generalized signature scheme of the previous simplified Fiat-Shamir signature scheme and briefly discuss the choice of the parameter k for a high level of security.

Hint: The Fiat-Shamir signature scheme was obtained from the Fiat-Shamir protocol. Proceed similarly from the Feige-Fiat-Shamir protocol. A version of this protocol is described in the textbook [56].

▷ Solution on page 224

Exercise 5   ⋆Authenticated Diffie-Hellman Key Agreement Protocol

Let us consider a public-key Diffie-Hellman key agreement protocol derived from the simple Diffie-Hellman protocol. In this protocol, we have the following public parameters:

- a large prime p

- a large prime factor q of $p-1$

- an element g of order q in $\mathbf{Z}_p^*$

Each user U has a random secret key $X_U \in \mathbf{Z}_q$ uniformly distributed and a public key $Y_U = g^{X_U} \bmod p$. All the users' public keys are stored in an authenticated database (e.g., using a trusted third party), which is publicly readable. We propose the following key agreement protocol between users A and B.

- A generates $a \in \mathbf{Z}_q$ using a pseudorandom number generator, computes $v = g^a \bmod p$, and sends v to B.

- B generates $b \in \mathbf{Z}_q$ using a pseudorandom number generator, computes $w = g^b \bmod p$ and sends w to A.

In the end, A and B share the secret key $K = g^{aX_B + bX_A} \bmod p$.

1 Explain how A can compute K.

2 Assume the pseudorandom number generator of B is biased in the sense that it only generates small numbers (e.g., of length around 40 bits) instead of generating numbers almost uniformly in $\mathbf{Z}_q$. Show how an adversary A^* can impersonate A to set up a key with B. Suggest a countermeasure.

3 Assume that $b = ac$ for some small c. Show that the adversary A^* can impersonate A and set up a key with B. Suggest a countermeasure.

▷ Solution on page 225

Exercise 6 Conference Key Distribution System

We study a synchronous Conference Key Distribution System (CKDS) for $m > 2$ users denoted by $U_0, U_1, \ldots, U_{m-1}$. Those m users are connected in a ring network (see Figure 11.2), such that U_i can only send messages to U_j, where $j = i+1 \bmod m$ for any $i \in \{0, 1, \ldots, m-1\}$. This means that U_i can receive messages from U_j only, where $j = i-1 \bmod m$, for any $i \in \{0, 1, \ldots, m-1\}$.

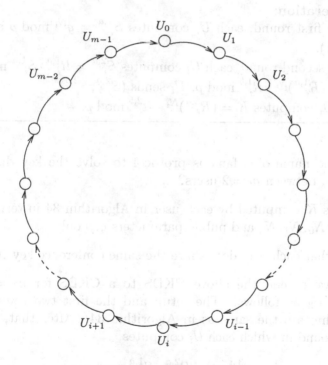

Figure 11.2. The CKDS ring network

The purpose of the CKDS is to derive one common communication key K for all users over authenticated channels, so that they can hold a confidential conference online. K is generated after several synchronized rounds among the users: during the kth round, U_i sends out two messages denoted by $(S_i^{k,a}, S_i^{k,b})$ and receives two messages $(R_i^{k,a}, R_i^{k,b})$.

Thus, according to the message transmission rule, we know that

$$\begin{cases} S_i^{k,a} &= R_j^{k,a} \\ S_i^{k,b} &= R_j^{k,b} \end{cases} \quad \text{where } j = i+1 \bmod m.$$

Let us first examine a CKDS for $m = 3$ users U_0, U_1, U_2. The protocol proceeds in 2 synchronized rounds as shown in Algorithm 34.

Algorithm 34 The key generation algorithm of the CKDS for three users

Public Parameters:
1: a large prime p, a generator g of $\mathbf{Z}_p^*$

Setup:
2: Each U_i chooses a random number $N_i \in \mathbf{Z}_p^*$ and keeps it secret.

Key Generation:
3: At the first round, each U_i computes $S_i^{1,a} = g^{N_i} \bmod p$ and sends $(S_i^{1,a}, 1)$.
4: At the second round, each U_i computes $S_i^{2,a} = R_i^{1,a} \cdot S_i^{1,a} \bmod p$ and $S_i^{2,b} = (R_i^{1,a})^{N_i} \cdot R_i^{1,b} \bmod p$. U_i sends $(S_i^{2,a}, S_i^{2,b})$.
5: Each U_i computes $K = (R_i^{2,a})^{N_i} \cdot R_i^{2,b} \bmod p$.

---

1 Give the name of a famous protocol to solve the key distribution problem between $m = 2$ users?

2 Express K computed by each user in Algorithm 34 in terms of user secrets N_0, N_1, N_2 and public parameters g, p only.

3 Prove that each user does share the same conference key K.

4 Now, we extend the above CKDS to a CKDS for $m = 4$ users $U_0, \ldots, U_3$ as follows. The setup and the first two rounds of the algorithm are the same as in Algorithm 34. After that, we add a third round in which each U_i computes

$$\begin{aligned} S_i^{3,a} &= R_i^{2,a} \cdot S_i^{1,a} \bmod p, \\ S_i^{3,b} &= (R_i^{2,a})^{N_i} \cdot R_i^{2,b} \bmod p, \end{aligned}$$

and sends $(S_i^{3,a}, S_i^{3,b})$. At the end, each U_i computes

$$K = (R_i^{3,a})^{N_i} \cdot R_i^{3,b} \bmod p. \tag{11.1}$$

Prove that K computed by each user in Equation (11.1) is the same.

5 We investigate the security of the above CKDS protocol for $m = 4$. Show that given $S_0^{2,b}, S_0^{3,b}, S_1^{3,b}, S_2^{2,b}$, the adversary (wire-tapper) can reconstruct K without the knowledge of user secrets N_i's.

6 For an arbitrary m-node CKDS communication network where all the channels are assumed to be authenticated (yet insecure), we define the Multi-Tap Resistance (MTR) by

$$\text{MTR} = \frac{\tau - 1}{m},$$

where τ is the minimum number of physical wires the wire-tapper needs to tap in order to recover K. From the previous question derive an upper bound of MTR for the above CKDS with $m = 4$.

7 Generalize the CKDS protocol for arbitrary number $m > 2$ of users $U_0, U_1, \ldots, U_{m-1}$ and justify your proposal. Give a general expression of the value K in terms of user secrets N_i's and public parameters g, p only. What is the exact total number of multiplications over $\mathbf{Z}_p^*$ that each user must compute to obtain K? And what is the exact total number of exponentiations over $\mathbf{Z}_p^*$ that each user must compute to obtain K? Determine an upper bound of the MTR for the above CKDS in terms of m.

▷ Solution on page 226

Solutions

Solution 1   ⋆Breaking the RDSA Identification Scheme

1 First, note that the generation of n, γ, and the secret key a is trivial.
   To generate the public parameters, one needs to generate a random
   prime of size t, which has a complexity of $\mathcal{O}(t^4)$ (this corresponds to
   performing a Miller-Rabin test on t different random numbers). Computing the public key is done via one modular exponentiation. The
   complexity is thus $\mathcal{O}((\log n)^2 \log a)$ which is $\mathcal{O}(s^2 t)$, using a square-
   and-multiply algorithm.

2 The parameters μ and λ are at most of the size of n while the size of
   e and r are at most of the size of q. The total bit length in the worst
   case is thus $2(s + t)$.

3 If both the prover and the verifier follow the protocol specifications
   we have

$$\gamma^r \alpha^e \lambda^q \equiv \gamma^r \alpha^e \gamma^{\ell \cdot q} \equiv \gamma^r \alpha^e \gamma^{x-r} \equiv \alpha^e \gamma^x \equiv \gamma^{a \cdot e} \gamma^{k - a \cdot e} \equiv \gamma^k \pmod{n}.$$

   Thus $\gamma^r \alpha^e \lambda^q \bmod n = \mu$, so that the test performed by the verifier
   should work.

4 If $e = 0$, then $x = k \in [0, q-1]$. Consequently, $\ell = 0$ and $r = k$. As
   $\ell = 0$, we have $\lambda = 1$. All these values are independent of the secret
   key a, so that the verifier does not recover any information about it
   in this case.

5 If $e = 1$, then $x = k - a$.

   - If $k \geq a$, then $x \in [0, q-1]$ and thus $\ell = 0$, $r = k - a$, and $\lambda = 1$.
   - If $k < a$, then $-x \in [0, q-1]$ and thus $\ell = -1$, $r = k - a + q$, and
     $\lambda = \gamma^{-1} \bmod n \neq 1$, which is different from 1 when $\gamma \neq 1$. As γ
     is uniformly distributed in $\mathbf{Z}_n^*$, this is almost always the case.

6 From the previous question, we see that when the verifier chooses
   $e = 1$, then λ is either 1 (when $k \geq a$) or something else (when $k < a$).
   For each new run of the protocol, a new random value is chosen for k.
   Clearly, if the verifier often receives $\lambda = 1$, it means that for several
   random values of k we have $k \geq a$, which only happens if a is "small".
   On the contrary, if the verifier often receives λ's different from 1, then
   a must be "large". As k and a are of the same size, the verifier can

conclude that the most significant bit of a is 0 (if he receives several λ's equal to 1) or 1 (if he receives several λ's different from 1).

7 As ℓ is the quotient of an Euclidean division,

$$\ell = \left\lfloor \frac{x}{q} \right\rfloor \quad \text{and thus} \quad \ell = \left\lfloor \frac{k - a \cdot e}{q} \right\rfloor = \left\lfloor \frac{-a \cdot e}{q} + \frac{k}{q} \right\rfloor.$$

As $0 \leq k/q < 1$, then either $\ell = \lfloor -(a \cdot e)/q \rfloor$ (when k/q is small), or $\ell = \lfloor -(a \cdot e)/q \rfloor + 1$ (when k/q is large enough, i.e., larger than or equal to $\lceil -(a \cdot e)/q \rceil - (-a \cdot e)/q$).

8 From the previous question, we deduce that

$$\log |\ell| \approx \log a + \log e - \log q.$$

As a and q roughly are of the same size, then $\log a \approx \log q$, so that ℓ and e approximately have the same size. Therefore, the verifier can make sure that ℓ will be small by choosing a small e. If he chooses a small enough value (say for example, of length $\delta = 30$ bits), he will be able to recover ℓ from the knowledge of λ and γ by using a simple exhaustive search.

9 We have $\ell \cdot q + r = k - a \cdot e$. Thus,

$$a - \frac{-\ell \cdot q}{e} = \frac{k - r}{e},$$

so that

$$\left| a - \frac{-\ell \cdot q}{e} \right| = \frac{|k - r|}{e} \leq \frac{|k| + |r|}{e} \leq \frac{2q}{e}.$$

10 By choosing a small enough e, the verifier can compute ℓ and thus $u = \frac{-\ell \cdot q}{e}$. From the previous question, we know that the distance between u and the private key a is not too large, namely, it is smaller than $\frac{2q}{e}$. As

$$\log \frac{2q}{e} \approx 1 + \log q - \log e = t - (\delta - 1),$$

and as $\log a \approx t$, it means that the $\delta - 1$ most significant bits of a and $\frac{-\ell \cdot q}{e}$ are the same (as their difference is of length $t - (\delta - 1)$). The verifier can thus recover the $\delta - 1$ most significant bits of the secret key a.

This attack is part of an article [18] of Pierre-Alain Fouque and Guillaume Poupard published at Eurocrypt'03.

Solution 2   ⋆A Blind Signature Protocol for a Variant of DSA

1 Using a square-and-multiply algorithm it takes $\mathcal{O}(\ell_p^2 \cdot \ell_q)$ operations to compute r. For computing s, one needs to perform a simple modular product which has a complexity of $\mathcal{O}(\ell_q^2)$.

2 We check
$$(g^{\frac{s}{H(m)}} y^{-\frac{r}{H(m)}} \bmod p) \bmod q = r.$$

This can be proved as follows:

$$
\begin{aligned}
(g^{\frac{s}{H(m)}} y^{-\frac{r}{H(m)}} \bmod p) \bmod q &= (g^{\frac{s-xr}{H(m)}} \bmod p) \bmod q \\
&= (g^k \bmod p) \bmod q \\
&= r.
\end{aligned}
$$

3 We must have $R \bmod q \neq 0$ as R must be invertible modulo q in step 8.

4 As (r, s) must be a valid DSA signature, it must satisfy relations similar to those satisfied by r and s in the signature generation. Consequently, R must be of the form $g^k \bmod p$, for some integer k. We can deduce from the definition of R that

$$k = k'\alpha + \beta \bmod q.$$

Replacing this value of k in the equation that s must satisfy, we obtain

$$
\begin{aligned}
s &= (k'\alpha + \beta)H(m) + xr \bmod q \\
&= k'\alpha H(m) + \beta H(m) + xr \bmod q.
\end{aligned}
$$

As the verifier does not know k', we must express the previous equation in terms of s' instead. We can show that

$$k'\alpha H(m) = (s'RR'^{-1} - xR) \bmod q = (s'RR'^{-1} - xr) \bmod q,$$

so that we finally obtain

$$s = s'RR'^{-1} + \beta H(m) \bmod q.$$

5 We have

$$m' = \alpha H(m)R'(R'^{-\alpha} \bmod p)(g^{-\beta} \bmod p) \bmod q.$$

For any legal $R', H(m)$, and nonzero α, we know that

$$\alpha H(m) R' (R'^{-\alpha} \bmod p) \bmod q$$

is nonzero. As $(g^\beta \bmod p) \bmod q$ is uniformly distributed over $\mathbf{Z}_q$, we know that $(g^\beta \bmod p) \bmod q$ and $(g^{-\beta} \bmod p) \bmod q$ are actually uniformly distributed over $\mathbf{Z}_q^*$ by the protocol. As multiplying a uniformly distributed group element by another group element results in a uniformly distributed random element, we are done. For the second part of the question, we distinguish two cases:

- if $m' = 0$, we must have $\alpha = 0$ and $H(m)$ is independent of m'.
- if $m' \neq 0$, we know α is invertible. So we can write

$$H(m) = m' \alpha^{-1} R'^{-1} (R'^\alpha \bmod p)(g^\beta \bmod p) \bmod q.$$

Similarly to what we had in the former half of the question, we deduce that $H(m)$ is uniformly distributed over $\mathbf{Z}_q^*$ for every invertible α given R', m'.

Both cases lead to the conclusion that B obtains no information about $H(m)$.

For more details about this blind signature protocol, the interested reader shall refer to [9].

Solution 3   ⋆Fiat-Shamir Signature I

1 If $p = q$, then we can easily recover p from n just by computing the square root of n which is fairly simple. Once an adversary has obtained p, he can forge a signature for any message.

2 For a valid signature (e, y), we have

$$
\begin{aligned}
w &\equiv y^2 v^e \pmod{n} \\
&\equiv (rs^e)^2 v^e \pmod{n} \\
&\equiv r^2 (s^2 v)^e \pmod{n} \\
&\equiv r^2 \pmod{n} \\
&\equiv x \pmod{n}.
\end{aligned}
$$

Thus we conclude that $w = x$ and $e = e'$.

3 Given m, the forger picks a random $r \in [1, n-1]$ and computes $x = r^2 \bmod n$, then checks if $e = H(m\|x)$ is zero or not. If $e = 0$

he just outputs the pair $(0, r)$ as the signature for m. Otherwise, he picks another $r \in [1, n-1]$ and repeats the above procedure. The probability of success for one round computation is $\frac{1}{2}$ assuming that H is an ideal hash function.

4 No! A similar attack works here with the difference that the forger checks if $e = H(m\|x)$ is even or not. The key idea of the attack is that as long as e is even, the forger can compute y without knowledge of the secret key s. For this, the adversary computes $y = r \cdot (v^{-1})^j \bmod p$, where $e = 2j$. Such a signature (e, y) is valid, since

$$ y \equiv rs^e \equiv r \cdot (v^{-1})^j \pmod{p}. $$

Solution 4   ⋆Fiat-Shamir Signature II

Below we present the Feige-Fiat-Shamir signature scheme.

Setup: The signer generates two random distinct primes p, q and computes $n = pq$. He keeps p, q secret. He then selects k distinct random integers $s_1, \ldots, s_k \in \mathbf{Z}_n^*$ and computes $v_j = s_j^{-2} \bmod n$, $1 \leq j \leq k$.

Secret Key: $s_1, \ldots, s_k$

Public Key: $v_1, \ldots, v_k, n$

Signature Generation: Given a message m, the signer picks a random $r \in [1, n-1]$ and computes $x = r^2 \bmod n$, $e = H(m\|x)$ which can be represented by the k-bit string $e_1 e_2 \cdots e_k$ and $y = r \prod_{j=1}^{k} s_j^{e_j} \bmod n$. His signature is the pair (e, y).

Verification: Upon the reception of signature (e, y) with the message m, the verifier computes $w = y^2 \prod_{j=1}^{k} v_j^{e_j} \bmod n$, then $e' = H(m\|w)$. He compares e' with e and accepts the signature if $e = e'$, otherwise rejects it.

The signature verification works, as it can be seen below

$$w \equiv y^2 \prod_{j=1}^{k} v_j^{e_j} \pmod{n}$$

$$\equiv r^2 \prod_{j=1}^{k} s_j^{2e_j} \prod_{j=1}^{k} v_j^{e_j} \pmod{n}$$

$$\equiv r^2 \prod_{j=1}^{k} (s_j^2 v_j)^{e_j} \pmod{n}$$

$$\equiv r^2 \pmod{n}$$

$$\equiv x \pmod{n}.$$

So, $w = x$ and $e = e'$.

About the choice of the parameter k, we can see that as long as the adversary succeeds in finding a lucky r such that $e = 0$ he can compute a valid signature on his own without knowledge of the secret keys. However, the complexity is equivalent to a preimage attack of the hash function, i.e., $\mathcal{O}(2^k)$. Henceforth, k should be very large to thwart such an attack. Typically, it suffices to have $k = 128$.

More details about the Feige-Fiat-Shamir signature scheme are given in [29].

Solution 5 ⋆Authenticated Diffie-Hellman Key Agreement Protocol

1 A can compute K as follows,

$$K = (g^{X_B})^a \cdot (g^b)^{X_A} \bmod p$$
$$= Y_B^a \cdot w^{X_A} \bmod p.$$

2 If user B happens to choose a small b, then the adversary A^* can perform an exhaustive search to find b from the pair (g, w). Once b is found, and as

$$K = Y_B^a (g^{X_A})^b \bmod p = Y_B^a Y_A^b \bmod p,$$

A^* can compute K without needing to know the secret key of A. Obviously, this attack is not feasible provided that the pseudorandom number generator used by B is unpredictable. In practice, B could for example use the ANSI X9.17 standard generator [1] based on 3DES.

3 If $b = ac$ for some small c, then

$$w \equiv g^b \equiv g^{ac} \equiv v^c \pmod{p}.$$

Consequently, the adversary A^* can recover c by an exhaustive search, testing whether $w = v^c \bmod p$ for each guess. Once A^* has recovered c, she can compute $K = Y_B^a Y_A^b \bmod p$. A possible countermeasure is to generate random primes instead of arbitrary numbers (note that the primes have to be large and uniformly distributed). This way b cannot be divisible by a.

Solution 6   Conference Key Distribution System

1 The famous Diffie-Hellman key agreement protocol solves the key distribution problem between $m = 2$ users.

2 From now on, for any $i, j \in \mathbf{Z}_m$, we let $i \ominus j = i - j \bmod m$. According to the protocol, for each U_i, we compute K as follows

$$
\begin{aligned}
K &= (S_{i\ominus 1}^{2,a})^{N_i} \cdot S_{i\ominus 1}^{2,b} \bmod p \\
&= (R_{i\ominus 1}^{1,a} \cdot g^{N_{i\ominus 1}})^{N_i} \cdot (R_{i\ominus 1}^{1,a})^{N_{i\ominus 1}} \bmod p \\
&= (S_{i\ominus 2}^{1,a} \cdot g^{N_{i\ominus 1}})^{N_i} \cdot (S_{i\ominus 2}^{1,a})^{N_{i\ominus 1}} \bmod p \\
&= (g^{N_{i\ominus 2}} \cdot g^{N_{i\ominus 1}})^{N_i} \cdot (g^{N_{i\ominus 2}})^{N_{i\ominus 1}} \bmod p \\
&= g^{N_{i\ominus 2}N_i + N_{i\ominus 1}N_i + N_{i\ominus 2}N_{i\ominus 1}} \bmod p.
\end{aligned}
$$

One can see that $\mathbf{Z}_3 = \{i \ominus 1, i \ominus 2, i \ominus 3\}$ and thus that

$$\{N_{i\ominus 1}, N_{i\ominus 2}, N_{i\ominus 3}\} = \{N_0, N_1, N_2\}$$

holds for any $i \in \mathbf{Z}_3$. Therefore we have

$$K = g^{N_0 N_1 + N_1 N_2 + N_0 N_2} \bmod p. \qquad (11.2)$$

3 From Equation (11.2), we immediately see that the value of K is independent of $i \in \mathbf{Z}_3$. Hence, each user U_i obtains the same conference key K.

4 For any subset $\mathcal{E} = \{e_1, e_2, \ldots, e_\ell\}$ of $\mathbf{Z}_m$ with cardinality $\ell \geq 2$, we define the function

$$f(e_1, e_2, \ldots, e_\ell) = \sum_{j > j', \text{ and } j, j' \in \mathcal{E}} N_j N_{j'}.$$

We shall first prove the following equations

$$S_i^{k,a} = g^{N_i+N_{i\ominus 1}+\cdots+N_{i\ominus(k-1)}} \bmod p \qquad (11.3)$$

$$S_i^{k,b} = g^{f(i,i\ominus 1,\ldots,i\ominus(k-1))} \bmod p \qquad (11.4)$$

for any $i \in \mathbf{Z}_4$ and any $k \in \{2,3,4\}$ by induction. We start by proving Equation (11.3). First with $k = 2$, it is easy to see that $S_i^{2,a} = g^{N_i+N_{i\ominus 1}} \bmod p$ for any $i \in \mathbf{Z}_4$ from the CKDS protocol, which verifies Equation (11.3). Assuming Equation (11.3) holds for $k = \ell$ and for any $i \in \mathbf{Z}_4$, we want to show it holds for $k = \ell+1$ and for any $i \in \mathbf{Z}_4$ as follows. From the protocol, we have

$$S_i^{\ell+1,a} = S_{i\ominus 1}^{\ell,a} \cdot g^{N_i} \bmod p.$$

By induction, we have

$$\begin{aligned}
S_i^{\ell+1,a} &= g^{N_{i\ominus 1}+\cdots+N_{i\ominus\ell}} \cdot g^{N_i} \bmod p \\
&= g^{N_i+N_{i\ominus 1}+\cdots+N_{i\ominus\ell}} \bmod p,
\end{aligned}$$

which completes our proof for Equation (11.3). Next, we would like to prove Equation (11.4). First, with $k = 2$, it is easy to see that $S_i^{2,b} = g^{N_i N_{i\ominus 1}} \bmod p$ for any $i \in \mathbf{Z}_4$ from the CKDS protocol, which verifies Equation (11.4). Assuming that Equation (11.4) holds for $k = \ell$ and any $i \in \mathbf{Z}_4$, we want to show it holds for $k = \ell+1$ as well for any $i \in \mathbf{Z}_4$ as follows. From Equation (11.3), we have

$$\begin{aligned}
S_i^{\ell+1,b} &= (S_{i\ominus 1}^{\ell,a})^{N_i} \cdot S_{i\ominus 1}^{\ell,b} \bmod p \\
&= g^{(N_{i\ominus 1}+\cdots+N_{i\ominus\ell})N_i} \cdot S_{i\ominus 1}^{\ell,b} \bmod p
\end{aligned}$$

By induction, we have

$$\begin{aligned}
S_i^{\ell+1,b} &= g^{(N_{i\ominus 1}+\cdots+N_{i\ominus\ell})N_i} \cdot g^{f(i\ominus 1,\ldots,i\ominus\ell)} \bmod p \\
&= g^{f(i,i\ominus 1,\ldots,i\ominus\ell)} \bmod p,
\end{aligned}$$

which completes our proof for Equation (11.4).

As it is clear that $K = S_i^{k,b}$ with $k = m = 4$, according to Equation (11.4), we immediately have

$$K = g^{f(i,i\ominus 1,\ldots,i\ominus(m-1))} \bmod p.$$

Moreover, we know that

$$\mathbf{Z}_m = \{i, i\ominus 1, \ldots, i\ominus(m-1)\}$$

for any $i \in \mathbf{Z}_m$. Consequently $K = g^{f(0,1,\ldots,m-1)} \bmod p$, which is independent of i. This completes our proof.

5 Given $S_0^{2,b}, S_0^{3,b}, S_1^{3,b}, S_2^{2,b}$, the adversary computes

$$\frac{S_0^{3,b} S_1^{3,b} S_2^{2,b}}{S_0^{2,b}} \bmod p,$$

which equals

$$\frac{g^{f(0,3,2)} \cdot g^{f(1,0,3)} \cdot g^{N_2 N_1}}{g^{N_0 N_3}} \bmod p$$

$$= \frac{g^{N_0 N_3 + N_0 N_2 + N_3 N_2} \cdot g^{N_1 N_0 + N_1 N_3 + N_0 N_3} \cdot g^{N_2 N_1}}{g^{N_0 N_3}} \bmod p$$

according to Equation (11.4). This quantity is obviously equal to $g^{f(0,1,2,3)} \bmod p = K$.

6 From the previous question, we see that $\tau \leq 3$ for the above CKDS with $m = 4$ because the adversary just needs to tap in the three wires connecting the user pairs $(U_0, U_1), (U_1, U_2)$ and (U_2, U_3) in order to find K. Therefore, by definition, we have

$$\mathrm{MTR} \leq \frac{3-1}{4} = \frac{1}{2}.$$

7 Algorithm 35 shows the generalized CKDS protocol for arbitrary number $m > 2$ of users $U_0, U_1, \ldots, U_{m-1}$. And the conference key $K = g^{f(0,1,\ldots,m-1)} \bmod p$. The proof follows exactly the same as in Question 4.

From Algorithm 35, we see that for the first round, computing $S_i^{1,a}$ takes one exponentiation for each user U_i. For each subsequent round $k \in \{2, \ldots, m-1\}$, computing $S_i^{k,a}$ takes one multiplication, computing $S_i^{k,b}$ takes one multiplication and one exponentiation for each user U_i. After $(m-1)$ rounds, computing K takes one multiplication and one exponentiation for each user U_i. Therefore, in total, each user computes m exponentiations and $2(m-2) + 1 = 2m - 3$ multiplications over $\mathbf{Z}_p^*$.

Regarding MTR for any $m > 2$, as long as $S_{i\ominus 1}^{m-2,b}$, $S_{i\ominus 1}^{m-1,b}$, $S_i^{m-1,b}$, $S_{i\ominus(m-1)}^{2,b}$ for some $i \in \mathbf{Z}_m$ are known, the adversary can always compute K by

$$\frac{S_{i\ominus 1}^{m-1,b} \cdot S_i^{m-1,b} \cdot S_{i\ominus(m-1)}^{2,b}}{S_{i\ominus 1}^{m-2,b}} \bmod p. \tag{11.5}$$

Algorithm 35 The key generation algorithm of the CKDS for m users

Public Parameters:

1: a large prime p, a generator g of $\mathbf{Z}_p^*$

Setup:

2: Each U_i chooses a random number $N_i \in \mathbf{Z}_p^*$ and keeps it secret.

Key Generation:

3: At the first round, each U_i computes $S_i^{1,a} = g^{N_i} \bmod p$ and sends $(S_i^{1,a}, 1)$.

4: **for** each round $k = 2, \ldots, m-1$ **do**

5:     Each U_i computes $S_i^{k,a} = R_i^{k-1,a} \cdot S_i^{1,a} \bmod p$ and $S_i^{k,b} = (R_i^{k-1,a})^{N_i} \cdot R_i^{k-1,b} \bmod p$. U_i sends $(S_i^{k,a}, S_i^{k,b})$.

6: **end for**

7: U_i computes $K = (R_i^{m-1,a})^{N_i} \cdot R_i^{m-1,b} \bmod p$.

For the proof, we would like to show that Equation (11.5) is equivalent to $S_i^{m,b} = K$. As

$$S_i^{m,b} = (S_{i\ominus 1}^{m-1,a})^{N_i} \cdot S_{i\ominus 1}^{m-1,b} \bmod p,$$

it suffices to show that

$$\frac{S_i^{m-1,b} \cdot S_{i\ominus(m-1)}^{2,b}}{S_{i\ominus 1}^{m-2,b}} \equiv (S_{i\ominus 1}^{m-1,a})^{N_i} \pmod{p}$$

to complete the proof. To prove this, we use Equation (11.4) to check the following

$$\frac{S_i^{m-1,b} \cdot S_{i\ominus(m-1)}^{2,b}}{S_{i\ominus 1}^{m-2,b}} \bmod p = \frac{g^{f(i,i\ominus 1,\ldots,i\ominus(m-2))}}{g^{f(i\ominus 1,\ldots,i\ominus(m-2))}} \cdot g^{N_{i\ominus(m-1)}N_i} \bmod p$$

$$= g^{N_i(N_{i\ominus 1}+\cdots+N_{i\ominus(m-1)})} \bmod p$$

which equals $(S_{i\ominus 1}^{m-1,a})^{N_i} \bmod p$ by Equation (11.3). As a matter of fact, Question 5 is the special case $i = 1, m = 4$. Thus, we conclude that the minimum number of physical wires for the adversary to tap in is less than or equal to 3 in order to find K. So, MTR $\leq \frac{2}{m}$, which goes towards 0, when m goes to infinity. In other words, the CKDS protocol is considered highly insecure when the user number m is large.

For more interesting studies on the above CKDS protocol, we refer to [21].

Chapter 12

FROM CRYPTOGRAPHY TO COMMUNICATION SECURITY

Exercises

Exercise 1   A Hybrid Cryptosystem Using RSA and DES

The boss of a small company wants to secure all digital exchanges among the computers of the employees. As he is stingy, he does not want to hire a cryptographer and decides to set up a complete system by himself (he borrowed a textbook in the library). More precisely, he wants to use RSA and DES in order to build a hybrid cryptosystem. Such a scheme assumes that each employee of the company has a private key and that the associated public key is known to all the other employees. Figure 12.1 illustrates an example of the setup of a secure communication between Alice and Bob (two employees of the company). The principle is first, to establish a DES secret key (the *session* key) to be used in a session, second, to encrypt every message of the session with this session key. We denote by (n_A, e_A) and (n_B, e_B) the RSA public keys of Alice and Bob respectively, and by d_A and d_B the corresponding private keys. The session key will simply be denoted k. As the boss of the company wants to achieve a high level of security, he decides to use 2048-bit RSA moduli.

1   What are the sizes of the two factors of an RSA modulus in this company? Explain why Bob wants to choose a *small* public exponent e_B.

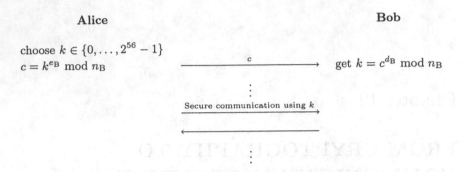

choose $k \in \{0, \ldots, 2^{56} - 1\}$

$c = k^{e_B} \bmod n_B$ $\xrightarrow{\hspace{2cm} c \hspace{2cm}}$ get $k = c^{d_B} \bmod n_B$

Secure communication using k

Figure 12.1. Alice and Bob using the hybrid cryptosystem to secure their communications

2 Bob chooses $e_B = 3$. Does this scheme provide good security in this case? Why?
Hint: Look at the size of k^{e_B}.

Bob now chooses $e_B = 2^{16} + 1$. Suppose that Eve (another employee of the company) can eavesdrop the communication and thus learn the value of c.

3 Give a brute force algorithm that would (in principle) allow Eve to recover k. What is its complexity? Can it display any wrong key (i.e., a key different from k)?

Suppose now that the DES key k chosen by Alice (considered as an integer of 56 bits) can be written as $k = k_1 \cdot k_2$ where k_1 and k_2 are both integers of 28 bits.

4 Eve decides to store in a table $T[\cdot]$ the value of $T[k_1] = k_1^{e_B} \bmod n_B$ for every possible value of k_1. Explain how she can mount a kind of meet-in-the-middle attack (using this table) in order to recover k.
Hint: Express $k_1^{e_B} \bmod n_B$ in terms of c, k_2, e_B, and n_B and exploit this relation.

5 What is the number of modular exponentiations needed to compute the table? What is the size of the table? Once the table is computed, how many modular exponentiations are required to recover the key?

In order to reduce the memory requirement, Eve decides to use a cryptographic hash function $h : \{0,1\}^* \rightarrow \{0,1\}^N$. Consequently, instead of storing the value of $k_1^{e_B} \bmod n_B$, she now stores $h(k_1^{e_B} \bmod n_B)$.

6 What is the size of this new table if the hash function that Eve decides to use is MD5? How many collision(s) should she expect?

In order to thwart the attack, the boss (who is a real geek) suggests to only use prime numbers for the DES keys, so that it is not possible to find two number to write k as $k_1 \cdot k_2$ (where k_1 and k_2 are 28 bits long).

7 Compute the approximate number of DES keys that satisfy this condition. What are the time and space complexities of a typical time-memory tradeoff against this scheme?

8 Obviously, the scheme is not very well designed. What could be done in order to obtain a better scheme?

▷ Solution on page 240

Exercise 2   SSL/TLS Cryptography

The Paranoid Client

We consider a paranoid client willing to connect to a TLS server. For some reasons, the client prefers to avoid cryptographic standards from the US Government and would like to rely on symmetric keys of at least 128 bits for his very secret transaction.

1 Select the only two cipher suites from the list below which satisfy the security policy of the client. Notice that one of the two requires to authenticate a public key. Identify which one.

```
TLS_NULL_WITH_NULL_NULL
TLS_RSA_WITH_NULL_MD5
TLS_RSA_WITH_NULL_SHA
TLS_RSA_EXPORT_WITH_RC4_40_MD5
TLS_RSA_WITH_RC4_128_MD5
TLS_RSA_WITH_RC4_128_SHA
TLS_RSA_EXPORT_WITH_RC2_CBC_40_MD5
TLS_RSA_WITH_IDEA_CBC_SHA
TLS_RSA_EXPORT_WITH_DES40_CBC_SHA
TLS_RSA_WITH_DES_CBC_SHA
TLS_RSA_WITH_3DES_EDE_CBC_SHA
TLS_DH_DSS_EXPORT_WITH_DES40_CBC_SHA
TLS_DH_DSS_WITH_DES_CBC_SHA
TLS_DH_DSS_WITH_3DES_EDE_CBC_SHA
TLS_DH_RSA_EXPORT_WITH_DES40_CBC_SHA
TLS_DH_RSA_WITH_DES_CBC_SHA
TLS_DH_RSA_WITH_3DES_EDE_CBC_SHA
TLS_DHE_DSS_EXPORT_WITH_DES40_CBC_SHA
TLS_DHE_DSS_WITH_DES_CBC_SHA
TLS_DHE_DSS_WITH_3DES_EDE_CBC_SHA
TLS_DHE_RSA_EXPORT_WITH_DES40_CBC_SHA
TLS_DHE_RSA_WITH_DES_CBC_SHA
TLS_DHE_RSA_WITH_3DES_EDE_CBC_SHA
TLS_DH_anon_EXPORT_WITH_RC4_40_MD5
TLS_DH_anon_WITH_RC4_128_MD5
TLS_DH_anon_EXPORT_WITH_DES40_CBC_SHA
TLS_DH_anon_WITH_DES_CBC_SHA
TLS_DH_anon_WITH_3DES_EDE_CBC_SHA
TLS_RSA_WITH_AES_128_CBC_SHA
TLS_DH_DSS_WITH_AES_128_CBC_SHA
```

```
TLS_DH_RSA_WITH_AES_128_CBC_SHA
TLS_DHE_DSS_WITH_AES_128_CBC_SHA
TLS_DHE_RSA_WITH_AES_128_CBC_SHA
TLS_DH_anon_WITH_AES_128_CBC_SHA
TLS_RSA_WITH_AES_256_CBC_SHA
TLS_DH_DSS_WITH_AES_256_CBC_SHA
TLS_DH_RSA_WITH_AES_256_CBC_SHA
TLS_DHE_DSS_WITH_AES_256_CBC_SHA
TLS_DHE_RSA_WITH_AES_256_CBC_SHA
TLS_DH_anon_WITH_AES_256_CBC_SHA
```

2 We consider the cipher suite which does not require public key authentication. Which kind of attack can threat the transaction? Recall the two related attacks. How do we make sure that the used subgroup has no proper subgroup? Show that we can use it in order to avoid one of the two attacks. Assuming that the client and the server can exchange messages over a secure channel with low bandwidth, propose a solution to avoid the other attack.

3 We consider the other cipher suite. We assume that an X.509 certificate is transmitted from the server to the client, but that the certificate authority is not known from the client. What happens? What is the typical reaction of the user?

4 Finally, how would you compare the security of the two cipher suites? Justify your answer.

A Specific Cipher Suite

We consider the TLS_DHE_RSA_WITH_AES_256_CBC_SHA cipher suite.

5 Recall the Merkle-Damgård construction and the HMAC construction.

6 Show that

- the total length of the 6 secrets obtained in the key derivation in SSL/TLS is 1088 bits,

- the length of the label "key expansion" is 104 bits.

7 Knowing that

- the length of the master_secret is 48 bytes,

- the length of nonce$_C$ and of nonce$_S$ is 80 bits,

study the PRF construction in order to determine the number of SHA-1 *compressions* that are performed to derive the 6 secrets from the master_secret and the two nonces.

8 We assume that all generated keys are erased when they are no longer used. We further assume that some information agency quietly records all communications. If the RSA secret key of the server leaks a long time after the transaction, can the agency decrypt the communications? How is this property called? Would we obtain the same with the authentication scheme RSA instead of DHE_RSA?

▷ Solution on page 241

Exercise 3   Secure Shell (SSH)

The SSH software enables a secure `telnet` session between two hosts. A simplified description of the protocol is given in Figure 12.2.

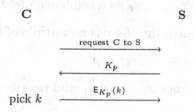

Figure 12.2. A simplified representation of the SSH protocol

- Upon a request from the client, the server sends his public key K_p in clear. The client stores it in his memory (if already stored, the client compares it with the stored one and warns the user if it has changed).

- The client picks a session key k and sends it to the server in an encrypted way.

- The server decrypts the session key k. The client and the server can now communicate with a common secret key k with symmetric encryption.

1 Why do we want to secure the session with symmetric encryption instead of asymmetric encryption?

2 Assuming that all the messages in the protocol given in Figure 12.2 are authenticated, explain why the subsequent connections are confidential and authenticated.

3 If the first connection is not authenticated, explain that an active adversary can impersonate the server.

4 Why does the client need to warn the user when the public key has changed?

5 Why is SSH useful?

▷ Solution on page 244

Exercise 4 Attack against RC5-CBC-PAD

RC5-CBC-PAD is specified in the informative Internet document RFC 2040. It describes how to pad digital messages (represented as a sequence of bytes) in order to be encrypted via block cipher RC5 in CBC mode. Here is how it works.

- Take the message $x_1, \ldots, x_\ell$ as a sequence of ℓ bytes.

- Take an integer p such that $\ell + p$ is a multiple of 8 and that $1 \leq p \leq 8$.

- Let $x_i = p$ for $i = \ell + 1, \ldots, \ell + p$.

- Take the byte sequence $x_1, \ldots, x_{\ell+p}$ and rewrite it as a *block* sequence $B_1, \ldots, B_{\frac{\ell+p}{8}}$.

- Encrypt the block sequence via RC5 in CBC mode and obtain the encrypted message $C_1, \ldots, C_{\frac{\ell+p}{8}}$.

1 Show that p is essentially unique by expressing its value in a mathematical formula.

2 Explain how the C_i's are computed.

3 We assume that the receiver of the encrypted message first decrypts in CBC mode then checks if the padding is correct and finally extracts the cleartext. Detail how all this is performed.

4 We assume we have access to an oracle $\mathcal{O}$ which, given a ciphertext $y = (C_1, \ldots, C_n)$, answers 1 if the padding check is correct after the RC5-CBC decryption or 0 otherwise. By using calls to the oracle $\mathcal{O}$, show that we can compute $\text{RC5}^{-1}(C)$ given a block C.
   Hint: Submit ciphertexts with the form (R, C) for a carefully chosen block R.

5 By using the previous question show how to decrypt any message by having access to $\mathcal{O}$ only.

6 Consider the following proposal to fix the scheme: we encrypt twice with RC5 in CBC mode, namely, we add an extra step in the previous

scheme by re-encrypting $C_1, \ldots, C_{\frac{\ell+p}{8}}$ in CBC mode and obtaining $C'_1, \ldots, C'_{\frac{\ell+p}{8}}$. Show that a similar attack works here: we can still decrypt any message by having an oracle which says whether the decrypted message is correctly padded or not.

▷ Solution on page 245

Exercise 5   Wired Equivalent Privacy (WEP)

In this exercise, we study some real security flaws in the Wired Equivalent Privacy (WEP) protocol used in 802.11 networks to protect the data at the link-layer during wireless transmission. WEP relies on a 40-bit secret key K shared between two communicating parties to protect the data of each transmitted frame. In this exercise, we assume that K is a permanent key which never changes its value. When the user A wants to send a frame of data to B, he proceeds in the following 3 steps

- CRC encoding: Given an n-bit message M (n is a constant), A computes the 32-bit parity check $L(M)$, where L is a linear function that does not depend on K (Note that the linear property of the function L satisfies $L(X \oplus Y) = L(X) \oplus L(Y)$ for any X, Y). The plaintext is $(n + 32)$-bit $P = M \| L(M)$.

- Encryption: A encrypts P with the stream cipher RC4 using the secret key K and a 24-bit initial vector IV assigned to each frame. The ciphertext is $C = P \oplus \mathsf{RC4}(\mathrm{IV}, K)$.

- Transmission: A sends (IV, C) in clear to B over the radio link.

1 Some marketing media advertise that WEP encryption enforces a total of $40 + 24 = 64$ bits security strength. What do you think about this statement? Justify your answer.

2 Explain how the receiver B uses K to extract the original message M upon receipt of (IV, C).

3 In some poor implementations, the 24-bit IV is assigned at random to each frame. Show that it leads to a serious security problem, when one user sends or receives a large amount of data. Propose a better solution.

4 Now we examine another security issue of WEP. Assume that an adversary sitting in-the-middle has intercepted one frame of traffic data (IV, C) from A destined for B. Show that the adversary, who

does not know K and does not bother to find K, can *easily* compute a valid C' ($C' \neq C$) such that he can send the modified data (IV, C') to B without fear of detection. How many different choices of such C' does he have? Which property of cryptography is violated here?

▷ Solution on page 246

Exercise 6   Forging X.509 Certificates

We consider X.509 certificates signed by the md5WithRSAEncryption. We want to submit an RSA public key (N_1, e_1) to the certificate authority for certification such that we can infer a fake certificate for another RSA public key (N_2, e_2). RSA moduli are assumed to be 2048-bit long. We also assume that $e_1 = e_2 = 65537$ and that all fields except the moduli parts in both certificates are identical.

We assume that we have filled all fields of the X.509 form, except the RSA modulus part (and the signature to be appended by the certificate authority). We assume that the length of the form (represented as a string) from the beginning of the form to the beginning of the modulus field is a multiple of 512 bits.

Preliminaries

1 Recall the Merkle-Damgård scheme for the MD5 hash function.

2 We denote by MD5′ the hash function obtained from MD5 by removing the padding scheme and replacing the standard initial vector IV by an arbitrary 128-bit string IV′. Show that there exists a vector IV′ such that, for any N_1 and N_2 with $\text{MD5}'(N_1) = \text{MD5}'(N_2)$, the strings to be signed in both certificates produce a collision for the standard MD5 hash function.

3 Briefly recall how strings are signed using md5WithRSAEncryption.

4 With the above IV′ and MD5′, deduce that if $\text{MD5}'(N_1) = \text{MD5}'(N_2)$, a valid signature for the certificate with N_1 is also a valid signature for the certificate with N_2.

Finding collisions on MD5′

We assume that we already find two different 1024-bit blocks b_1 and b_2 such that $\text{MD5}'(b_1) = \text{MD5}'(b_2)$ (we actually can, very efficiently! cf. [58]).

5 Show that for any 1024-bit string b, we have

$$\text{MD5}'(b_1 \| b) = \text{MD5}'(b_2 \| b).$$

Constructing N_1 and N_2

By using the previous notations, it remains to find b such that $N_1 = b_1 \| b$ and $N_2 = b_2 \| b$ are valid RSA moduli for which we know the factorization.

6 Recall what it a valid RSA modulus.

7 Let p_1 and p_2 be two different arbitrary 512-bit prime numbers. Using the Chinese Remainder Theorem, show that we can compute an integer b_0 between 0 and $p_1 p_2$ such that p_1 divides $b_1 2^{1024} + b_0$, and p_2 divides $b_2 2^{1024} + b_0$.

8 By taking $b = b_0 + k p_1 p_2$ for $k = 0, 1, 2, \ldots$, (heuristically) show that we are likely to find k such that $(b_1 2^{1024} + b)/p_1$ and $(b_2 2^{1024} + b)/p_2$ are both primes. Conclude.

Discussions

9 To what extent is the above attack devastating?

10 We now assume that given two vectors IV' and IV'' defining MD5' and MD5'' we can find two 1024-bit blocks b_1 and b_2 such that $MD5'(b_1) = MD5''(b_2)$. Can we now derive a more dangerous attack?

11 We now assume that given a vector IV' defining MD5' and a 1024-bit block b_1 we can find another 1024-bit block b_2 such that $MD5'(b_1) = MD5'(b_2)$. Can we now derive an even more dangerous attack?

▷ Solution on page 247

Solutions

Solution 1   A Hybrid Cryptosystem Using RSA and DES

1 The prime factors of a 2048-bit RSA modulus are both 1024 bits long. Encrypting with Bob's public key is a modular exponentiation that has a complexity of $\mathcal{O}((\log n_B)^2 \log e_B)$. Using a small public exponent e_B (i.e., much smaller that n_B) such as 3 or $2^{16}+1$ (which is a prime number) allows to reduce the complexity to $\mathcal{O}((\log n_B)^2)$.

2 The size of k^{e_B} is given by

$$\log(k^{e_B}) = e_B \log k \approx 3 \times 56 \ll \log n_B,$$

as n_B is a 2048-bit modulus. Therefore

$$c = k^{e_B} \bmod n_B = k^{e_B},$$

as $k^{e_B} < n_B$. This implies that computing the e_B-root of c allows to recover k. In other words, the log is not discrete anymore, which makes it easy to compute.

3 The exhaustive key search made in Algorithm 36 allows to recover the key. Its worst case complexity is 2^{56} modular exponentiations,

---

Algorithm 36 Exhaustive key search against the hybrid cryptosystem

Input: the RSA public key (n_B, e_B) of Bob and the ciphertext c
Output: the key k
Processing:
1: **for** $\widetilde{k} = 0, \ldots, 2^{56} - 1$ **do**
2:      $\widetilde{c} \leftarrow \widetilde{k}^{e_B} \bmod n_B$
3:      **if** $\widetilde{c} = c$ **then**
4:          output $\widetilde{k}$ and exit
5:      **end if**
6: **end for**

---

its average complexity is 2^{55} modular exponentiations. It does not display any wrong key. Indeed, because of the bijectivity nature of RSA, k is the only number (smaller than n_B) such that $c = k^{e_B} \bmod n_B$.

4 We have

$$c \equiv k^{e_B} \equiv k_1^{e_B} \cdot k_2^{e_B} \pmod{n_B}$$

so that
$$c \cdot k_2^{-e_B} \bmod n_B = k_1^{e_B} \bmod n_B.$$

The meet-in-middle attack then uses the table $T[\cdot]$ of all possible $k_1^{e_B} \bmod n_B$ and, for all possible k_2, checks if $c \cdot k_2^{-e_B} \bmod n_B$ is in the table. If such a value exists, the candidate $k_1 \cdot k_2$ is the correct key.

5 There are 2^{28} different values of k_1 and thus, 2^{28} modular exponentiations are needed to compute table $T[\cdot]$. A table entry is at most of the size of n_B, which is 2048 bits long. The table would thus require $2^{28} \cdot 2^{11} \cdot 2^{-3} = 64\text{GB}$ in memory. Once the table is computed, the algorithm loops on all possible values of k_2 and thus performs 2^{28} supplementary modular exponentiations.

6 If MD5 can be used to reduce each table entry from 2048 bits down to 128 bits. The size of the table is now equal to $2^{28} \cdot 2^7 \cdot 2^{-3} = 4\text{GB}$. By the Birthday Paradox, $2^{128/2} = 2^{64}$ different inputs of MD5 are needed in order to obtain a collision with a good probability. As there only are 2^{28} different values hashed in our case, no collision is expected. Consequently, it may be a good idea to further reduce the hash size in order further decrease the size of table.

7 The number of DES keys satisfy the condition is the number of primes between 2^{55} and 2^{56} (which is well approximated by the number of primes smaller than 2^{56}), and is given by $2^{56}/\log 2^{56} \approx 2^{51}$. A typical time-memory tradeoff against a 2^{51} bits key would approximately have a $2^{2 \times 51/3} = 2^{28}$ time and memory complexity.

8 The trouble comes from the fact that plain RSA is used, and this is usually not a good idea. A solution is to pad the input prior the encryption. For example, one should use RSA-OAEP instead.

Solution 2 SSL/TLS Cryptography

1 The only two ciphers that satisfy the security policy of the client are TLS_RSA_WITH_RC4_128_MD5 and TLS_DH_anon_WITH_RC4_128_MD5. The suite that requires a public key authentication is the one using RSA, namely TLS_RSA_WITH_RC4_128_MD5.

2 We consider the TLS_DH_anon_WITH_RC4_128_MD5 cipher suite. The Diffie-Hellman protocol faces two *man-in-the-middle* attacks:

- If the messages between the client and the server are not authenticated, an active adversary can sit in the middle of the protocol and impersonate both the client and the server. At the end, the adversary shares two different keys, one with the client, the other with the server. Both honest parties believe they share a common secret key, which is not the case. Afterwards, the adversary carries on with an active attack.

- In a more subtle attack, both the client and the server share the same key, which is known to the adversary. This attack can be carried on if the order of the group (from which the Diffie-Hellman parameters are chosen) can be written as bw, where b is smooth (i.e., all its prime factors are smaller than a given small bound).

In order to avoid the second attack, it is sufficient to choose a generator that generates a group of prime order, and to check that received Diffie-Hellman public keys are different from 1 (and 0 of course). If the two parties share a secure channel with low bandwidth, the first attack can be avoided by authenticating the secret key obtained at the end of the protocol. For example the client could hash the secret key and transmit the hash value to the server through the secure channel. The server should then check that the value corresponds to the hashed value of its own secret key.

3 We consider TLS_RSA_WITH_RC4_128_MD5. Commonly, if the certificate authority is not known to the client browser, some window will let it know to the user, who can then chose to reject the certificate (in which case, the transaction is stopped), or accept it (either once or forever). Usually, the client will simply accept the certificate, regardless of all the security issues.

4 Provided that the authority certification is known to the browser of the client, TLS_RSA_WITH_RC4_128_MD5 is the best alternative. Indeed, an anonymous Diffie-Hellman is clearly exposed to a basic man-in-the-middle attack. Nevertheless, if as in the previous question, the RSA public key cannot be clearly authenticated, both suites provides the same (weak) security. The security provided by the TLS_RSA_WITH_RC4_128_MD5 cipher suite may be overestimated, which can be dangerous.

5 The Merkle-Damgård construction is represented on Figure 12.3. It consists of the iteration of a *compression* function f which takes a $(\ell+n)$-bit string as an input and returns a n-bit string as an output. Before it is hashed, the message must be padded. We refer to the textbook [56] for further details.

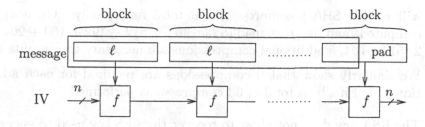

Figure 12.3. The Merkle-Damgård Construction

HMAC builds a MAC using a hash function H as a black-box. Basically, the MAC of a message m under the key K is given by

$$H(K \oplus \mathtt{opad} \| H(K \oplus \mathtt{ipad}) \| m),$$

where $\mathtt{opad}$ and $\mathtt{ipad}$ are two fixed bitstrings. We refer to the textbook [56] for further details on the HMAC construction.

6 Both AES encryption keys are 256 bits long, the IV's are of AES block size, that is 128 bits. That makes a total of 768 bits. Finally the authentication key used in HMAC has the size of the hash function output, that is 160 bits. The total length of the 6 secrets is thus 1088 bits. As each character of the string "key expansion" is encoded on 8 bits, the total length of the string is 104 bits.

7 Let $\mathtt{master\_secret} = S1 \| S2$, where $S1$ and $S2$ have a length of 24 bytes. Let $\alpha = $ "key expansion"$\| \mathtt{nonce}_C \| \mathtt{nonce}_S$. The length of α is thus 264 bits. We must compute

$$\mathtt{key\_block} = \mathrm{PRF}(\mathtt{master\_secret}, \alpha)$$

where $\mathtt{key\_block}$ is of length 1088 bits, and where

$$\mathrm{PRF}(\mathtt{master\_secret}, \alpha) = \mathrm{P\_MD5}(S1, \alpha) \oplus \mathrm{P\_SHA1}(S2, \alpha).$$

By definition

$$\mathrm{P\_SHA1}(S2, \alpha) = r_1, r_2, r_3, \ldots$$

As we need an output of at least 1088 bits, we must generate r_1 up to r_7, as each one is 160 bits long.

We now compute the number of compressions performed in order to compute r_1. We have

$$r_1 = \mathrm{HMAC}_{\mathsf{SHA\text{-}1}}(S2, a_1, \alpha) \quad \text{with} \quad a_1 = \mathrm{HMAC}_{\mathsf{SHA\text{-}1}}(S2, \alpha).$$

As $(K \oplus \mathtt{ipad} \| S2 \| \alpha)$ is $512 + 192 + 264 = 512 + 456$ bits long,

$$\mathrm{HMAC}_{\mathsf{SHA\text{-}1}}(S2, \alpha) = \mathsf{SHA\text{-}1}(K \oplus \mathtt{opad} \| \mathsf{SHA\text{-}1}(K \oplus \mathtt{ipad} \| S2 \| \alpha))$$

will need 4 SHA-1 compressions in total for a_1 only. Once a_1 is computed, and as $(K \oplus \mathrm{ipad}\|S2\|a_1\|\alpha)$ is $512 + 192 + 160 + 264 = 2 \cdot 512 + 104$, 5 additional compressions are necessary to compute r_1.

We similarly show that 9 compressions are required for each additional r_i. Finally, a total of 63 compressions performed.

8 The RSA key does not allow to recover the AES key used to encrypt the communications, so that the agency cannot decrypt the communications. This property is called *forward secrecy*. If we replace DHE_RSA by RSA, the property does not hold because if the agency finds the RSA secret key, it can derive the pre_master_secret and thus break the whole scheme.

Solution 3   Secure Shell (SSH)

1 Symmetric encryption is faster than asymmetric encryption. Here, the latter is only used for exchanging symmetric keys.

2 If the first connection is authenticated, the client is ensured to receive the server's public key. Then, this allows the client and the server to agree on a symmetric key only known to themselves (we assume that the public key cryptosystem is secure). In the subsequent connections, we note that breaking the confidentiality corresponds to breaking the symmetric encryption scheme. We also notice that impersonating one of the players requires the ability of producing encrypted meaningful messages. Thus, assuming that encryption is secure and all encrypted messages are meaningful, all subsequent connections are also secure.

3 An active adversary can impersonate the server and send his own public key. Then the client will communicate with the adversary who can have simultaneous communications with the server. Therefore the adversary can play with both the client and the server by forwarding all messages in decryption-reencryption. This is a man-in-the-middle attack.

4 If the key is changed and the user is not aware of it, then this key may not be authenticated. Therefore the man-in-the-middle can just claim that the key has changed and attack the scheme as in the previous question. If the user is warned that the key has changed, he can decide to accept the new key or not (in most cases, he will accept it, so the previous attack is applicable anyway).

5 Despite the previous attack, SSH is better than nothing. When used by mature users, it provides good protection provided that the first connection is authenticated. When used by novice users, it provides protection against passive adversaries.

Solution 4   Attack against RC5-CBC-PAD

1 We have $p = 8 - (\ell \bmod 8)$.

2 Let $k = \frac{\ell + p}{8}$ (note that k is an integer from the previous question). For the block sequence of messages $B_1, B_2, \ldots, B_k$, we compute the ciphertexts $C_1, C_2, \ldots, C_k$ this way,

$$
\begin{aligned}
C_1 &= \text{RC5}(B_1 \oplus \text{IV}), \\
C_2 &= \text{RC5}(B_2 \oplus C_1), \\
&\ \vdots \qquad\quad \vdots \\
C_k &= \text{RC5}(B_k \oplus C_{k-1}),
\end{aligned}
$$

where IV is the initial value used for the CBC mode.

3 First, we decrypt in CBC mode by computing

$$
\begin{aligned}
B_1 &= \text{RC5}^{-1}(C_1) \oplus \text{IV}, \\
B_2 &= \text{RC5}^{-1}(C_2) \oplus C_1, \\
&\ \vdots \qquad\quad \vdots \\
B_k &= \text{RC5}^{-1}(C_k) \oplus C_{k-1}.
\end{aligned}
$$

Second, we check if B_k ends by exactly i byte(s) equal to i for some $i \in \{1, 2, \ldots, 8\}$. Finally if the padding check succeeds, we extract the plaintext, which corresponds to $B_1, B_2, \ldots, B_{k-1}$ concatenated with the first $(8 - i)$ bytes of B_k.

4 We do an exhaustive trial on all the 256 values of the last byte of R for the submission of (R, C) until the oracle answers that padding is right. We get the last byte of $\text{RC5}^{-1}(C)$ equals $\texttt{0x01} \oplus \texttt{LastByte}(R)$ as well as the value of p. Next, we modify the last byte of R to be the last byte of $\text{RC5}^{-1}(C)$ XORed with the byte $\texttt{0x02}$. We similarly try exhaustively on all the 256 values of the second last byte of R for the submission of (R, C) until the oracle answers that padding is correct. Then we know that the second last byte of $\text{RC5}^{-1}(C)$ equals $\texttt{0x02} \oplus \texttt{SecondLastByte}(R)$. This way, after a maximum of $8 \times 256 = 2^{11}$ oracle calls, we have $\text{RC5}^{-1}(C)$. This is much more

efficient than an exhaustive search effort, which needs $256^8 = 2^{64}$ trials.

5 For any k-block ciphertext $C_1, C_2, \ldots, C_k$, we can compute

$$\text{RC5}^{-1}(C_k), \text{RC5}^{-1}(C_{k-1}), \ldots, \text{RC5}^{-1}(C_1)$$

using previous technique. The description of the CBC decryption mode then allows to recover $B_1, B_2, \ldots, B_k$.

6 Since we know how to compute $\text{RC5}^{-1}(C)$ for any block C by calling the oracle from previous question, we first compute $\text{RC5}^{-1}(C'_k)$, $\text{RC5}^{-1}(C'_{k-1})$, ..., $\text{RC5}^{-1}(C'_1)$. Then we compute

$$
\begin{aligned}
C_1 &= \text{RC5}^{-1}(C'_1) \oplus \text{IV}, \\
C_2 &= \text{RC5}^{-1}(C'_2) \oplus C'_1, \\
\vdots\; &= \quad \vdots \\
C_k &= \text{RC5}^{-1}(C'_k) \oplus C'_{k-1}.
\end{aligned}
$$

Last, we repeat above procedure to decrypt $C_1, C_2, \ldots, C_k$ and get $B_1, B_2, \ldots, B_k$.

For details and the experimental results of the attack, see [10].

Solution 5   Wired Equivalent Privacy (WEP)

1 It is wrong to compute the key size by summing up the sizes of the two inputs of the cipher, because only one input is kept secret. So, the real key size is only 40 bits, not 64 bits.

2 First B reconstructs the plaintext $P' = C \oplus \text{RC4}(\text{IV}, K)$. Then B divides P' into two parts $P' = M' \| Q$, where M' is n bits and Q is 32 bits. Next, B computes $L(M')$ and compares it with Q'. B accepts the message M' if $L(M') = Q'$, otherwise rejects M'.

3 By the Birthday Paradox, randomizing IV for each frame implies that every $2^{\frac{24}{2}} \approx 5000$ frames, we expect to discover a collision on two IV's out of 5000 IV's sent to and from the same user. When this occurs, we will have a collision on the corresponding two keystreams, which helps us to deduce some information about the two plaintexts from the ciphertexts (see [56] for example). One better solution is to increment IV for each frame.

4 Let $M' = M \oplus \Delta$ be the new message, where Δ is any n-bit string. We compute the difference between the corresponding new ciphertext C' and C as follows:

$$
\begin{aligned}
C' \oplus C &= (P' \oplus \mathsf{RC4}(\mathrm{IV}, K)) \oplus (P \oplus \mathsf{RC4}(\mathrm{IV}, K)) \\
&= P' \oplus P \\
&= (M \oplus M') \| (L(M) \oplus L(M')) \\
&= \Delta \| L(\Delta).
\end{aligned}
$$

Thus, for any nonzero Δ, the adversary knows that the ciphertext $C' = C \oplus (\Delta \| L(\Delta))$ passes the CRC parity check at the receiver's end. Consequently, he has $(2^n - 1)$ different choices of Δ (and C'). The property of *message integrity* is violated herein. One important conclusion we draw from this problem is that the linear (and unkeyed) error-correcting CRC encoding only protects the random transmission error (a.k.a. the noise) generated by the communication channel itself, *not* by a malicious adversary.

For more details about the security of WEP, see [8].

Solution 6   Forging X.509 Certificates

Preliminaries

1 MD5 is an iterative hash function which proceeds by first padding the message with a string which only depends on its length so that the padded string has a length multiple of 512 bits, then splitting it in a sequence of 512-bit blocks. Every block is then iteratively hashed by using a compression function C. More precisely, we define a sequence H by $H_0 = \mathrm{IV}$ where IV is a standard initial vector and $H_i = C(H_{i-1}, X_i)$ where X_i is the ith block to be hashed. The last H_i value is the hash of the message.

2 The filled part of the certificate consists of an integral sequence of 512-bit blocks $X_1, \ldots, X_i$. By appending the RSA modulus N_j we have two new blocks such that $X_{i+1}^j \| X_{i+2}^j = N_j$. By taking $\mathrm{IV}' = H_i$, we have $\mathsf{MD5}'(N_j) = H_{i+2}^j$, so $\mathsf{MD5}'(N_1) = \mathsf{MD5}'(N_2)$ is equivalent to $H_{i+2}^1 = H_{i+2}^2$. The remaining part of the filled (padded) certificate appends a final sequence of constant blocks.

3 Basically, the message is first hashed by using MD5, then put in a specific format, then signed by using the plain RSA signature scheme.

4 Since the signature only depends on the hashed value, a collision on the hash function makes that a valid signature on the first message is also a valid signature for the second message.

Finding collisions on MD5′

5 By iteratively hashing the 2-block sequence b_1 or b_2, if we already have a collision on H_2, then we continue to have collisions if we iteratively hash the same sequence of blocks.

Constructing N_1 and N_2

6 An RSA modulus is a product of two different large prime integers.

7 Since p_1 and p_2 are different primes, they are coprime. Hence, from the Chinese Remainder Theorem, for any $x_1 = -b_1 2^{1024}$ and any $x_2 = -b_2 2^{1024}$, we can find b_0 between 0 and $p_1 p_2$ such that $b_0 \equiv x_1$ (mod p_1) and $b_0 \equiv x_2$ (mod p_2). We deduce that p_1 divides $b_1 2^{1024} + b_0$ and that p_2 divides $b_2 2^{1024} + b_0$.

8 Assuming that $b = b_0 + k p_1 p_2$ looks like a random integer, we can further assume that $(b_1 2^{1024} + b)/p_1$ and $(b_2 2^{1024} + b)/p_2$ also look like random independent integers. Eventually, both will be prime. We obtain $q_1 = (b_1 2^{1024} + b)/p_1$ and $q_2 = (b_2 2^{1024} + b)/p_2$ so $b_1 \| b$ and $b_2 \| b$ are two RSA moduli N_1 and N_2 with factorization $N_1 = p_1 q_1$ and $N_2 = p_2 q_2$.

Discussions

9 This attack produces certificates with all fields (except the RSA modulus) in common. So this does not really forge a certificate for an entity which is unknown by the certificate authority. It is just weird that the authority does not see the right public key it is signing. The attack is not so devastating.

10 If we knew how to make collisions with two different arbitrary initial vectors, we could have changed the fields before the modulus part. This could be much more devastating: we could request a certificate for a fake company and transform it into a valid certificate for another one with another public key.

11 If we knew how to make second preimage attacks, we could use an existing valid certificate from a company and change its public key. This would be a disaster for the public key infrastructure.

This exercise was inspired by the memo [25] "Colliding X.509 Certificates" by Arjen Lenstra, Xiaoyun Wang, and Benne de Weger.

References

[1] ANSI X9.17. American National Standard Institute. Financial Institution Key Management (Wholesale). ASC X9 Secretariat, American Bankers Association, 1986.

[2] I. Biehl, J. Buchmann, S. Hamdy, and A. Meyer. A signature scheme based on the intractability of computing roots. *Designs, Codes and Cryptography*, 25(3):223–236, 2002.

[3] E. Biham. Cryptanalysis of multiple modes of operation. *Journal of Cryptology*, 11(1):45–58, 1998.

[4] E. Biham. Cryptanalysis of triple modes of operation. *Journal of Cryptology*, 12(3):161–184, 1999.

[5] E. Biham and A. Shamir. Differential cryptanalysis of DES-like cryptosystems (extended abstract). In A. Menezes and S. Vanstone, editors, *Advances in Cryptology – CRYPTO '90, 10th Annual International Cryptology Conference, Santa Barbara, California, USA, August 11-15, 1990. Proceedings*, volume 537 of *Lecture Notes in Computer Science*, pages 2–21. Springer-Verlag, 1990.

[6] E. Biham and A. Shamir. Differential fault analysis of secret key cryptosystems. In B. Kaliski, editor, *Advances in Cryptology – CRYPTO '97: 17th Annual International Cryptology Conference, Santa Barbara, California, USA, August 1997. Proceedings*, volume 1294 of *Lecture Notes in Computer Science*, pages 513–525. Springer-Verlag, 1997.

[7] Bluetooth™. *Bluetooth Specifications, version 1.2*, 2003. Available on https://www.bluetooth.org.

[8] N. Borisov, I. Goldberg, and D. Wagner. Intercepting mobile communications: the insecurity of 802.11. In *MOBICOM 2001, Proceedings of the Seventh Annual International Conference on Mobile Computing and Networking, July 16-21, 2001, Rome, Italy*, pages 180–189. ACM Press, 2001.

[9] J. L. Camenisch, J.-M. Piveteau, and M. A. Stadler. Blind signatures based on the discrete logarithm problem. In A. DeSantis, editor, *Advances in Cryptology*

– EUROCRYPT '94: Workshop on the Theory and Application of Cryptographic Techniques, Perugia, Italy, May 1994. Proceedings, volume 950 of Lecture Notes in Computer Science, pages 428–434. Springer-Verlag, 1994.

[10] B. Canvel, A. Hiltgen, S. Vaudenay, and M. Vuagnoux. Password interception in a SSL/TLS channel. In D. Boneh, editor, Advances in Cryptology – CRYPTO 2003, 23rd Annual International Cryptology Conference, Santa Barbara, California, USA, August 17-21, 2003. Proceedings, volume 2729 of Lecture Notes in Computer Science, pages 583–599. Springer-Verlag, 2003.

[11] D. Catalano, R. Gennaro, N. Howgrave-Graham, and P. Q. Nguyen. Paillier's cryptosystem revisited. In Proceedings of the 8th ACM conference on Computer and Communications Security, Philadelphia, PA, U.S.A., pages 206–214. ACM Press, 2001.

[12] D. Catalano, P. Q. Nguyen, and J. Stern. The hardness of Hensel lifting: The case of RSA and discrete logarithm. In Y. Zheng, editor, Advances in Cryptology - ASIACRYPT '02: 8th International Conference on the Theory and Application of Cryptology and Information Security, Queenstown, New Zealand, December 2002, Proceedings, volume 2501 of Lecture Notes in Computer Science, pages 299–310. Springer-Verlag, 2002.

[13] J. Daemen and V. Rijmen. The Design of Rijndael: AES - The Advanced Encryption Standard. Information Security and Cryptography. Springer-Verlag, 2002.

[14] D. W. Davies. Some regular properties of the DES. In A. Gersho, editor, Advances in Cryptology: a report on CRYPTO'81, IEEE Workshop on Communication Security, Santa Barbara, August 24–26, 1981. U.C. Santa Barbara, Dept. of Elec. and Computer Eng., ECE Report No 82-84, page 41, 1982.

[15] J. M. DeLaurentis. Weakness in common modulus protocol for the RSA. Cryptologia, 8(3):253–259, 1984.

[16] S. Dreyfus. Underground. Random House Australia, 1997. Available on http://www.underground-book.com.

[17] P. Flagolet and A. Odlyzko. Random mappings statistics. In J. J. Quisquater and J. Vandewalle, editors, Advances in Cryptology - EUROCRYPT '89: Workshop on the Theory and Application of Cryptographic Techniques, Houthalen, Belgium, April 1989. Proceedings, volume 434 of Lecture Notes in Computer Science, pages 329–354. Springer-Verlag, 1990.

[18] P.-A. Fouque and G. Poupard. On the security of RDSA. In E. Biham, editor, Advances in Cryptology – EUROCRYPT '03: International Conference on the Theory and Application of Cryptographic Techniques, Warsaw, Poland, May 2003. Proceedings, volume 2656 of Lecture Notes in Computer Science, pages 462–476. Springer-Verlag, 2003.

[19] H. Gilbert, D. Gupta, A Odlyzko, and J.-J. Quisquater. Attacks on Shamir's "RSA for paranoids". Information Processing Letters, 68(4):197–199, 1998.

[20] D. Hong, J Sung, S. Hong, W. Lee, S. Lee, J. Lim, and O. Yi. Known-IV attacks on triple modes of operation of block ciphers. In C. Boyd, editor, Advances in

Cryptology - ASIACRYPT *'01: 7th International Conference on the Theory and Application of Cryptology and Information Security, Gold Coast, Australia, December 2001, Proceedings*, volume 2248 of *Lecture Notes in Computer Science*, pages 208–221. Springer-Verlag, 2001.

[21] I. Ingemarsson, D. T. Tang, and C. K. Wong. A conference key distribution system. In *IEEE Trans. on Information Theory*, volume IT-28, pages 714–720, September 1982.

[22] K. Ireland and M. Rosen. *A Classical Introduction to Modern Number Theory*. Number 84 in Graduate Texts in Mathematics. Springer-Verlag, second edition, 1990.

[23] A. Joux. Multicollisions in iterated hash functions. Application to cascaded constructions. In M. Franklin, editor, *Advances in Cryptology – CRYPTO 2004, 24th Annual International Cryptology Conference, Santa Barbara, California, USA, August 15-19, 2004. Proceedings*, volume 3152 of *Lecture Notes in Computer Science*, pages 306–316. Springer-Verlag, 2004.

[24] L. Knudsen. The security of Feistel ciphers with six rounds or less. *Journal of Cryptology*, 15(3):207–222, 2002.

[25] A. Lenstra, X. Wang, and B. de Weger. Colliding X.509 certificates. Cryptology ePrint Archive, Report 2005/067, 2005. http://eprint.iacr.org/.

[26] J. Massey. SAFER-K: a byte-oriented block-ciphering algorithm. In R. Anderson, editor, *Fast Software Encryption, Cambridge Security Workshop, Cambridge, UK, December 9-11, 1993. Proceedings*, volume 809 of *Lecture Notes in Computer Science*, pages 1–17. Springer-Verlag, 1994.

[27] Mathworld. http://mathworld.wolfram.com.

[28] M. Matsui. Linear cryptanalysis method for DES cipher. In T. Helleseth, editor, *Advances in Cryptology – EUROCRYPT '93: Workshop on the Theory and Application of Cryptographic Techniques, Lofthus, Norway, May 1993. Proceedings*, volume 765 of *Lecture Notes in Computer Science*, pages 386–397. Springer-Verlag, 1993.

[29] A. Menezes, P. Van Oorschot, and S. Vanstone. *Handbook of applied cryptography*. The CRC Press series on discrete mathematics and its applications. CRC-Press, 1997.

[30] D. Naccache, D. M'Raïhi, S. Vaudenay, and D. Raphaeli. Can DSA be improved? Complexity trade-offs with the digital signature standard. In A. De Santis, editor, *Advances in Cryptology – EUROCRYPT '94: Workshop on the Theory and Application of Cryptographic Techniques, Perugia, Italy, May 1994. Proceedings*, volume 950 of *Lecture Notes in Computer Science*, pages 77–85. Springer-Verlag, 1995.

[31] D. Naccache and J. Stern. A new public-key cryptosystem based on higher residues. In *Proceedings of the 5th ACM conference on Computer and Communications Security, San Francisco, California, U.S.A.*, pages 59–66. ACM Press, 1998.

[32] J. Nakahara, P. Barreto, B. Preneel, J. Vandewalle, and Y. Kim. Square attacks on reduced-round PES and IDEA block ciphers. In B. Macq and J.-J. Quisquater, editors, *Proceedings of 23rd Symposium on Information Theory in the Benelux, Louvain-la-Neuve, Belgium, May 29-31, 2002*, pages 187–195, 2002.

[33] National Institute of Standards and Technology, U. S. Department of Commerce. *Advanced Encryption Standard (AES) - FIPS 197*, 26 November 2001.

[34] U. Okamoto and S. Uchiyama. A new public-key cryptosystem as secure as factoring. In K. Nyberg, editor, *Advances in Cryptology – EUROCRYPT '98: International Conference on the Theory and Application of Cryptographic Techniques, Espoo, Finland, May/June 1998. Proceedings*, volume 1403 of *Lecture Notes in Computer Science*, pages 308–318. Springer-Verlag, 1998.

[35] H. Ong, C. P. Schnorr, and A. Shamir. An efficient signature scheme based on quadratic equations. In R. DeMillo, editor, *Proceedings of the sixteenth annual ACM symposium on Theory of computing, Washington D.C., U.S.A.*, pages 208–216. ACM Press, 1984.

[36] P. Paillier. Public-key cryptosystems based on composite degree residuosity classes. In J. Stern, editor, *Advances in Cryptology – EUROCRYPT '99: International Conference on the Theory and Application of Cryptographic Techniques, Prague, Czech Republic, May 1999. Proceedings*, volume 1592 of *Lecture Notes in Computer Science*, pages 223–238. Springer-Verlag, 1999.

[37] T. Peyrin. Bluetooth security. Diploma Project, CPE Lyon, September 2004.

[38] T. Peyrin and S. Vaudenay. The pairing problem with user interaction. In Security and Privacy in the Age of Ubiquitous Computing IFIP TC11 20th International Information Security Conference (SEC'05), Chiba, Japan, 2005.

[39] J. M. Pollard and C. P. Schnorr. An efficient solution of the congruence $x^2 + ky^2 = m \pmod{n}$. *IEEE Transactions on Information Theory*, IT-33(5):702–709, 1987.

[40] M. O. Rabin. Digitalized signatures and public-key functions as intractable as factorization. Technical Report MIT/LCS/TR-212, MIT, 1979.

[41] R. L. Rivest. Remarks on a proposed cryptanalytic attack on the M.I.T. public-key cryptosystem. *Cryptologia*, 2(1):62–65, 1978.

[42] R. L. Rivest and A. Shamir. PayWord and MicroMint: two simple micropayment schemes. In M. Lomas, editor, *Proceedings of 1996 International Workshop on Security Protocols*, number 1189 in Lecture Notes in Computer Science, pages 69–87, 1997.

[43] R. L. Rivest, A. Shamir, and L. M. Adleman. A method for obtaining digital signatures and public-key cryptosystem. *Communications of the ACM*, 21(2):120–126, 1978.

[44] R. L. Rivest, A. Shamir, and Y. Tauman. How to leak a secret. In C. Boyd, editor, *Advances in Cryptology - ASIACRYPT '01: 7th International Conference on the Theory and Application of Cryptology and Information Security, Gold*

Coast, Australia, December 2001, Proceedings, volume 2248 of *Lecture Notes in Computer Science*, pages 552–565. Springer-Verlag, 2001.

[45] R. L. Rivest and R. Silverman. Are "strong" primes needed for RSA. Cryptology ePrint Archive, Report 2001/007, 2001. http://eprint.iacr.org/.

[46] T. Satoh, M. Haga, and K. Kurosawa. Towards secure and fast hash functions. In *IEICE Trans.*, volume E82-A, 1999.

[47] C. Schnorr and S. Vaudenay. Black box cryptanalysis of hash networks based on multipermutations. In A. De Santis, editor, *Advances in Cryptology – EU-ROCRYPT'94: Workshop on the Theory and Application of Cryptographic Techniques, Perugia, Italy, May 1994. Proceedings*, volume 950 of *Lecture Notes in Computer Science*, pages 47–57. Springer-Verlag, 1995.

[48] A. Shamir. RSA for paranoids. *Cryptobytes*, 1(3):1–4, 1995.

[49] G. J. Simmons. A "weak" privacy protocol using the RSA crypto algorithm. *Cryptologia*, 7(2):180–182, 1983.

[50] G. J. Simmons and M. J. Norris. Preliminary comments on the M.I.T public-key cryptosystem. *Cryptologia*, 1(4):406–414, 1977.

[51] S. Singh. *The Code Book: The secret history of codes and code-breaking*. Fourth Estate Ltd., 2000.

[52] J. Stern and S. Vaudenay. CS-Cipher. In S. Vaudenay, editor, *Fast Software Encryption, 5th International Workshop, FSE'98, Paris, France, March 23-25, 1998. Proceedings*, volume 1372 of *Lecture Notes in Computer Science*, pages 189–205. Springer-Verlag, 1998.

[53] S. Vaudenay. On the need for multipermutations: cryptanalysis of MD4 and SAFER. In B. Preneel, editor, *Fast Software Encryption: Second International Workshop. Leuven, Belgium, 14-16 December 1994. Proceedings*, volume 1008 of *Lecture Notes in Computer Science*, pages 286–297. Springer-Verlag, 1995.

[54] S. Vaudenay. On the Lai-Massey scheme. In K. Lam , T. Okamoto, and C. Xing, editors, *Advances in Cryptology – ASIACRYPT'99: International Conference on the Theory and Application of Cryptology and Information Security, Singapore, November 14-18, 1999. Proceedings*, volume 1716 of *Lecture Notes in Computer Science*, pages 8–19. Springer-Verlag, 2000.

[55] S. Vaudenay. Decorrelation: a theory for block cipher security. *Journal of Cryptology*, 16(4):249–286, 2003.

[56] S. Vaudenay. *A Classical Introduction to Cryptography: Applications for Communications Security*. Springer-Verlag, 2005.

[57] D. Wagner. Cryptanalysis of the Yi-Lam hash. In T. Okamoto, editor, *Advances in Cryptology – ASIACRYPT 2000: 6th International Conference on the Theory and Application of Cryptology and Information Security, Kyoto, Japan, December 3-7, 2000. Proceedings*, volume 1976 of *Lecture Notes in Computer Science*, pages 483–488. Springer-Verlag, 2000.

[58] W. Xiaoyun and Y. Hongbo. How to break MD5 and other hash functions. In R. Cramer, editor, *Advances in Cryptology* – EUROCRYPT *'05: International Conference on the Theory and Application of Cryptographic Techniques, Aarhus, Denmark, May 2005. Proceedings*, volume 3494 of *Lecture Notes in Computer Science*, pages 19–35. Springer-Verlag, 2005.